WITHDRAWN

# Also by the Editors at America's Test Kitchen

## For a Full Listing of All Our Books
CooksIllustrated.com

AmericasTestKitchen.com

# Praise for Other America's Test Kitchen Titles

Selected as the Cookbook Award Winner of 2017 in the Baking category

**INTERNATIONAL ASSOCIATION OF CULINARY PROFESSIONALS (IACP) ON *BREAD ILLUSTRATED***

"The editors at America's Test Kitchen pack decades of baking experience into this impressive volume of 250 recipes. . . . You'll find a wealth of keeper recipes within these pages."

**LIBRARY JOURNAL (STARRED REVIEW) ON *THE PERFECT COOKIE***

Selected as one of Amazon's Best Books of 2015 in the Cookbooks and Food Writing category

**AMAZON ON *THE COMPLETE VEGETARIAN COOKBOOK***

"With 1,000 photos and the expertise of the America's Test Kitchen editors, this title might be the definitive book on bread baking."

**PUBLISHERS WEEKLY ON *BREAD ILLUSTRATED***

"This book is a comprehensive, no-nonsense guide . . . a well-thought-out, clearly explained primer for every aspect of home baking."

**THE WALL STREET JOURNAL ON *THE COOK'S ILLUSTRATED BAKING BOOK***

"Cooks with a powerful sweet tooth should scoop up this well-researched recipe book for healthier takes on classic sweet treats."

**BOOKLIST ON *NATURALLY SWEET***

"A terrifically accessible and useful guide to grilling in all its forms that sets a new bar for its competitors on the bookshelf. . . . The book is packed with practical advice, simple tips, and approachable recipes."

**PUBLISHERS WEEKLY (STARRED REVIEW) ON *MASTER OF THE GRILL***

"This encyclopedia of meat cookery would feel completely overwhelming if it weren't so meticulously organized and artfully designed. This is *Cook's Illustrated* at its finest."

**THE KITCHN ON *THE COOK'S ILLUSTRATED MEAT BOOK***

"The 21st-century *Fannie Farmer Cookbook* or *The Joy of Cooking*. If you had to have one cookbook and that's all you could have, this one would do it."

**CBS SAN FRANCISCO ON *THE NEW FAMILY COOKBOOK***

"The go-to gift book for newlyweds, small families, or empty nesters."

**ORLANDO SENTINEL ON *THE COMPLETE COOKING FOR TWO COOKBOOK***

"The sum total of exhaustive experimentation . . . anyone interested in gluten-free cookery simply shouldn't be without it."

**NIGELLA LAWSON ON *THE HOW CAN IT BE GLUTEN-FREE COOKBOOK***

"A one-volume kitchen seminar, addressing in one smart chapter after another the sometimes surprising whys behind a cook's best practices. . . . You get the myth, the theory, the science, and the proof, all rigorously interrogated as only America's Test Kitchen can do."

**NPR ON *THE SCIENCE OF GOOD COOKING***

"Another winning cookbook from ATK. . . . The folks at America's Test Kitchen apply their rigorous experiments to determine the facts about these pans."

**BOOKLIST ON *COOK IT IN CAST IRON***

"The perfect kitchen home companion. . . . The practical side of things is very much on display . . . cook-friendly and kitchen-oriented, illuminating the process of preparing food instead of mystifying it."

**THE WALL STREET JOURNAL ON *THE COOK'S ILLUSTRATED COOKBOOK***

"An exceptional resource for novice canners, though preserving veterans will find plenty here to love as well."

**LIBRARY JOURNAL (STARRED REVIEW) ON *FOOLPROOF PRESERVING***

"Some 2,500 photos walk readers through 600 painstakingly tested recipes, leaving little room for error."

**ASSOCIATED PRESS ON *THE AMERICA'S TEST KITCHEN COOKING SCHOOL COOKBOOK***

# DINNER

## *illustrated*

### 175 MEALS READY IN 1 HOUR OR LESS

the editors at America's Test Kitchen

Library of Congress Cataloging-in-Publication Data

Names: America's Test Kitchen (Firm), editor.
Title: Dinner illustrated : 175 meals ready in 1 hour or less / the editors at America's Test Kitchen.
Description: Boston, MA : America's Test Kitchen, [2018] | Includes index.
Identifiers: LCCN 2017055764 | ISBN 9781945256301 (paperback)
Subjects: LCSH: Dinner and dining. | Quick and easy cooking. | BISAC: COOKING / Courses & Dishes / General. | COOKING / Methods / General. | COOKING / Reference. | LCGFT: Cookbooks.
Classification: LCC TX737 .D526 2018 | DDC 641.5/12--dc23
LC record available at https://lccn.loc.gov/2017055764

— AMERICA'S —
**TEST KITCHEN** ®

**America's Test Kitchen**
21 Drydock Avenue, Boston, MA 02210
Manufactured in Canada
**10 9 8 7 6 5 4 3 2 1**

Distributed by Penguin Random House Publisher Services
Tel: 800.733.3000

Pictured On Front Cover: Grilled Beef Skewers with Arugula Salad and Heirloom Tomatoes (page 102)
Pictured On Back Cover: Tk (page 000)

Chief Creative Officer **Jack Bishop**
Editorial Director, Books **Elizabeth Carduff**
Executive Editor **Julia Collin Davison**
Executive Editor **Adam Kowit**
Executive Food Editor **Suzannah McFerran**
Senior Editors **Stephanie Pixley and Anne Wolf**
Associate Editors **Leah Colins, Rachel Greenhaus, Lawman Johnson, and Nicole Konstantinakos**
Test Cooks **Kathryn Callahan, Afton Cyrus, Joseph Gitter, and Katherine Perry**
Editorial Assistant **Alyssa Langer**
Design Director, Books **Carole Goodman**
Deputy Art Directors **Allison Boales and Jen Kanavos Hoffman**
Designer **Katie Barranger**
Production Designer **Reinaldo Cruz**
Photography Director **Julie Bozzo Cote**
Photography Producer **Mary Ball**
Senior Staff Photographer **Daniel J. Van Ackere**
Staff Photographer **Steve Klise**
Additional Photography **Keller + Keller and Carl Tremblay**
Food Styling **Daniel Cellucci, Catrine Kelty, Kendra McKnight, Marie Piraino, Elle Simone Scott, and Sally Staub**
Photoshoot Kitchen Team
  Manager **Timothy McQuinn**
  Associate Editor **Daniel Cellucci**
  Assistant Test Cooks **Mady Nichas and Jessica Rudolph**
Production Director **Guy Rochford**
Senior Production Manager **Jessica Lindheimer Quirk**
Production Manager **Christine Spanger**
Imaging Manager **Lauren Robbins**
Production and Imaging Specialists **Heather Dube, Dennis Noble, and Jessica Voas**
Copy Editor **Cheryl Redmond**
Proofreader **Elizabeth Wray Emery**
Indexer **Elizabeth Parson**

# Contents

# Welcome to America's Test Kitchen

**This book has been tested, written, and edited by the folks at America's** Test Kitchen. Located in Boston's Seaport District in the historic Innovation and Design Building, it features 15,000 square feet of kitchen space including multiple photography and video studios. It is the home of *Cook's Illustrated* magazine and *Cook's Country* magazine and is the workday destination for more than 60 test cooks, editors, and cookware specialists. Our mission is to test recipes over and over again until we understand how and why they work and until we arrive at the best version.

We start the process of testing a recipe with a complete lack of preconceptions, which means that we accept no claim, no technique, and no recipe at face value. We simply assemble as many variations as possible, test a half-dozen of the most promising, and taste the results blind. We then construct our own recipe and continue to test it, varying ingredients, techniques, and cooking times until we reach a consensus. As we like to say in the test kitchen, "We make the mistakes so you don't have to." The result, we hope, is the best version of a particular recipe, but we realize that only you can be the final judge of our success (or failure). We use the same rigorous approach when we test equipment and taste ingredients.

All of this would not be possible without a belief that good cooking, much like good music, is based on a foundation of objective technique. Some people like spicy foods and others don't, but there is a right way to sauté, there is a best way to cook a pot roast, and there are measurable scientific principles involved in producing perfectly beaten, stable egg whites. Our ultimate goal is to investigate the fundamental principles of cooking to give you the techniques, tools, and ingredients you need to become a better cook. It is as simple as that.

To see what goes on behind the scenes at America's Test Kitchen, check out our social media channels for kitchen snapshots, exclusive content, video tips, and much more. You can watch us work (in our actual test kitchen) by tuning in to *America's Test Kitchen* or *Cook's Country from America's Test Kitchen* on public television or on our websites. Listen in to test kitchen experts on public radio (SplendidTable.org) to hear insights that illuminate the truth about real home cooking. Want to hone your cooking skills or finally learn how to bake—with an America's Test Kitchen test cook? Enroll in one of our online cooking classes. However you choose to visit us, we welcome you into our kitchen, where you can stand by our side as we test our way to the best recipes in America.

**Getting Started**

# How to Use This Book

**Welcome to your new go-to guide to fast, stress-free weeknight cooking.**

This book has been designed from the ground up to provide foolproof, fully illustrated instructions for getting dinner on the table every night. It's packed with quick, easy, delicious meals; from meatless options to comfort foods, you can do it all in under an hour with our streamlined recipes. We've even included nutritional information in the back of the book to help inform your choices. We like to think of *Dinner Illustrated* as a meal kit plan for busy people who love to be in the kitchen but need a little help with timing and inspiration (and would rather do their own shopping and skip the wasteful packaging). This book empowers you to shop, prep, and cook efficiently without stifling your creativity or limiting your tastes.

Every recipe in this book has been designed and tested to ensure that it can be made in an hour or less. We obsessively timed ourselves as we developed the recipes and then rounded up to 30 minutes, 45 minutes, or 60 minutes based on how long they took, from gathering our ingredients to trying that first bite. We had our kitchen interns make each recipe to double-check the timing, and then we sent recipes to our home cook recipe testers to triple-check. In order to meet our under-60-minutes promise, we're assuming a few things about how you're going to cook these weeknight recipes: In general, we expect you to be reasonably focused (not folding laundry in between chopping ingredients), but you don't need to have pro-level skills and you don't need to rush—nor should you.

Since we designed our ingredient lists to work as shopping lists, this means that sometimes we call for "1 lemon" or "fresh parsley" since that's what you would want to pick up from the grocery store or dig up from your crisper drawer; however, the recipe might only require 1 tablespoon of lemon juice or a few teaspoons of minced herbs. If you want to check exactly how much of an ingredient you need, just read through the recipe.

In order to get a full dinner on the table in less than an hour, we've reinvented the way we present recipes. Once you're ready to cook, each recipe is engineered for maximum efficiency. We tell you exactly when to prep each ingredient during the cooking process, with detailed photos illustrating every step along the way. The only advance work required before you start a recipe is washing and drying your produce. We know that your time is valuable, so when it makes more sense to trim the steaks while the oven preheats but save the sauce prep for while the meat is in the oven, that's how we wrote the recipe. Then, while the cooked steaks rest, it's time to make the salad. There's less wasted downtime, less chance of skipping a key ingredient, and less fuss between you and your meal. This fresh approach recreates how seasoned chefs really cook at home and works with the way many of us actually tackle dinner on a busy evening.

# 5 Habits of an Efficient Cook

## 1 Set Yourself Up for Success

Before you start cooking, read the recipe carefully. Identify any unusual tools you need to hunt down from a hidden cabinet or terms you want to look up. Also think about what plates, platters, serving dishes, and utensils you will need in order to serve the food when it's done and assemble them for later. And, of course, gather all your ingredients.

## 2 Prep Smart

Prepping your ingredients as you go (instead of all at the beginning) is a great way to eliminate wasted downtime and make your cooking more efficient. Think about what order you want to prep your ingredients in to make the smallest amount of mess. (Beets always get prepped last!) And be aware of food safety if you're prepping meat, poultry, or seafood; prep other ingredients first to avoid contamination, or keep a second cutting board specifically for these ingredients.

## 3 Keep Clean as You Go

Keep a container of hot, soapy water on your counter so you can soak dirty tools and utensils and then just give them a quick rinse before you use them again. (Utensils that touch raw meat should be washed separately in the sink to avoid cross-contamination.) Keep a plastic bag or empty container handy for scraps and other waste that accumulate as you cook; keeping it off your board makes it easier to work and is also safer.

## 4 Get the Most Out of Your Board

Flip the cutting board over if you need a new, clean surface rather than dirtying another board or taking the time to clean and dry the one you're using.

## 5 Have Fun and Go with Your Gut

Keep in mind that the recipes in this book were designed using methods and techniques that are straightforward, relatively unfussy, and forgiving; so relax, have fun, and try not to get bogged down with any particular step. The most important thing is that you make food that you want to eat, so if you like your curry a little spicier, or your steak rarer, or your dressing with less lemon juice, you should adapt the recipes accordingly. And always, always taste the dish before serving and adjust the seasonings to taste.

## Bonus

### Know What to Do When Seasonings Go Awry

Sometimes you finish a dish and it just doesn't quite taste perfect. While salt and pepper are always a consideration for final tweaks, our test cooks also look to a range of other pantry ingredients that can help bring a dish into the right balance. Just a small quantity of one of these finishing touches (from a pinch to a few tablespoons) is a good starting place.

| If your food is | Add | Such as |
| --- | --- | --- |
| Too salty | An acid or sweetener | Lemon juice, lime juice, or vinegar; sugar, honey, maple syrup, or fruit jam |
| Too sweet | An acid or seasonings | Lemon juice, lime juice, or vinegar; chopped fresh herbs, citrus zest, or a dash of cayenne (for savory dishes), liqueur or instant espresso (for sweet dishes) |
| Too spicy or acidic | A fat or sweetener | Butter, olive oil, heavy cream, cheese, or sour cream; sugar, honey, maple syrup, or fruit jam |
| Too rich | An acid | Lemon juice, lime juice, or vinegar; pickled vegetables (such as jalapeños) |
| Too flat | A salty and/or savory boost | Worcestershire sauce, soy sauce, fish sauce, miso, Parmesan cheese, anchovies, tomato paste, mushrooms, sherry |

# Tools That Speed Up Dinner

Most of the equipment that we used to make the recipes in this book is pretty basic, but there are a few tools we rely on more than others. At the top of this list is a skillet that can go from the stovetop to the oven for recipes that take advantage of multiple cooking methods, like Crispy Chicken with Sautéed Radishes, Spinach, and Bacon (page 194) or Broccoli and Feta Frittata with Watercress Salad (page 350). Rimmed baking sheets are also really convenient vessels for making meals with multiple components that all cook at the same time, especially with an assist from a wire rack set inside the pan.

There are a few gadgets that can help speed up and streamline your weeknight dinner prep. For instance, use a rasp grater to mince garlic to a paste instead of putting all the pressure on your knife skills, or use a garlic press for a larger quantity of cloves. A handheld manual citrus juicer makes it a breeze to get every drop of juice out of lemons and limes with minimal effort. And a reliable vegetable peeler lets you fly through a pile of carrots in a flash.

Of course, a good, sharp chef's knife is your most vital tool; not only does it make prep work easier, it also makes it faster and safer. You'll also want a big cutting board that has room to do all the necessary prep. When it comes to where to put all those perfectly prepped ingredients, we love using small prep bowls to hold them; they're not just for TV chefs! Using little bowls helps keep your cutting board clean and makes it easy to add an ingredient to the pan all at once. We prefer glass bowls, since they're sturdy, microwave-safe, and easy to clean.

# Stocking Your Kitchen for Dinner Success

If having a set of dependable, foolproof, delicious weeknight recipes to work with is the first step to dinner happiness, another key is having a well-stocked kitchen full of ingredients that lend themselves to quick, flavorful meals (and we're not just talking about boneless, skinless chicken breasts and dried spaghetti). Using powerhouse ingredients with unique flavor profiles can also help save you from the monotony of familiar go-to recipes.

## Bulk It Up

### Rice
This is a side dish you can basically ignore while you do other things—just set a timer.

### Canned Beans
Great for your emergency bomb shelter, great for quick and easy weeknight dinners! We like chickpeas, black beans, and small white beans such as cannellini.

### Eggs
Put an egg on it—whether fried, poached, or hard-cooked—and you have a simple meal.

### Frozen Shrimp
Buy individually quick-frozen shell-on shrimp and defrost as needed—it only takes a few minutes under running water.

## Balance It Out

### Tender Greens
Baby spinach, baby kale, baby arugula . . . just put something green on your plate. Think how proud your mom would be.

### Frozen Peas
Just be sure to add these at the last minute to keep them from getting mushy.

### Cherry Tomatoes
These little tomatoes need almost no prep but pack high-impact flavor.

## Worth the Splurge

### Cheese
Even if you're only using a small amount, a high-quality Parmesan or feta will make all the difference.

### Lettuce
Buy the high-quality triple-washed stuff to save yourself time and effort.

### Whole-Milk Greek Yogurt
Real strained Greek yogurt with no artificial thickeners has a beautiful thick texture and tangy flavor that can't be beat.

## Amp Up the Flavor

### Seasoned Rice Vinegar
This shortcut product already contains salt and sugar for extra flavor.

### Kimchi
The powerful flavor in this crunchy Korean vegetable condiment is as result of fermentation. Make sure you don't throw away the flavorful pickling liquid!

### Za'atar
You can use this aromatic blend of wild thyme, oregano, sumac, and sesame seeds as a seasoning or a condiment.

### Pomegranate Molasses
The unique sweet-sour flavor and thick texture of this ingredient make it great for glazing chicken, fish, vegetables, and more.

### Tahini
A versatile paste made from toasted sesame seeds, tahini is great for sauces, dips, baking, and more.

## Spice Up Your Life

### Harissa
We like this traditional North African chile-garlic paste for flavoring sauces and dressings.

### Chipotle Chiles in Adobo
Both the smoky dried chiles and the tangy sauce they come in are flavor powerhouses.

### Gochujang
This spicy Korean fermented chile bean paste is great as an ingredient or a condiment.

# DIY Dinner Helpers

For quick, approachable recipes, we tried to keep the ingredient lists short. To make sure this didn't leave us short on flavor, we relied on a number of versatile, high-impact ingredients to add complex flavor to our recipes. Depending on where you live, some of the more unfamiliar international ingredients in our dinner pantry may be difficult to find at your local supermarket, but luckily they're relatively easy to make at home.

### Harissa
MAKES ABOUT ½ CUP

*Harissa is potent, so just a dollop adds a jolt of bright, spicy flavor to everything from soups and stews to sautéed vegetables and fried eggs. If you can't find Aleppo pepper, substitute ¾ teaspoon paprika plus ¾ teaspoon finely chopped red pepper flakes.*

**6 tablespoons extra-virgin olive oil**
**6 garlic cloves, minced**
**2 tablespoons paprika**
**1 tablespoon ground coriander**
**1 tablespoon ground dried Aleppo pepper**
**1 teaspoon ground cumin**
**¾ teaspoon caraway seeds**
**½ teaspoon salt**

Combine ingredients in bowl and microwave until bubbling and very fragrant, about 1 minute, stirring halfway through microwaving; let cool to room temperature. (Harissa can be refrigerated for up to 4 days.)

### Pomegranate Molasses
MAKES ⅓ CUP

*Pomegranate molasses can be whisked into vinaigrette, drizzled over vegetables, brushed onto roasted meats, or pureed into dips. Reducing the pomegranate juice at a simmer, rather than at a boil, drives off fewer flavor compounds and results in fresher, more complex flavor. To speed up evaporation, we use a 12-inch skillet, which offers more surface area.*

**2 cups unsweetened pomegranate juice**
**½ teaspoon sugar**
**Pinch salt**

Bring ingredients to simmer in 12-inch skillet over high heat. Reduce heat to low and simmer, stirring and scraping thickened juice from sides of skillet occasionally, until mixture is thick and syrupy and measures ⅓ cup, 12 to 15 minutes. Let cool slightly before transferring to container. (Once cooled, syrup can be refrigerated for up to 1 month.)

### Za'atar
MAKES ABOUT ½ CUP

*Try sprinkling za'atar over olive oil as a dip for bread. You can also use it in grain dishes or as a flavorful topping for hummus or other dips.*

**½ dried thyme**
**2 tablespoon sesame seeds, toasted**
**1½ tablespoons ground sumac**

Grind thyme in spice grinder or with mortar and pestle until finely ground and powdery. Transfer to bowl and stir in sesame seeds and sumac. (Za'atar can be stored at room temperature in airtight container for up to 1 year.)

### Tahini
To make a homemade version of tahini, grind sesame seeds in a blender with just enough peanut or vegetable oil to make a fairly smooth mixture. (Use an amount of sesame seeds equal to the amount of tahini you want to make.) Add 1 teaspoon toasted sesame oil (or more to taste), if you have some on hand.

# Prep Tips from the Pros

There are certain kinds of ingredient prep that you are going to do over and over (and over and over) in your cooking life. Knowing the best, most efficient ways to do them will save you time and effort (and also make you look and feel like a kitchen star). Here are our notes on our favorite ways to approach a few of the most common prep tasks in this book and in basic cooking more generally.

## Chopping Onions

1 Halve onion through root end, then peel onion and trim top. Make several horizontal cuts from one end of onion to other but don't cut through root end.

2 Make several vertical cuts. Be sure to cut up to but not through root end.

3 Rotate onion so root end is in back; slice onion thinly across previous cuts. As you slice, onion will fall apart into chopped pieces.

## Peeling and Mincing Garlic

## Peeling Ginger

1 Trim off root ends of garlic clove, then crush clove gently between side of chef's knife and cutting board to loosen papery skin. Remove skin.

2 Using two-handed chopping motion, run knife over garlic repeatedly to mince it.

To quickly peel a knob of ginger, use edge of dinner spoon to scrape away its thin brown skin.

## Cutting Up Bell Peppers

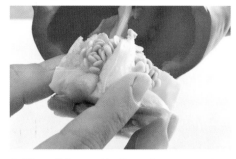

**1** Slice off top and bottom of pepper and remove seeds and stem, then slice down through side of pepper.

**2** Lay pepper flat, trim away remaining ribs and seeds, then cut into strips or pieces as required.

## Mincing Herbs

Grip handle of knife with one hand and rest fingers of other hand lightly on knife tip. Use up-and-down rocking motion to mince herbs. Pivot knife through pile of food as you work.

## Cutting Up Avocado

**1** Slice avocado in half around pit. Lodge edge of knife in pit and twist to remove pit. Use wooden spoon to pry pit safely off knife.

**2** Use dish towel to hold avocado steady. Make ½-inch crosshatch incisions in flesh of each avocado half with knife, cutting down to, but not through, skin.

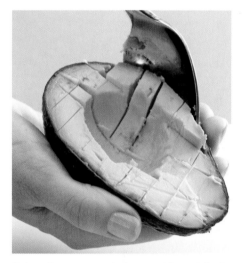

**3** Insert soupspoon between skin and flesh and gently scoop out avocado cubes.

## Peeling and Deveining Shrimp

**1** Break shell under swimming legs. Leave tail end intact if desired, or tug tail end to remove shell.

**2** Use paring knife to make shallow cut along back of shrimp to expose vein. Use tip of knife to lift vein out. Discard vein by wiping knife blade on paper towel.

## Chopping Nuts

Shape damp dish towel into ring on cutting board to contain nuts, leaving enough room for nuts and knife blade. Chop nuts.

# Dinner on the Grill

If you have access to it, grilling is an excellent cooking technique for quick and easy weeknight dinners. In particular, a gas grill takes very little time to set up and preheat. We have written and tested all of the grilling recipes in this book for a gas grill. Charcoal grilling is slightly less quick and easy, but if you want to use charcoal for our recipes, here are some basic guidelines for translating our gas grill instructions to charcoal setups.

For a list of all the grilling recipes in this book, see the index. Note: One thing that can slow you down when you're grilling is running back and forth to the grill if you're worried about leaving the lit grill unattended. If you'd rather keep an eye on the grill and the weather permits, try setting up a mini prep station next to your grill with your cutting board and knife so you can do the rest of your ingredient prep right there.

To prepare a charcoal grill, open the bottom vent and light a large chimney starter filled with the required amount of charcoal briquettes. For high heat, use a full chimney of charcoal (6 quarts). For medium-high heat, use ¾ chimney of charcoal (4½ quarts). For medium heat, use ½ chimney of charcoal (3 quarts).

When the top coals are partially covered with ash, add them to the grill. For a single-level fire, pour the coals evenly over the grill.

For a two-level fire with a hotter side and a cooler side, divide the charcoal between the two sides of the grill when you add it: two-thirds on one side (this will be the hotter side) and one-third on the opposite side (this will be the cooler side).

Once you add the coals, you need to set the cooking grate in place, cover the grill, and open the lid vent. Heat the grill until it's hot, about 5 minutes.

Whether you're using gas or charcoal, always make sure you clean the cooking grate before cooking in order to remove any burnt-on residue. Once the grill is hot, scrape the grate clean with a grill brush.

Once the cooking grate is clean, oil it by using a wad of paper towels dipped in vegetable oil. Use tongs to wipe the grate several times with the paper towels. For really delicate foods such as fish, we recommend slicking down the grate as many as 10 times.

# Meatless and Gluten-Free Recipes

The recipes in this book have been developed with many different palates, preferences, and diets in mind. For those looking for vegetarian, vegan, or gluten-free options, whether all the time or just tonight, we've put together these lists to make navigation a little easier.

## Gluten-Free Recipes

*Make sure to use gluten-free soy sauce, hoisin sauce, and oyster sauce when necessary.*

# Chicken and Arugula Salad with Figs and Warm Spices

serves 6; total time 45 minutes

## notes for the cook

This salad is light and fresh but still packs a protein punch with chickpeas, almonds, and chicken breasts.

Figs have a subtle, seductive flavor that comfortably swings between the sweet and savory sides of the menu, so they're right at home in this sophisticated salad. If you can't find fresh figs, you can substitute dried figs; they have a chewier texture and deeper caramel flavor.

We tried a variety of spice combinations in the dressing and finally settled on coriander for its light citrus note, along with smoked paprika for depth.

Note that you'll need ½ cup of parsley, so shop accordingly.

Salt and pepper
4 (6- to 8-ounce) boneless, skinless chicken breasts
1 lemon
1 (15-ounce) can chickpeas
Fresh parsley
1 shallot
8 fresh figs
½ cup whole almonds
6 tablespoons extra-virgin olive oil
1 teaspoon ground coriander
½ teaspoon smoked paprika
1 teaspoon honey
5 ounces (5 cups) baby arugula

**1** **Poach Chicken** Dissolve ¼ cup salt in 4 quarts cold water in Dutch oven. Trim chicken, cover with plastic wrap, and pound thick ends until ¾ inch thick. Arrange breasts in steamer basket. Submerge basket in salt water. Heat pot over medium heat until water registers 175 degrees, about 20 minutes. Turn off heat, cover pot, and let sit until chicken registers 160 degrees, 15 to 20 minutes. Transfer chicken to large plate; set aside.

**2** **Prep Ingredients** While chicken cooks, squeeze 3 tablespoons lemon juice. Drain and rinse chickpeas. Pick ½ cup parsley leaves. Halve shallot through root end and slice thin. Stem and quarter figs.

**3** **Toast Nuts** Toast almonds in 10-inch skillet over medium heat, shaking occasionally, until golden and fragrant, 3 to 5 minutes; transfer to small bowl to cool, then chop cooled nuts.

**4 Make Dressing** Microwave 1 tablespoon oil, coriander, and paprika in large bowl until fragrant, about 30 seconds. Whisk honey, lemon juice, remaining 5 tablespoons oil, ½ teaspoon salt, and ¼ teaspoon pepper into spice mixture until incorporated.

**5 Shred Chicken** Once chicken is cool enough to handle, shred into bite-size pieces using 2 forks.

**6 Finish Salad** Add shredded chicken, chickpeas, parsley, shallot, and arugula to dressing in bowl and gently toss to combine. Transfer salad to serving dish, arrange figs over top, and sprinkle with almonds. Serve.

# Kale Caesar Salad with Chicken

serves 4; total time 1 hour

## notes for the cook

This play on a traditional chicken Caesar uses hearty, healthy kale rather than romaine but otherwise keeps all the savory punch of the classic salad.

Kale is notorious for being fibrous and tough, but a short massage turns the leaves completely silky.

To stand up to the assertive flavor of the kale, we made our dressing extra-potent, with a stronger dose of lemon juice and anchovies than is typical in Caesar salad.

We prefer curly kale in this recipe, but you can substitute Lacinato kale; just decrease the massaging time in step 2 to 1 minute.

A demi-baguette is usually about 12 inches long (versus 24 inches for a full baguette).

1 demi-baguette
¼ cup extra-virgin olive oil
Salt and pepper
12 ounces curly kale
1 ounce Parmesan cheese
1 lemon
3 anchovy fillets
1 garlic clove
⅓ cup mayonnaise
2 teaspoons white wine vinegar
2 teaspoons Worcestershire sauce
2 teaspoons Dijon mustard
4 (3- to 4-ounce) chicken cutlets, ½ inch thick

**1 Make Croutons** Adjust oven rack to middle position and heat oven to 350 degrees. Cut baguette into ¾-inch cubes and transfer to rimmed baking sheet. Drizzle with 1 tablespoon oil, sprinkle with ¼ teaspoon pepper and ⅛ teaspoon salt, and toss to combine. Spread into even layer and bake until golden and crisp, about 15 minutes. Let croutons cool completely on sheet.

**2 Prep and Massage Kale** While croutons are baking, stem kale by cutting away leafy green portion from either side of stalk, then chop leaves into 1-inch pieces. Transfer to large bowl and vigorously squeeze and massage kale with your hands until leaves are uniformly darkened and slightly wilted, about 2 minutes.

**3 Prep Dressing Ingredients** Grate Parmesan (½ cup). Squeeze 1 tablespoon lemon juice. Rinse anchovy fillets. Mince garlic.

**4** **Make Dressing** Process mayonnaise, vinegar, Worcestershire, mustard, ¼ cup Parmesan, lemon juice, anchovies, garlic, ¼ teaspoon salt, and ¼ teaspoon pepper in blender until smooth, about 30 seconds. With blender running, slowly add 2 tablespoons oil until incorporated.

**5** **Cook Chicken** Trim chicken, pat dry with paper towels, and season with salt and pepper. Heat remaining 1 tablespoon oil in 12-inch nonstick skillet over medium-high heat until just smoking. Add chicken and cook until golden brown and registers 160 degrees, about 3 minutes per side. Transfer chicken to cutting board, tent with aluminum foil, and let rest.

**6** **Finish Salad** While chicken rests, add dressing, croutons, and remaining ¼ cup Parmesan to bowl with kale and toss until well coated. Divide salad among individual serving dishes. Slice chicken thin and arrange over salads. Serve.

# Beet and Carrot Noodle Salad with Pan-Seared Chicken

serves 4; total time 1 hour

## notes for the cook

This colorful dish uses homemade beet and carrot noodles for the appeal of pasta salad with the freshness of raw vegetables.

You will need a spiralizer to make the beet and carrot noodles; if you don't have one, use precut store-bought vegetable noodles. You'll need about 12 ounces of each.

Generously sized vegetables spiralize more easily, so use beets that are at least 1½ inches in diameter and carrots that are at least ¾ inch across at the thinnest end and 1½ inches across at the thickest end.

You can use smooth or chunky peanut butter in the dressing for this recipe.

If you can't find tahini, you can make your own (see page 7).

2 limes
Fresh ginger
2 garlic cloves
5 scallions
¼ cup peanut butter
3 tablespoons tahini
1 tablespoon soy sauce
1 tablespoon honey
½ teaspoon toasted sesame oil
Salt and pepper
1 pound beets
1 pound carrots
4 (3- to 4-ounce) chicken cutlets, ½ inch thick
1 tablespoon vegetable oil
Fresh cilantro

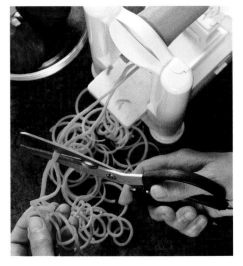

**1 Prep Ingredients** Squeeze 2 tablespoons lime juice from 1 lime and cut remaining lime into wedges. Peel and grate 1 tablespoon ginger. Mince garlic. Slice scallions thin on bias.

**2 Make Dressing** Whisk peanut butter, tahini, soy sauce, honey, toasted sesame oil, lime juice, ginger, garlic, and ½ teaspoon salt in large bowl until well combined. Whisking constantly, add hot water, 1 tablespoon at a time (up to 6 tablespoons), until dressing has consistency of heavy cream.

**3 Prep and Spiralize Vegetables** Trim and peel beets and carrots. Using spiralizer, cut into ⅛-inch-thick noodles, cutting noodles into 6- to 8-inch lengths with kitchen shears as you spiralize (about every 2 to 3 revolutions).

**4** **Dress Salad** Add beet and carrot noodles and scallions to dressing and toss well to combine.

**5** **Cook Chicken** Trim chicken, pat dry with paper towels, and season with salt and pepper. Heat vegetable oil in 12-inch nonstick skillet over medium-high heat until just smoking. Add chicken and cook until golden brown and registers 160 degrees, about 3 minutes per side. Transfer chicken to cutting board, tent with aluminum foil, and let rest.

**6** **Finish Salad** While chicken rests, pick ¼ cup cilantro leaves. Divide noodles among individual serving dishes. Slice chicken thin and arrange over salads. Sprinkle with cilantro and serve with lime wedges.

# Chicken Salad with Whole-Grain Mustard Vinaigrette

serves 4; total time 45 minutes

## notes for the cook

Fresh lemon juice brightens this light and summery version of chicken salad, while sugar snap peas and red grapes add a juicy crunch.

Whole-grain mustard helps make a thick, hearty vinaigrette for this salad. The whole seeds also add subtle, tangy mustard flavor and a pleasant pop of texture.

You can substitute more delicate Bibb lettuce for the red leaf lettuce if you prefer.

Salt and pepper
4 (6- to 8-ounce) boneless, skinless chicken breasts
1 small head red leaf lettuce (8 ounces)
8 ounces sugar snap peas
1 cup red grapes
Fresh chives
1 lemon
⅓ cup whole-grain mustard
3 tablespoons extra-virgin olive oil

**1 Poach Chicken** Dissolve ¼ cup salt in 4 quarts cold water in Dutch oven. Trim chicken, cover with plastic wrap, and pound thick ends until ¾ inch thick. Arrange breasts in steamer basket. Submerge basket in salt water. Heat pot over medium heat until water registers 175 degrees, about 20 minutes. Turn off heat, cover pot, and let sit until chicken registers 160 degrees, 15 to 20 minutes. Transfer chicken to large plate; set aside.

**2 Prep Fruit and Vegetables** While chicken poaches, tear lettuce into bite-size pieces. Remove strings from snap peas and halve crosswise on bias. Cut grapes in half. Mince 3 tablespoons chives.

**3 Make Dressing** Squeeze 3 tablespoons lemon juice into large bowl. Whisk in mustard, ¼ teaspoon pepper, and ⅛ teaspoon salt. Whisking constantly, slowly drizzle in oil until incorporated.

**4 Shred and Dress Chicken** Once chicken is cool enough to handle, shred into bite-size pieces using 2 forks. Measure ¼ cup of vinaigrette and toss with chicken until well coated.

**5 Dress Salad** Add lettuce, snap peas, grapes, and chives to remaining vinaigrette in bowl and toss until combined. Season with salt and pepper to taste.

**6 Finish Salad** Divide salad among individual serving dishes and top with chicken. Serve.

# Grilled Thai Beef Salad

serves 4; total time 45 minutes

## notes for the cook

Our version of this Thai dish known as *nam tok* captures the cuisine's five signature flavors—hot, sour, salty, sweet, and bitter.

Note that you'll need 1½ cups each of mint and cilantro, so shop accordingly.

If fresh Thai chiles are unavailable, substitute half of a serrano chile.

Don't skip the toasted rice; it's integral to the texture and flavor of the dish. Toasted rice powder (*kao kua*) can also be found in many Asian markets; if you have that on hand, substitute 1 tablespoon for the ground toasted rice.

A mini food processor or mortar and pestle can be used to grind the toasted rice in step 2 if you don't have a spice grinder.

1 teaspoon paprika
1 teaspoon cayenne pepper
1 tablespoon white rice
1 English cucumber
4 shallots
Fresh mint
Fresh cilantro
1 Thai chile
1 (1½-pound) flank steak
Salt and white pepper
2 limes
2 tablespoons fish sauce
½ teaspoon sugar

**1 Heat Grill** Turn all burners to high, cover, and heat grill until hot, about 15 minutes. Leave primary burner on high and turn off other burner(s).

**2 Toast Spices and Rice** While grill heats, toast paprika and cayenne in 8-inch skillet over medium heat, shaking pan, until fragrant, about 1 minute; transfer to small bowl. Wipe skillet clean, then return to medium-high heat; add rice and toast, stirring constantly, until deep golden brown, about 5 minutes. Transfer to small bowl and let cool for 5 minutes. Grind rice with spice grinder until it resembles fine meal, 10 to 30 seconds.

**3 Prep Vegetables** Slice cucumber ¼ inch thick on bias. Slice shallots thin. Tear 1½ cups mint leaves into bite-size pieces. Pick 1½ cups cilantro leaves. Stem and seed chile, then slice thin into rounds.

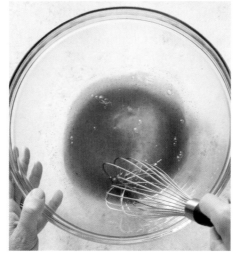

**4** **Season and Grill Steak** Trim steak, pat dry with paper towels, and season with salt and pepper. Clean and oil cooking grate. Place steak on hotter side of grill, cover, and cook until beads of moisture appear on edges of meat, 5 to 6 minutes. Flip steak and continue to cook until meat registers 120 to 125 degrees (for medium-rare), about 5 minutes. Transfer to carving board, tent with aluminum foil, and let rest.

**5** **Make Dressing** While steak rests, squeeze 3 tablespoons lime juice into large bowl. Whisk in 2 tablespoons water, fish sauce, sugar, and ¼ teaspoon toasted paprika mixture until incorporated.

**6** **Finish Salad** Line large platter with cucumber slices. Slice steak thin against grain on bias into ¼-inch-thick slices. Transfer sliced steak to bowl with fish sauce mixture; add shallots, mint, cilantro, chile, and half of rice powder; and toss to combine. Arrange steak mixture over cucumber-lined platter. Serve, passing remaining rice powder and toasted paprika mixture separately.

# Wedge Salad with Steak Tips

serves 4; total time 45 minutes

## notes for the cook

The pairing of crunchy iceberg lettuce, tangy blue cheese, and crispy bacon is what makes this classic salad so popular. To turn it into dinner, we added meaty steak tips in a nod to its steakhouse roots.

We prefer Stilton in this salad, but you can substitute any high-quality blue cheese.

Sirloin steak tips, also known as flap meat, can be sold as whole steaks, cubes, and strips. To ensure uniform pieces, we prefer to purchase whole steaks and cut them ourselves.

This salad is best when the iceberg wedges are cold, so leave the lettuce in the fridge until the steak is done cooking.

4 slices bacon
3 ounces Stilton cheese
1 garlic clove
¾ cup plain yogurt
1 teaspoon red wine vinegar
Salt and pepper
1½ pounds sirloin steak tips
1 head iceberg lettuce (9 ounces)
10 ounces cherry tomatoes
Fresh chives

**1 Cook Bacon** Cut bacon into ½-inch pieces. Cook bacon in 12-inch skillet over medium heat, stirring frequently, until crisp and fat is well rendered, 6 to 8 minutes. Transfer bacon to paper towel–lined plate and remove skillet from heat (do not wipe out skillet).

**2 Make Dressing** Crumble Stilton (¾ cup). Mince garlic. Whisk yogurt, vinegar, ½ cup Stilton, garlic, ¼ teaspoon salt, and ¼ teaspoon pepper together in bowl to combine.

**3 Prep Steak** Trim steak and cut into 2-inch pieces. Pat steak dry with paper towels and season with salt and pepper.

**Cook Steak** Heat bacon fat in skillet over medium-high heat until just smoking. Add steak and cook until well browned on all sides and meat registers 125 degrees (for medium-rare), about 7 minutes. Transfer to plate, tent with aluminum foil, and let rest.

**Prep Salad** While steak rests, cut lettuce into 8 wedges and remove cores. Halve tomatoes and mince 2 tablespoons chives.

**Finish Salad** Arrange lettuce wedges and steak tips on individual serving dishes and drizzle with dressing. Top with tomatoes, bacon, and remaining ¼ cup Stilton. Sprinkle with chives and season with salt and pepper to taste. Serve.

# Arugula Salad with Pears, Prosciutto, and Chickpeas

serves 4; total time 30 minutes

## notes for the cook

Peppery arugula paired with an array of sweet and salty ingredients makes the perfect light but filling dinner salad.

Toasting the almonds helps release their essential oils and makes them more flavorful. This is a great trick for any type of nut you're adding to a salad (or pretty much any other dish).

In this salad and many of the others in this chapter, we mix the dressing right in the serving bowl and then add the rest of the ingredients to save on dishes and streamline the process of dressing the salad.

An apple can be substituted for the pear, if you prefer.

½ cup sliced almonds
2 ounces thinly sliced prosciutto
¼ cup extra-virgin olive oil
1 Bosc or Bartlett pear
1 (15-ounce) can chickpeas
2 ounces Parmesan cheese
3 tablespoons balsamic vinegar
1 tablespoon honey
Salt and pepper
8 ounces (8 cups) baby arugula

**1** **Toast Nuts** Toast almonds in 10-inch nonstick skillet over medium heat, shaking pan occasionally, until golden and fragrant, 3 to 5 minutes; transfer to small bowl to cool.

**2** **Cook Prosciutto** Cut prosciutto slices crosswise into ¼-inch-wide ribbons. Heat 1 tablespoon oil in now-empty skillet over medium heat until shimmering. Add prosciutto and cook, stirring frequently, until crisp, about 7 minutes. Using slotted spoon, transfer prosciutto to paper towel–lined plate and set aside.

**3** **Prep Pear and Chickpeas** Halve and core pear, then slice thin. Drain and rinse chickpeas.

4 **Prep Parmesan** Shave Parmesan into thin strips using vegetable peeler.

5 **Make Dressing** Whisk vinegar, honey, and remaining 3 tablespoons oil together in large bowl until incorporated.

6 **Finish Salad** Add pear, chickpeas, and arugula to vinaigrette and toss to combine. Season with salt and pepper to taste. Divide salad among individual serving dishes. Top with prosciutto, toasted almonds, and Parmesan. Serve.

# Arugula Salad with Steak Tips and Gorgonzola

serves 4; total time 30 minutes

## notes for the cook

Dressing spicy arugula with a simple vinaigrette and fortifying it with tender steak tips makes for a quick and elegant dinner salad.

Sirloin steak tips, also known as flap meat, can be sold as whole steaks, cubes, and strips. To ensure uniform pieces, we prefer to purchase whole steaks and cut them ourselves.

You can substitute any blue cheese for the Gorgonzola in this recipe.

Make sure to slice the cooked steak against the grain—perpendicular to the fibers in the meat—to make the steak tender and easier to chew.

1½ pounds sirloin steak tips
Salt and pepper
6 tablespoons extra-virgin olive oil
1 shallot
2 garlic cloves
2 tablespoons cider vinegar
1 teaspoon Dijon mustard
1 teaspoon honey
6 ounces Gorgonzola cheese
10 ounces (10 cups) baby arugula

**1 Prep Steak** Trim steak and cut into 3-inch pieces. Pat dry with paper towels and season with salt and pepper.

**2 Cook Steak** Heat 2 tablespoons oil in 12-inch skillet over medium-high heat until just smoking. Cook steak until well browned on all sides and meat registers 125 degrees (for medium-rare), 8 to 10 minutes. Transfer to plate, tent with aluminum foil, and let rest.

**3 Make Dressing** While steak rests, mince shallot and garlic and transfer to large bowl. Add vinegar, mustard, honey, ¼ teaspoon salt, and ¼ teaspoon pepper. Whisking constantly, slowly drizzle in remaining ¼ cup oil until incorporated.

**4** **Crumble Gorgonzola**
Crumble Gorgonzola into small pieces (1½ cups).

**5** **Make Salad** Add arugula and crumbled Gorgonzola to vinaigrette and toss to combine. Season with salt and pepper to taste.

**6** **Slice Steak and Finish Salad**
Cut steak against grain into ¼-inch-thick slices. Divide salad among individual serving dishes and top with sliced steak. Serve.

# Salmon, Avocado, Grapefruit, and Watercress Salad

serves 4; total time 45 minutes

## notes for the cook

Peppery watercress balances the sweetness of the grapefruit and the richness of the avocado and salmon in this light, bright dinner salad.

If you buy bunched watercress, be sure to wash it thoroughly. You'll also need to trim the tough stems. It's fine to leave some thinner stems near the leaves intact.

Starting the salmon on a preheated baking sheet creates an initial blast of heat that firms up the exterior. The fish then gently cooks through in a low oven.

The doneness notes in step 2 are for farmed salmon; if you're using leaner wild-caught salmon, cook it until the center of the fillet registers 120 degrees for best results.

2 (8-ounce) skin-on salmon fillets

3 tablespoons plus 1 teaspoon extra-virgin olive oil

Salt and pepper

2 grapefruits

1 small shallot

1 teaspoon white wine vinegar

1 teaspoon Dijon mustard

¼ cup skinned hazelnuts

4 ounces (4 cups) watercress

1 avocado

Fresh mint

**1 Prep Salmon** Adjust oven rack to lowest position, place aluminum foil–lined rimmed baking sheet on rack, and heat oven to 500 degrees. Pat salmon dry with paper towels, rub with 1 teaspoon oil, and season with salt and pepper.

**2 Roast Salmon** Once oven reaches 500 degrees, reduce oven temperature to 275 degrees. Remove sheet from oven and carefully place salmon, skin side down, on hot sheet. Roast until center is still translucent when checked with tip of paring knife and registers 125 degrees (for medium-rare), 9 to 13 minutes. Let salmon cool on sheet to room temperature, about 20 minutes.

**3 Prep Grapefruits** While salmon cools, cut away peel and pith from grapefruits. Holding fruit over bowl, use paring knife to slice between membranes to release segments. Measure out 2 tablespoons grapefruit juice and transfer to separate bowl.

**4** **Make Dressing** Mince shallot. Whisk vinegar, mustard, shallot, and ½ teaspoon salt into grapefruit juice. Whisking constantly, slowly drizzle in remaining 3 tablespoons oil until incorporated.

**5** **Toast Nuts and Prep Salad Ingredients** Toast hazelnuts in 10-inch skillet over medium heat, shaking pan occasionally, until golden and fragrant, 3 to 5 minutes; transfer to small bowl to cool, then chop cooled nuts. Tear watercress into bite-size pieces. Halve avocado, remove pit, and cut into ¼-inch-thick slices. Coarsely chop ¼ cup mint.

**6** **Flake Salmon and Finish Salad** Arrange watercress in even layer on platter. Using 2 forks, flake salmon into large 2-inch pieces. Arrange salmon pieces, grapefruit segments, and avocado on top of watercress. Drizzle dressing over top, then sprinkle with mint and hazelnuts. Serve.

# Smoked Salmon Niçoise Salad

serves 4; total time 1 hour

## notes for the cook

This take on the classic French *salade niçoise* swaps out the usual tuna for flavor-packed smoked salmon but keeps the traditional hard-cooked eggs, green beans, potatoes, and olives.

Starting the potatoes first and adding the green beans later ensures that both vegetables finish cooking at the same time.

For even cooking, use small red potatoes measuring 1 to 2 inches in diameter.

If you don't have a steamer basket, use a spoon or tongs to gently place the eggs directly in the boiling water.

4 large eggs
1 pound small red potatoes
8 ounces green beans
Salt and pepper
Fresh dill
½ cup pitted kalamata olives
1 lemon
⅔ cup sour cream
10 ounces (10 cups) mesclun
8 ounces sliced smoked salmon

**1 Hard-Cook Eggs** Bring 2 quarts water to boil in large saucepan over medium-high heat. Meanwhile, bring 1 inch water to rolling boil in medium saucepan over high heat. Place eggs in steamer basket and transfer to medium saucepan. Cover, reduce heat to medium-low, and cook eggs for 13 minutes.

**2 Prep Vegetables** While eggs are cooking, combine 2 cups ice cubes and 2 cups cold water in bowl. Cut potatoes in half (do not peel), and trim green beans. When eggs are finished cooking, transfer them to ice bath; let sit for 15 minutes.

**3 Cook Vegetables** Add potatoes and 1½ tablespoons salt to large saucepan of boiling water, return to boil, and cook for 10 minutes. Add green beans and continue to cook until both vegetables are tender, about 4 minutes. Drain vegetables well and set aside to cool slightly.

4 **Prep Remaining Ingredients** While vegetables cool, chop 1 tablespoon dill. Cut olives in half. Peel and halve cooled hard-cooked eggs.

5 **Make Dressing** Squeeze 2 tablespoons lemon juice into bowl. Whisk in 2 tablespoons water, sour cream, dill, ¼ teaspoon salt, and ⅛ teaspoon pepper until incorporated.

6 **Finish Salad** Toss mesclun and ¼ cup dressing together in large bowl. Divide dressed mesclun among individual serving dishes. Top with potatoes, green beans, eggs, olives, and salmon. Drizzle salads with remaining dressing. Serve.

# Mediterranean Couscous Salad with Smoked Trout

serves 4 to 6; total time 30 minutes

## notes for the cook

The tangy vinaigrette on this couscous salad is a refreshing pairing with the smoky richness of the smoked trout.

We use brine from the pepperoncini in our dressing to deepen the flavors of the salad and also to take advantage of an ingredient that often goes to waste.

Tossing the cooked couscous with the dressing while it's still warm helps it absorb the dressing as it cools in the refrigerator.

Some smoked trout comes with pinbones in it and some does not. Make sure to check your fish for pinbones before flaking it into pieces in step 5.

Note that you'll need ½ cup of parsley, so shop accordingly.

1½ cups couscous

Salt and pepper

1 cup pepperoncini, plus its brine

1 garlic clove

⅓ cup extra-virgin olive oil

8 ounces cherry tomatoes

Fresh parsley

3 scallions

1 lemon

8 ounces smoked trout

**1** **Cook Couscous** Bring 2 cups water to boil in medium saucepan. Remove pot from heat. Stir in couscous and ¾ teaspoon salt. Cover and let sit for 10 minutes. Fluff couscous with fork.

**2** **Make Dressing** While couscous cooks, measure out 3 tablespoons pepperoncini brine. Mince garlic. Whisk oil, brine, and garlic together in large bowl.

**3** **Dress Couscous** Transfer couscous to bowl with dressing and toss to combine. Refrigerate couscous mixture until room temperature, about 10 minutes.

**4** **Prep Vegetables and Herbs**
While couscous cools, halve cherry tomatoes. Pick ½ cup parsley leaves. Slice scallions thin. Slice lemon into wedges. Stem pepperoncini and slice thin into rings.

**5** **Prep Smoked Trout** Remove skin (and pinbones, if necessary) from trout. Using 2 forks, flake into bite-size pieces.

**6** **Finish Salad** Add cherry tomatoes, parsley, scallions, and pepperoncini rings to cooled couscous and gently toss to combine. Season with salt and pepper to taste, and drizzle with extra oil to taste. Divide salad among individual serving dishes. Top with smoked trout and serve with lemon wedges.

# Fennel and Bibb Salad with Scallops and Hazelnuts
serves 4; total time 45 minutes

## notes for the cook

Fresh scallops cook in minutes and add substance to this simple, elegant salad.

Using a hot skillet and just-smoking oil are the keys to perfectly seared scallops.

We recommend buying "dry" scallops, which don't have chemical additives and taste better than "wet" scallops, which do. Dry scallops will look ivory or pinkish; wet scallops are bright white.

Hazelnuts bring out the natural sweet nuttiness of the scallops, and tarragon emphasizes the anise flavor of the fennel.

Using lemon zest along with the juice amps up flavor without adding too much acidity.

You can substitute Boston lettuce for the Bibb lettuce.

¼ cup skinned hazelnuts

2 heads Bibb lettuce (1 pound)

1 fennel bulb

4 radishes

Fresh tarragon

1 small shallot

1 lemon

1 teaspoon Dijon mustard

Salt and pepper

7 tablespoons extra-virgin olive oil

1½ pounds large sea scallops

**1 Toast Nuts** Toast hazelnuts in 12-inch nonstick skillet over medium heat, stirring frequently, until golden and fragrant, 3 to 5 minutes; transfer to small bowl to cool, then chop cooled nuts.

**2 Prep Vegetables** Tear lettuce into bite-size pieces. Mince 1 tablespoon fennel fronds. Discard stalks, halve bulb, remove core, and slice thin. Trim radishes and slice thin. Chop 2 tablespoons tarragon.

**3 Make Dressing** Mince shallot. Grate ½ teaspoon lemon zest and squeeze 1½ tablespoons juice into large bowl. Whisk in mustard, shallot, ¼ teaspoon salt, and ¼ teaspoon pepper until combined. Whisking constantly, slowly drizzle in 5 tablespoons oil until incorporated.

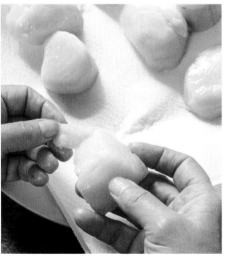

**4 Prep Scallops** Remove tendons from scallops. Pat dry with paper towels and season with salt and pepper.

**5 Sear Scallops** Heat 1 tablespoon oil in now-empty skillet over high heat until just smoking. Add half of scallops in single layer and cook, without moving, until well browned, 1½ to 2 minutes. Flip and cook until sides are firm and centers are opaque, 30 to 90 seconds (remove scallops as they finish cooking). Transfer scallops to plate and tent with aluminum foil. Wipe skillet clean and repeat with remaining oil and scallops.

**6 Finish Salad** Add lettuce, fennel, and radishes to vinaigrette and toss to combine. Season with salt and pepper to taste. Divide salad among individual serving dishes. Top with scallops and sprinkle with hazelnuts, tarragon, and fennel fronds. Serve.

# Shrimp and Wilted Spinach Salad with Bacon-Pecan Vinaigrette

serves 4; total time 45 minutes

## notes for the cook

A warm bacon vinaigrette provides just enough heat to gently wilt the spinach in this shrimp-topped salad.

We toast pecans in the rendered bacon fat while the bacon cooks, a shortcut which also reinforces the flavor profile of the salad.

Letting the cooked shrimp sit in a few tablespoons of the vinaigrette base after they come off the heat helps infuse them with deep flavor.

If you're using frozen shrimp, make sure to thaw them before starting the recipe.

Serve this salad immediately to make sure the spinach and shrimp don't get cold.

2 heads Belgian endive (8 ounces)
10 ounces (10 cups) baby spinach
1 shallot
1 Fuji or Honeycrisp apple
6 tablespoons red wine vinegar
2 tablespoons whole-grain mustard
1½ teaspoons sugar
Salt and pepper
½ cup pecans
6 slices bacon
1 pound extra-large shrimp (21 to 25 per pound)
1 tablespoon vegetable oil

**1 Prep Fruit and Vegetables** Halve and core endive, then cut into ½-inch strips; place in large bowl along with spinach. Halve shallot through root end and slice thin. Halve and core apple, then slice thin.

**2 Make Dressing and Marinate Shallot** Whisk vinegar, mustard, sugar, and ¼ teaspoon salt together in bowl. Measure out 2 tablespoons vinegar mixture and set aside in medium bowl. Add shallot to remaining vinegar mixture, cover, and microwave until steaming, 30 to 60 seconds. Stir briefly to submerge shallot; uncover and set aside to cool.

**3 Prep Pecans, Bacon, and Shrimp** Chop pecans coarse. Cut bacon into ½-inch pieces. Peel and devein shrimp. Pat shrimp dry with paper towels and season with ¼ teaspoon salt and ⅛ teaspoon pepper.

**4** **Sauté Shrimp** Heat oil in 12-inch nonstick skillet over high heat until just smoking. Add shrimp to skillet in single layer and cook, without stirring, until spotty brown and edges turn pink on first side, about 1 minute. Off heat, flip shrimp and let sit until opaque throughout, about 30 seconds. Transfer shrimp to bowl with reserved 2 tablespoons vinegar mixture and cover to keep warm.

**5** **Cook Bacon and Pecans** Cook bacon and pecans in now-empty skillet over medium heat, stirring frequently, until bacon is crisp and well rendered, 8 to 10 minutes.

**6** **Finish Salad** Off heat, whisk shallot mixture into skillet until combined. Pour warm vinaigrette over spinach and endive and toss until spinach is wilted slightly. Add apple and gently toss to combine. Divide salad among individual serving dishes. Using slotted spoon, top with shrimp. Season with salt and pepper to taste. Serve immediately.

# Shrimp and White Bean Salad with Garlic Toasts

serves 4; total time 45 minutes

## notes for the cook

Quick-cooking shrimp are a great ingredient to use for fast weeknight dinners. In this recipe, the shrimp are perfectly cooked—seared on the outside and moist on the inside—in less than 2 minutes. Keeping frozen shrimp in your freezer is a great shortcut to a quick meal.

If you're using frozen shrimp, make sure to thaw them before starting the recipe.

The sweetness of mild, creamy cannellini beans is a perfect foil to the briny shrimp in this salad.

Quick homemade garlic toasts complement the simple flavors of this dinner.

1 red bell pepper
1 small red onion
3 garlic cloves
2 (15-ounce) cans cannellini beans
1 lemon
1 pound extra-large shrimp (21 to 25 per pound)
Salt and pepper
1 loaf rustic bread
5 tablespoons extra-virgin olive oil
¼ teaspoon red pepper flakes
2 ounces (2 cups) baby arugula

**1 Prep Vegetables and Beans** Adjust oven rack 6 inches from broiler element and heat broiler. Stem and seed bell pepper, then chop fine. Chop onion fine and mince 2 garlic cloves. Drain and rinse cannellini beans. Squeeze 2 tablespoons lemon juice.

**2 Prep Shrimp** Peel and devein shrimp. Pat shrimp dry with paper towels and season with ¼ teaspoon salt and ⅛ teaspoon pepper.

**3 Toast Bread** Slice four ¾-inch-thick slices of bread and spread out evenly over rimmed baking sheet. Broil, flipping as needed, until well toasted on both sides, about 4 minutes. Peel remaining 1 garlic clove and rub 1 side of each toast with garlic, then drizzle with 1 tablespoon oil and season with salt and pepper to taste.

4 **Cook Vegetables and Beans** Heat 3 tablespoons oil in 12-inch nonstick skillet over medium heat until shimmering. Add bell pepper, onion, and ¼ teaspoon salt. Cook until softened, about 5 minutes. Stir in pepper flakes and minced garlic. Cook until fragrant, about 30 seconds. Add beans and ¼ cup water and cook until heated through, about 5 minutes. Transfer mixture to serving bowl and cover to keep warm.

5 **Sauté Shrimp** Wipe skillet clean with paper towels. Heat remaining 1 tablespoon oil in now-empty skillet over high heat until just smoking. Add shrimp to skillet in single layer and cook, without stirring, until spotty brown and edges turn pink on first side, about 1 minute. Off heat, flip shrimp and let sit until opaque throughout, about 30 seconds.

6 **Finish Salad** Add shrimp, arugula, and lemon juice to beans and gently toss to combine. Season with salt and pepper to taste, and drizzle with extra oil to taste. Serve with garlic toasts.

# Farro Salad with Sugar Snap Peas and White Beans

serves 4 to 6; total time 1 hour

## notes for the cook

This hearty, fresh grain salad makes a perfect light dinner.

Cooking the nutty farro in plenty of water and then draining it like pasta speeds up the cooking time and yields perfectly tender results with no presoak required.

We found a wide range of cooking times among various brands of farro, so start checking for doneness after 10 minutes.

We prefer the flavor and texture of whole-grain farro; pearled farro can be used, but the texture may be softer. Do not use quick-cooking farro in this recipe.

Convenient canned beans are an easy way to turn a grain salad into a substantial meal.

12 ounces sugar snap peas
Salt and pepper
1½ cups whole farro
6 ounces cherry tomatoes
⅓ cup pitted kalamata olives
Fresh dill
1 (15-ounce) can cannellini beans
1 shallot
1 lemon
1 teaspoon Dijon mustard
3 tablespoons extra-virgin olive oil

**1 Cook Snap Peas** Bring 4 quarts water to boil in large pot. Remove strings from snap peas and cut in half crosswise. Add snap peas and 1 tablespoon salt to boiling water and cook until crisp-tender, about 2 minutes. Using slotted spoon, transfer snap peas to large plate and let cool completely.

**2 Cook Farro** While snap peas cool, add farro to water, return to boil, and cook until grains are tender with slight chew, 15 to 30 minutes.

**3 Prep Vegetables** While farro cooks, halve cherry tomatoes and chop olives. Chop 2 tablespoons dill. Drain and rinse beans.

4 **Cool Farro** Drain farro well, then spread on rimmed baking sheet, and let cool completely, about 15 minutes.

5 **Make Dressing** While farro cools, mince 2 tablespoons shallot. Squeeze 2 tablespoons lemon juice into large bowl. Whisk in mustard, shallot, ¼ teaspoon salt, and ¼ teaspoon pepper until combined. Whisking constantly, slowly drizzle in oil until incorporated.

6 **Finish Salad** Add cooled snap peas, cooled farro, tomatoes, olives, dill, and beans to bowl with dressing and toss to combine. Season with salt and pepper to taste. Serve.

# Quinoa Taco Salad

serves 4; total time 1 hour

## notes for the cook

This is taco salad for the 21st century. We've replaced the usual beef with quinoa, which gets simmered in a flavorful broth doctored with chipotle chiles in adobo, tomato paste, and cumin to give it deep, spiced flavor.

We like the convenience of prewashed quinoa; rinsing removes the quinoa's bitter protective coating (called saponin). If you buy unwashed quinoa, rinse it and then spread it out on a clean dish towel to dry for 15 minutes.

Escarole is a leafy green with a mildly bitter flavor that makes a perfect base for our rich quinoa, black beans, and cheese.

¾ cup prewashed white quinoa

Canned chipotle chile in adobo sauce

3 tablespoons extra-virgin olive oil

2 teaspoons tomato paste

½ teaspoon ground cumin

1 cup chicken or vegetable broth

1 lime

Salt and pepper

1 head escarole (1 pound)

Fresh cilantro

8 ounces cherry tomatoes

1 avocado

1 (15-ounce) can black beans

2 ounces queso fresco

**1 Toast Quinoa** Toast quinoa in medium saucepan over medium-high heat, stirring frequently, until quinoa is very fragrant and makes continuous popping sound, 5 to 7 minutes; transfer to bowl.

**2 Cook Quinoa** Mince 2 teaspoons chipotle. Heat 1 tablespoon oil in now-empty saucepan over medium heat until shimmering. Stir in tomato paste, cumin, and chipotle and cook until fragrant, about 30 seconds. Stir in broth and toasted quinoa, increase heat to medium-high, and bring to simmer. Cover, reduce heat to low, and simmer until quinoa is tender and liquid has been absorbed, 18 to 22 minutes, stirring once halfway through cooking.

**3 Make Dressing** While quinoa cooks, squeeze 2 tablespoons lime juice into large bowl. Whisk in remaining 2 tablespoons oil, ¼ teaspoon salt, and ¼ teaspoon pepper until incorporated.

4 **Cool Quinoa** Remove pan from heat and let sit, covered, for 10 minutes. Spread quinoa onto rimmed baking sheet and let cool for 20 minutes.

5 **Prep Salad** While quinoa cools, trim escarole and slice thin. Chop ½ cup cilantro. Quarter tomatoes. Halve avocado, remove pit, and cut into ½-inch pieces. Drain and rinse beans. Crumble queso fresco (½ cup).

6 **Finish Salad** Add escarole and ¼ cup cilantro to dressing and toss to combine. Gently fold in tomatoes, avocado, and beans. Top with quinoa, queso fresco, and remaining ¼ cup cilantro. Serve.

# Bistro Salad with Fried Egg

serves 4; total time 30 minutes

## notes for the cook

Thick-cut bacon, sautéed mushrooms, and a fried egg add heft to greens in this classic French salad.

The eggs' runny yolks coat the lettuce and mingle with the other ingredients to enrich and balance the acidic red wine vinaigrette.

If you like your fried eggs less runny, use the following resting times in step 5: Let sit 45 to 60 seconds for soft but set yolks, or about 2 minutes for medium-set yolks.

Sautéing the mushrooms in reserved bacon fat helps deepen the flavors of the dish.

You can substitute 8 cups of mixed greens for the frisée and romaine, if you like.

1 small shallot

8 ounces cremini mushrooms

1 head frisée (6 ounces)

1 romaine lettuce heart (6 ounces)

2 tablespoons red wine vinegar

1½ teaspoons Dijon mustard

Salt and pepper

3 tablespoons extra-virgin olive oil

6 slices thick-cut bacon

4 large eggs

**1 Prep Vegetables** Mince shallot. Trim mushrooms and halve if small or quarter if large. Cut frisée and romaine into 1-inch pieces.

**2 Make Dressing** Whisk vinegar, mustard, shallot, ⅛ teaspoon salt, and ⅛ teaspoon pepper together in large bowl. Whisking constantly, slowly drizzle in oil until incorporated.

**3 Cook Bacon** Cut bacon into 1-inch pieces. Cook in 12-inch nonstick skillet over medium heat until crisp, about 8 minutes. Using slotted spoon, transfer bacon to paper towel–lined plate. Pour off and reserve 5 teaspoons fat from skillet; discard any remaining fat.

**4** **Sauté Mushrooms** Add 1 tablespoon reserved bacon fat back to skillet and heat over medium-high heat until shimmering. Add mushrooms and ¼ teaspoon salt and cook, stirring occasionally, until liquid has released, about 3 minutes. Increase heat to high and continue to cook until liquid has evaporated and mushrooms begin to brown, about 5 minutes. Transfer mushrooms to bowl and cover to keep warm.

**5** **Fry Eggs** Crack eggs into 2 small bowls (2 eggs per bowl) and season with salt and pepper. Add remaining 2 teaspoons reserved fat to now-empty skillet and heat over medium-high heat until shimmering. Pour 1 bowl of eggs in 1 side of pan and second bowl in other side. Cover and cook for 1 minute. Remove skillet from heat. Let sit, covered, 15 to 45 seconds for runny yolks (white around edge of yolk will be barely opaque).

**6** **Finish Salad** Toss frisée and romaine in bowl with dressing and season with salt and pepper to taste. Divide salad among individual serving dishes. Top with mushrooms, bacon, and fried eggs. Serve.

# Pita Bread Salad with Tomatoes, Cucumber, and Chickpeas (Fattoush)

serves 4; total time 45 minutes

## notes for the cook

This Middle Eastern salad combines fresh veggies with crisp pita chips and bright herbs. The addition of chickpeas brings it into dinner territory.

The success of fattoush depends on ripe, in-season tomatoes. Save this recipe for when you know you can get the real thing.

Serve this salad as soon as you're done making it so the pita doesn't get too soggy.

Don't fuss about evenly coating the pita with oil; the oil will spread during baking.

The baked and cooled pitas can be stored in a zipper-lock bag for 24 hours if you want to get a head start on this salad.

Note that you'll need ½ cup of mint, so shop accordingly.

2 (8-inch) pita breads
½ cup extra-virgin olive oil
Salt and pepper
1 garlic clove
2 lemons
1 (15-ounce) can chickpeas
1 pound tomatoes
1 English cucumber
1 cup baby arugula
Fresh mint
4 scallions

**1 Prep Pita** Adjust oven rack to middle position and heat oven to 375 degrees. Using kitchen shears, cut around perimeter of each pita and separate into 2 thin rounds. Cut each round in half. Place pitas, smooth side down, on wire rack set in rimmed baking sheet. Brush ¼ cup oil over surface of pitas. Season with salt and pepper to taste.

**2 Bake Pita** Bake until pitas are crisp and golden brown, 10 to 12 minutes. Set aside to cool.

**3 Make Dressing** While pitas bake, mince garlic. Grate ½ teaspoon lemon zest and squeeze ¼ cup juice into large bowl. Whisk in remaining ¼ cup oil, garlic, and ¼ teaspoon salt until incorporated.

**Marinate Chickpeas** Drain and rinse chickpeas and add to dressing. Let sit for 10 minutes.

**Prep Vegetables** While chickpeas marinate, core tomatoes and cut into ¾-inch pieces. Peel cucumber and slice into ⅛-inch-thick slices. Chop arugula coarse. Chop ½ cup mint. Slice scallions thin.

**Finish Salad** Add tomatoes, cucumber, arugula, mint, and scallions to bowl with dressing and chickpeas. Break pitas into ½-inch pieces and add to bowl with vegetables. Toss to combine all ingredients. Season with salt and pepper to taste. Serve immediately.

# Marinated Tofu and Vegetable Salad

serves 4; total time 30 minutes

## notes for the cook

This Asian-inspired salad combines a bright dressing with crunchy cabbage, snow peas, and bell pepper, plus a hefty dose of protein from quick-marinated tofu.

Even a short marinade can do wonders for raw tofu. Here, our Sriracha-based salad dressing does double-duty as a marinade, adding a touch of heat and tons of flavor.

Firm tofu is tender and supple when eaten raw, but still sturdy. Do not substitute other varieties in this recipe.

Apart from briefly toasting the sesame seeds, this recipe is entirely no-cook.

28 ounces firm tofu
¼ cup rice vinegar
2 tablespoons Sriracha sauce
2 teaspoons honey
Salt and pepper
3 tablespoons toasted sesame oil
2 tablespoons sesame seeds
½ small head napa cabbage (12 ounces)
6 ounces snow peas
1 red bell pepper
2 scallions

1 **Prep Tofu** Cut tofu into ¾-inch cubes. Gently press tofu cubes dry with paper towels.

2 **Make Dressing** Whisk vinegar, Sriracha, honey, oil, and ¼ teaspoon salt together in large bowl until incorporated.

3 **Marinate Tofu** Gently toss tofu in dressing until evenly coated, then cover and refrigerate for 20 minutes.

**4 Toast Sesame Seeds** While tofu marinates, toast sesame seeds in 8-inch skillet over medium heat, shaking pan occasionally, until golden and fragrant, 3 to 5 minutes. Set aside to cool.

**5 Prep Vegetables** Remove core from cabbage, then slice thin. Remove strings from snow peas and cut in half crosswise. Stem and seed bell pepper, then cut into ½-inch pieces. Slice scallions thin on bias.

**6 Finish Salad** Add cabbage, snow peas, and bell pepper to bowl with tofu and gently toss to combine. Season with salt and pepper to taste, sprinkle with scallions and sesame seeds, and serve.

# Chopped Winter Salad with Butternut Squash

serves 4; total time 1 hour

## notes for the cook

To accentuate the flavor of the butternut squash in this hearty salad, we cut it into small pieces and toss the pieces with balsamic vinegar and oil before roasting them. The caramelized balsamic perfectly complements the earthy squash.

Texture is a big element of this salad. Chopped, toasted hazelnuts and raw apple add a crunchy contrast to the leafy greens while the roasted squash and feta cheese provide a richer, creamier element.

There's no need to peel the apple for this dish. We prefer Fuji, but any sweet apple will work here.

1 small (1½- to 2-pound) butternut squash

¼ cup extra-virgin olive oil

3 tablespoons balsamic vinegar

Salt and pepper

½ cup skinned hazelnuts

1 head radicchio (6 ounces)

1 romaine lettuce heart (6 ounces)

1 Fuji apple

1 tablespoon Dijon mustard

2 ounces feta cheese

**1 Prep Squash** Adjust oven rack to lowest position and heat oven to 450 degrees. Peel and seed squash, then cut into ½-inch cubes (about 4½ cups). Toss squash with 1 tablespoon oil, 1½ teaspoons vinegar, ¼ teaspoon salt, and ¼ teaspoon pepper.

**2 Roast Squash** Spread squash in single layer on aluminum foil–lined rimmed baking sheet and roast until well browned and tender, 20 to 25 minutes, stirring halfway through roasting. Remove squash from oven and let cool for 5 to 10 minutes.

**3 Toast Nuts** While squash cooks, toast hazelnuts in 10-inch skillet over medium heat, shaking pan occasionally, until golden and fragrant, 3 to 5 minutes; transfer to small bowl to cool, then chop cooled nuts.

4 **Prep Radicchio, Romaine, and Apple** Trim and core radicchio and slice into ½-inch-thick pieces. Cut romaine into 1-inch pieces. Halve and core apple, then cut into ½-inch cubes.

5 **Make Dressing** Whisk mustard, remaining 2½ tablespoons vinegar, ⅛ teaspoon salt, and ⅛ teaspoon pepper together in large bowl. Whisking constantly, slowly drizzle in remaining 3 tablespoons oil until incorporated.

6 **Finish Salad** Add radicchio, romaine, and apple to bowl with dressing and toss to combine. Divide salad among individual serving dishes. Top with squash and sprinkle with hazelnuts. Crumble feta (½ cup) over top. Season with salt and pepper to taste. Serve.

# Thai Chicken Soup

serves 4; total time 45 minutes

## notes for the cook

For a simple shortcut to a Thai flavor profile (avoiding a laundry list of hard-to-find ingredients), we turned to prepared Thai red curry paste, which delivers authentic flavors in a superconcentrated form.

If you prefer a soup with a bit more heat, add more red curry paste to taste.

If you want a soup with less fat, you can substitute light coconut milk for half or all of the regular coconut milk.

3 scallions

Fresh cilantro

1 medium sweet potato (12 ounces)

1½ pounds boneless, skinless chicken breasts

Salt and pepper

1 tablespoon vegetable oil

2 tablespoons red curry paste

4 cups chicken broth

4 teaspoons fish sauce

2 (14-ounce) cans coconut milk

2 limes

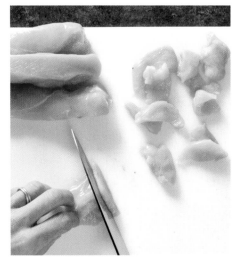

1 **Prep Vegetables** Mince scallion whites and slice scallion greens thin; keep whites and greens separate. Mince 6 tablespoons cilantro. Peel sweet potato, then quarter lengthwise and slice thin.

2 **Prep Chicken** Trim chicken and halve each breast lengthwise, then slice crosswise ¼ inch thick. Season with salt and pepper.

3 **Build Flavor Base** Heat oil in large saucepan over medium heat until shimmering. Add curry paste, scallion whites, and 3 tablespoons cilantro and cook until fragrant, about 1 minute.

**4** **Simmer Broth** Stir in broth, 2 teaspoons fish sauce, and coconut milk and bring to boil over high heat. Cover, reduce heat to low, and simmer for 5 minutes.

**5** **Cook Chicken and Sweet Potato** Increase heat to medium-high, add sweet potato and chicken, and cook until chicken is cooked through and potato is tender, about 5 minutes.

**6** **Juice Limes and Finish Soup** While chicken cooks, squeeze 3 tablespoons lime juice. Off heat, stir lime juice and remaining 2 teaspoons fish sauce into soup. Portion soup into individual serving bowls and sprinkle with scallion greens and remaining 3 tablespoons cilantro. Serve.

# Garlicky Chicken and Orzo Soup

serves 6; total time 1 hour

## notes for the cook

This elevated version of classic chicken and rice soup gets supercharged aromatic flavor from 12 full cloves of garlic.

To keep this soup fast, we substituted quick-cooking orzo for the usual white rice.

Cutting the chicken into small pieces and then cooking it right in the broth makes for a smooth, streamlined process.

A few handfuls of tender baby spinach added at the end of cooking give this soup a fresh finish.

You can mince the garlic by hand, with a garlic press, or by pulsing it in a food processor.

12 garlic cloves

2 carrots

1 onion

1 celery rib

Fresh thyme

2 tablespoons extra-virgin olive oil

Salt and pepper

6 cups chicken broth

Fresh parsley

1½ pounds boneless, skinless chicken breasts

½ cup orzo

4 ounces (4 cups) baby spinach

1 **Prep Vegetables** Mince garlic. Peel carrots and slice ¼ inch thick. Chop onion fine and mince celery. Mince 2 teaspoons thyme.

2 **Sauté Garlic and Vegetables** Heat oil and garlic in Dutch oven over medium-low heat, stirring occasionally, until garlic is light golden, about 3 minutes. Add carrots, onion, celery, and ¼ teaspoon salt; increase heat to medium; and cook, stirring occasionally, until vegetables are softened, 5 to 7 minutes.

3 **Add Thyme and Broth** Stir in thyme and cook until fragrant, about 30 seconds. Stir in broth, scraping up any browned bits, and bring to simmer.

**4 Prep Parsley and Chicken** While broth comes up to simmer, mince 2 tablespoons parsley. Trim chicken, cut into ¾-inch pieces, and season with salt and pepper.

**5 Cook Orzo and Chicken** Stir orzo into broth, return to simmer, cover, and cook over medium-low heat, adjusting heat as needed to maintain simmer, until orzo is just tender, about 6 minutes. Stir chicken into soup and cook, stirring occasionally, until chicken is cooked through and orzo is tender, 3 to 5 minutes.

**6 Add Spinach and Finish Soup** Stir in spinach and cook until spinach is wilted, 1 to 2 minutes. Off heat, stir in parsley and season with salt and pepper to taste. Serve.

# Chicken Tortilla Soup with Greens

serves 6; total time 1 hour

## notes for the cook

A flavorful broth, tender chicken, subtle heat, and crispy tortilla strips make this soup an easy crowd-pleaser.

Different brands of corn tortillas come in varying thicknesses; the cooking time for the tortilla strips may vary based on how thick yours are.

We give a range for the amount of adobo sauce that should be added in step 3 so that you can tweak the heat level to match your preference; the more sauce you use, the more heat in the soup.

8 (6-inch) corn tortillas

2 tablespoons vegetable oil

Salt

1 onion

Canned chipotle chile in adobo sauce

1 (14.5-ounce) can diced tomatoes

2 garlic cloves

12 ounces Swiss chard

1 avocado

Fresh cilantro

1½ pounds boneless, skinless chicken breasts

1 tablespoon tomato paste

8 cups chicken broth

**1 Make Tortilla Strips** Adjust oven rack to middle position and heat oven to 425 degrees. Cut tortillas into ½-inch-wide strips. Toss tortilla strips with 1 tablespoon oil and spread evenly on rimmed baking sheet. Bake, stirring occasionally, until strips are deep golden brown and crisped, 8 to 12 minutes. Season lightly with salt.

**2 Prep Ingredients** While tortilla strips bake, chop onion fine. Mince 2 teaspoons chipotle. Drain diced tomatoes. Mince garlic. Stem chard by cutting away leafy green portion from either side of stalk, then chop leaves coarse. Halve avocado, remove pit, and cut into ½-inch pieces. Mince 2 tablespoons cilantro. Trim chicken.

**3 Sauté Aromatics** Heat remaining 1 tablespoon oil in Dutch oven over medium heat until shimmering. Add onion and ¼ teaspoon salt and cook until just beginning to soften, about 3 minutes. Stir in tomato paste, minced chipotle chile plus 1 to 3 teaspoons adobo sauce, and drained tomatoes and cook until onion is softened and mixture has darkened, 5 to 7 minutes. Stir in garlic and cook until fragrant, about 30 seconds.

**4 Simmer Chicken and Chard**
Add broth and chicken to pot, cover, and bring to boil. Reduce heat to medium-low and simmer until chicken registers 160 degrees, 12 to 14 minutes. Transfer chicken to plate and let cool slightly. Stir chard leaves into broth and cook until chard is mostly tender, about 5 minutes.

**5 Shred Chicken** Once chicken is cool enough to handle, shred into bite-size pieces using 2 forks. Stir chicken into broth and cook until chicken is warmed through and chard is fully tender, about 5 minutes.

**6 Finish Soup** Season soup with salt to taste. Divide tortilla strips among individual serving bowls and ladle soup over strips. Serve with avocado and cilantro.

# Quick Turkey Chili
serves 4; total time 45 minutes

## notes for the cook

This no-fuss turkey chili has a hearty flavor profile built on pinto beans and aromatics (but no tomato products).

Pureeing half the beans in broth helps thicken this chili and gives it a silky texture.

We add the raw turkey straight to the chili so it stays in large chunks.

Be sure to use 93 percent lean ground turkey in this recipe, not 99 percent fat-free ground turkey breast. It has enough fat to flavor the chili and stay moist.

Ground chicken is a fine substitute for turkey in this chili.

1 red bell pepper
1 onion
3 garlic cloves
2 (15-ounce) cans pinto beans
1½ cups chicken broth
2 tablespoons vegetable oil
2 tablespoons chili powder
1 tablespoon ground cumin
1 teaspoon sugar
1 (4-ounce) can chopped green chiles
12 ounces ground turkey
Fresh cilantro
½ cup sour cream

**1** **Prep Vegetables** Stem and seed bell pepper then cut into 1-inch pieces. Chop onion fine. Mince garlic.

**2** **Process Portion of Beans** Drain and rinse beans. Process half of beans and ½ cup broth in food processor to coarse paste, about 10 seconds; set aside.

**3** **Sauté Vegetables** Heat oil in Dutch oven over medium-high heat until just smoking. Add bell pepper and onion cook until softened, about 5 minutes. Stir in chili powder, cumin, sugar, and garlic and cook until fragrant, about 1 minute.

**Add Chiles, Beans, and Broth**
Stir green chiles, pureed bean-broth mixture, remaining whole beans, and remaining 1 cup broth into pot.

**Add Turkey** Add turkey to pot in 2-inch chunks. Bring to boil, reduce heat to medium-low, and simmer, stirring occasionally, until chili is slightly thickened, 15 to 20 minutes.

**Finish Chili** While chili cooks, chop 3 tablespoons cilantro. Off heat, stir half of cilantro into chili. Serve, topping individual bowls with dollops of sour cream and sprinkling with remaining cilantro.

# Ginger Beef and Ramen Noodle Soup

serves 4; total time 45 minutes

## notes for the cook

In Japan, ramen noodle soup is serious business, with whole restaurants specializing in the dish. Our simplified take on this soup uses lime zest and ginger simmered in chicken broth to build a deeply flavored base.

To smash the ginger pieces, use the flat side of a chef's knife.

Slicing flank steak against the grain before serving (that is, perpendicular to the orientation of the muscle fibers) makes this relatively tough cut much more tender.

Supermarket ramen noodles work well here; just be sure to discard the dusty flavoring packets.

1 (1-pound) flank steak

Salt and pepper

1 (2-inch) piece ginger

1 lime

5 scallions

8 cups chicken broth

1 teaspoon vegetable oil

Fresh cilantro

4 (3-ounce) packages ramen noodles, seasoning packets discarded

¼ cup soy sauce

**1 Season Steak** Trim steak, pat dry with paper towels, and season with salt and pepper.

**2 Prep Aromatics** Peel ginger, cut in half lengthwise, and smash pieces. Peel three 2½-inch-long strips of zest from lime. Squeeze 1 tablespoon lime juice. Slice scallions thin.

**3 Build Broth** Bring broth, ginger, and lime zest to boil in Dutch oven over medium-high heat. Reduce heat to medium-low, cover, and simmer, stirring occasionally, for 10 minutes.

**4** **Cook Steak** Meanwhile, heat oil in 12-inch skillet over medium-high heat until just smoking. Add steak and cook until well browned and meat registers 120 to 125 degrees (for medium-rare), 6 to 8 minutes per side. Transfer to cutting board, tent with aluminum foil, and let rest.

**5** **Pick Cilantro and Slice Steak** While steak rests, pick ¼ cup cilantro leaves. Slice steak in half lengthwise, then slice thin against grain.

**6** **Cook Noodles and Finish Soup** Discard ginger and lime zest from broth. Add noodles and cook, stirring often, until tender, about 3 minutes. Stir in soy sauce, lime juice, and scallions. Ladle noodles and broth into individual serving bowls and top with steak and cilantro. Serve.

# Rioja-Style Potatoes with Chorizo and Peas

serves 4; total time 1 hour

## notes for the cook

This light, brothy stew gets its characteristic robust flavor from the chorizo sausage, a hard, cured, usually smoked pork sausage seasoned with paprika, garlic, and salt that is typical of the Rioja region of Spain.

Other varieties of hard, cured sausage (such as linguiça) can be substituted for the Spanish chorizo; we do not recommend using fresh chorizo. In this recipe, we particularly like the sweet (*dulce*) version.

To wash sliced leeks, put them in a bowl of cold water and rub the pieces together until the layers separate. Let the grit settle for 1 minute, then lift the leeks from the water and transfer them to a colander to drain.

If you prefer a milder dish, omit the red pepper flakes.

1 leek

1 red bell pepper

4 garlic cloves

8 ounces sweet Spanish-style chorizo sausage

2 tablespoons extra-virgin olive oil

Salt and pepper

1½ pounds Yukon Gold potatoes

1 teaspoon smoked sweet paprika

¼ teaspoon red pepper flakes

1 cup dry white wine

2 cups chicken broth

Fresh parsley

1 loaf crusty bread

1¼ cups frozen peas

**1 Prep Vegetables and Chorizo** Cut dark green leaves from leek and discard. Trim ends and halve leek lengthwise, then slice thin and wash thoroughly. Stem and seed bell pepper, then chop into ½-inch pieces. Mince garlic. Slice chorizo in half lengthwise, then slice crosswise ½ inch thick.

**2 Sauté Vegetables** Heat oil in Dutch oven over medium heat until shimmering. Stir in leek, bell pepper, and ¼ teaspoon salt. Cover, reduce heat to medium-low, and cook, stirring occasionally, until vegetables are softened, 5 to 7 minutes.

**3 Add Chorizo and Potatoes** While vegetables soften, peel potatoes and cut into ¾-inch pieces. Stir paprika, pepper flakes, garlic, and chorizo into pot and cook, uncovered, stirring frequently, until chorizo is softened and fragrant, about 2 minutes. Stir potatoes into chorizo mixture and cook over medium heat until edges are translucent, 2 to 4 minutes.

**4 Cook Potatoes** Stir in wine, scraping up any browned bits, and cook, stirring occasionally, until wine is reduced by half, about 2 minutes. Stir in broth and bring to simmer over high heat. Reduce heat to medium-low, cover, and simmer vigorously, stirring occasionally and adjusting heat as needed, until potatoes are tender, about 20 minutes.

**5 Mince Parsley and Slice Bread** While stew cooks, mince 2 tablespoons parsley. Slice bread.

**6 Finish Dish** Off heat, stir in peas and parsley. Cover pot and let sit until peas are heated through, about 2 minutes. Season with salt and pepper to taste. Adjust consistency as needed with hot water. Serve with bread, drizzling stew with extra oil to taste.

# Kimchi Beef and Tofu Soup

serves 4 to 6; total time 1 hour

## notes for the cook

This traditional Korean dish has a double dose of hearty protein from beef and tofu, plus tons of tangy flavor from kimchi, a spicy pickled vegetable condiment.

Make sure to save the kimchi brine when draining and measuring the kimchi; we use the brine to add extra zing to our broth.

Sirloin steak tips, also known as flap meat, can be sold as whole steaks, cubes, and strips. To ensure uniform pieces, we prefer to buy whole steaks and cut them ourselves.

Note that the flavor and spiciness of kimchi can vary from brand to brand and will slightly affect the flavor of the soup.

For supple, tender bites of tofu, we chose firm tofu. You can also use extra-firm.

1 pound sirloin steak tips

Salt and pepper

1 tablespoon vegetable oil

Fresh ginger

3 cups kimchi, plus its brine

½ cup mirin

2 cups beef broth

8 ounces firm tofu

4 scallions

1 tablespoon soy sauce

1 tablespoon toasted sesame oil

**1 Sear Beef** Trim beef and cut into ½-inch pieces. Pat beef dry with paper towels and season with salt and pepper. Heat oil in Dutch oven over medium-high heat until just smoking. Brown beef on all sides, 8 to 10 minutes.

**2 Prep Ginger and Kimchi** While beef cooks, peel and grate 1 tablespoon ginger. Drain kimchi, chop coarse, and measure out 1 cup reserved kimchi brine (add water if needed to make this amount).

**3 Sauté Aromatics and Deglaze Pan** Stir ginger into pot with beef and cook until fragrant, about 30 seconds. Slowly stir in mirin, scraping up any browned bits.

**4** **Add Kimchi and Simmer Soup**
Stir in broth, 3 cups water, kimchi, and kimchi brine and bring to boil. Reduce heat to low, cover, and simmer until meat is tender, 25 to 30 minutes.

**5** **Prep Tofu and Scallions** While soup is simmering, cut tofu into ½-inch cubes. Gently press tofu cubes dry with paper towels. Slice scallions thin.

**6** **Finish Soup** Off heat, stir soy sauce, sesame oil, tofu, and scallions into soup. Season with salt and pepper to taste. Serve.

# Sicilian Fish Stew

serves 4 to 6; total time 45 minutes

## notes for the cook

This classic dish from Sicily has a pleasant combination of sweet, sour, and salty flavors.

To finish our stew, we put together a twist on gremolata, a classic Italian condiment. We swapped the usual lemon zest for orange zest and parsley for mint to underline the sweet and fragrant flavors in the dish and stirred in toasted pine nuts for added crunch.

To prevent the fish from overcooking, add it when the stew is nearly done and let it finish cooking using residual heat with the stove off and the pot covered.

Tuna and halibut are good substitutes for the swordfish.

2 onions
4 garlic cloves
1 orange
Fresh mint
1 (28-ounce) can whole peeled tomatoes
2 tablespoons capers
2 tablespoons extra-virgin olive oil
Salt and pepper
Pinch red pepper flakes
½ cup dry white wine
2 (8-ounce) bottles clam juice
¼ cup golden raisins
¼ cup pine nuts
1½ pounds skinless swordfish steaks, 1 to 1½ inches thick
1 baguette

**1 Prep Aromatics and Tomatoes** Chop onions fine and mince garlic. Grate 1 teaspoon orange zest. Chop ¼ cup mint. Drain tomatoes, reserving juice, then chop tomatoes coarse. Rinse capers.

**2 Sauté Aromatics** Heat oil in Dutch oven over medium heat until shimmering. Add onions, ½ teaspoon salt, and ¼ teaspoon pepper and cook until softened, about 5 minutes. Stir in pepper flakes and three-quarters of garlic and cook until fragrant, about 30 seconds.

**3 Simmer Broth** Stir in wine and reserved tomato juice, bring to simmer, and cook until reduced by half, about 4 minutes. Stir in clam juice, raisins, tomatoes, and capers and bring to simmer. Cook until flavors meld, about 15 minutes.

4 **Toast Nuts** While broth simmers, toast pine nuts in 10-inch nonstick skillet over medium heat, shaking pan occasionally, until golden and fragrant, 3 to 5 minutes. Transfer to small bowl to cool.

5 **Cook Fish** Cut swordfish into 1-inch pieces. Pat dry with paper towels and season with salt and pepper. Nestle swordfish into pot and spoon some cooking liquid over top. Bring to simmer and cook for 4 minutes. Remove pot from heat, cover, and let sit until swordfish flakes apart when gently prodded with paring knife, about 3 minutes.

6 **Make Gremolata and Finish Stew** While swordfish cooks, combine remaining garlic, orange zest, mint, and cooled pine nuts in bowl. Slice bread. Season soup with salt and pepper to taste. Serve with bread, sprinkling individual serving bowls with pine nut mixture.

# Thai-Style Hot and Sour Soup with Shrimp and Rice Vermicelli

serves 4; total time 45 minutes

## notes for the cook

To create a quick and pantry-friendly version of Thai *tom yum* soup, we substituted an easy-to-find jalapeño chile for traditional Thai chiles and lime juice for harder-to-find kaffir lime leaves.

We built an intensely aromatic soup while making the most of our short ingredient list by infusing a combination of chicken broth and water with tomatoes, mushroom stems, jalapeño chiles, garlic, ginger, shrimp shells, cilantro stems, fish sauce, and sugar.

To smash the ginger pieces, use the flat side of a chef's knife.

If you can't find cremini mushrooms, white mushrooms can be used in their place.

4 ounces rice vermicelli
3 cups chicken broth
8 ounces cremini mushrooms
2 tomatoes
1 jalapeño chile
2 garlic cloves
1 (½-inch) piece ginger
1 pound large shrimp (26 to 30 per pound)
Fresh cilantro
2 tablespoons fish sauce
1 teaspoon sugar
3 limes

**1 Heat Broth and Prepare Noodles** In large saucepan, bring 2 quarts water to boil over high heat. Off heat, add noodles to hot water, and let stand until tender, about 5 minutes. Drain noodles in colander and rinse under cold running water until cooled and water runs clear. Drain well and set aside.

**2 Prep Vegetables and Shrimp** In second large saucepan, bring broth and 3 cups water to boil over medium-high heat. While broth and water come to boil, stem and quarter mushrooms, reserving stems separately. Core tomatoes and chop coarse. Stem and seed jalapeño, then slice crosswise into ¼-inch rings. Lightly crush garlic cloves. Peel ginger, then cut in half and smash pieces. Peel and devein shrimp, reserving shells separately.

**3 Simmer Broth** Stir 2 sprigs cilantro, fish sauce, sugar, mushroom stems, half of tomatoes, half of jalapeño rings, garlic, ginger, and shrimp shells into broth mixture and return to boil. Reduce heat to low, cover, and simmer gently for 20 minutes.

**4** **Squeeze Lime Juice, Chop Cilantro, and Strain Broth** While broth simmers, squeeze 3 tablespoons lime juice from 2 limes. Cut remaining lime into wedges. Coarsely chop ¼ cup cilantro. Strain broth through fine-mesh strainer set over large bowl, pushing on solids to extract as much liquid as possible.

**5** **Cook Mushrooms and Shrimp** Return broth to now-empty saucepan and bring to simmer over medium-high heat. Add quartered mushrooms and remaining jalapeño rings and cook for 2 minutes. Stir in shrimp and cook for 1 minute.

**6** **Finish Soup** Off heat, stir in lime juice and season with salt and pepper to taste. Divide noodles, remaining chopped tomatoes, and chopped cilantro among individual serving bowls and ladle soup over top. Serve with lime wedges.

# Chickpea and Kale Soup

serves 4; total time 45 minutes

## notes for the cook

The traditional Italian pairing of mild chickpeas with hearty greens and fennel gives this rustic soup tons of heartiness and complex flavor.

A short simmer takes tough kale leaves from chewy to tender and adds heft.

The mild anise bite of the sautéed fennel complements the nutty chickpeas and salty Pecorino Romano cheese.

You can use chicken broth instead of vegetable broth, if you like.

1 onion
1 fennel bulb
3 garlic cloves
1 (15-ounce) can chickpeas
6 ounces kale
2 tablespoons extra-virgin olive oil
Salt and pepper
¼ teaspoon red pepper flakes
4 cups vegetable broth
1 ounce Pecorino Romano cheese
Fresh parsley

**1 Prep Aromatics** Chop onion. Discard fennel stalks, halve bulb, core, and chop. Mince garlic. Drain and rinse chickpeas.

**2 Stem Kale** Stem kale by cutting away leafy green portion from either side of stalk, then chop leaves into 1-inch pieces.

**3 Sauté Aromatics** Heat oil in Dutch oven over medium-high heat until shimmering. Add onion, fennel, ½ teaspoon salt, and ½ teaspoon pepper and cook until vegetables have softened and are starting to brown, about 8 minutes. Stir in pepper flakes and garlic and cook until fragrant, about 30 seconds.

4  **Add Broth and Cook Vegetables**
Add broth, chickpeas, and kale and bring to boil. Reduce heat to medium-low, cover, and simmer until kale is tender, about 15 minutes.

5  **Grate Pecorino and Mince Parsley**
While soup simmers, grate Pecorino (½ cup). Mince 2 tablespoons parsley.

6  **Finish Soup** Off heat, stir in parsley and season with salt and pepper to taste. Serve, sprinkling individual serving bowls with Pecorino and drizzling with extra oil to taste.

# Turkish Tomato, Bulgur, and Red Pepper Soup

serves 6; total time 1 hour

## notes for the cook

A pair of powerhouse ingredients—smoked paprika and fire-roasted tomatoes—give this simple soup a big punch of flavor with minimal effort (and no open flame required).

The addition of quick-cooking, hearty bulgur makes this flavorful soup perfect for dinner.

You can use chicken broth instead of vegetable broth, if you like.

When shopping, don't confuse bulgur with cracked wheat, which has a much longer cooking time and will not work in this recipe.

2 red bell peppers

1 onion

3 garlic cloves

2 tablespoons extra-virgin olive oil

Salt and pepper

½ teaspoon smoked paprika

1 teaspoon dried mint

1 tablespoon tomato paste

½ cup dry white wine

1 (28-ounce) can diced fire-roasted tomatoes

¾ cup medium-grind bulgur

4 cups vegetable broth

Fresh mint

1 loaf rustic bread

**1 Prep Vegetables** Stem and seed bell peppers, then chop. Chop onion and mince garlic.

**2 Sauté Vegetables** Heat oil in Dutch oven over medium heat until shimmering. Add bell peppers, onion, ¾ teaspoon salt, and ¼ teaspoon pepper and cook until softened and lightly browned, 6 to 8 minutes.

**3 Sauté Aromatics** Stir in paprika and garlic, then crumble in dried mint and cook until fragrant, about 30 seconds. Stir in tomato paste and cook for 1 minute.

**4** **Simmer Wine and Tomatoes** Stir in wine, scraping up any browned bits, and simmer until reduced by half, about 1 minute. Add tomatoes and their juice and cook, stirring occasionally, until tomatoes soften and begin to break apart, about 10 minutes.

**5** **Cook Bulgur** Rinse bulgur, then stir into tomato mixture along with broth and 2 cups water and bring to simmer. Reduce heat to low, cover, and simmer gently until bulgur is tender, about 20 minutes.

**6** **Finish Soup** While soup simmers, chop ⅓ cup fresh mint. Slice bread. Season soup with salt and pepper to taste. Sprinkle individual serving bowls with fresh mint, and serve with bread.

# Quinoa and Vegetable Stew
serves 6 to 8; total time 1 hour

## notes for the cook

Quinoa stews are one-pot meals beloved in several South American regions.

We like the convenience of prewashed quinoa; rinsing removes the quinoa's bitter protective coating. If you buy unwashed quinoa, rinse it and then spread it out on a clean dish towel to dry for 15 minutes.

This stew tends to thicken as it sits; add more warm broth as needed before serving to loosen.

If you can't find queso fresco, crumbled feta makes a good substitute.

You can use chicken broth instead of vegetable broth, if you like.

You can use fresh corn if it's in season; for 1 cup of kernels, use 1 large ear of corn.

1 red bell pepper

1 onion

5 garlic cloves

1 pound red potatoes

2 tablespoons vegetable oil

Salt and pepper

1 tablespoon paprika

1½ teaspoons ground cumin

6 cups vegetable broth

2 tomatoes

1 cup prewashed white quinoa

1 cup frozen corn

1 avocado

Fresh cilantro

4 ounces queso fresco

**1** **Prep Vegetables** Stem and seed bell pepper, then cut into ½-inch pieces. Chop onion and mince garlic. Cut potatoes into ½-inch pieces.

**2** **Sauté Aromatics and Bell Pepper** Heat oil in Dutch oven over medium heat until shimmering. Add bell pepper, onion, and ¼ teaspoon salt and cook until softened, about 5 minutes. Stir in paprika, cumin, and garlic and cook until fragrant, about 30 seconds.

**3** **Cook Potatoes** Stir in broth and potatoes and bring to boil over high heat. Reduce heat to medium-low and simmer gently for 10 minutes.

**4 Prep Tomatoes and Cook Quinoa**
While potatoes simmer, core tomatoes and chop coarse. Stir in quinoa and simmer for 8 minutes. Stir in corn and simmer until potatoes and quinoa are just tender, 5 to 7 minutes.

**5 Prep Toppings** While quinoa cooks, halve avocado, remove pit, and dice. Mince ½ cup cilantro. Crumble queso fresco into small bowl (1 cup).

**6 Finish Soup** Stir in tomatoes and let heat through, about 2 minutes. Off heat, season with salt and pepper to taste. Serve, sprinkling individual serving bowls with avocado, cilantro, and queso fresco.

# Caribbean-Style Swiss Chard and Butternut Squash Stew

serves 4; total time 1 hour

## notes for the cook

This dish is inspired by an earthy, spicy Caribbean stew that pairs the local callaloo leaves with squash in a rich, coconut-infused broth. Swiss chard is a good substitute for the earthy callaloo leaves.

While you can omit it if you want, we found that a dash of Angostura cocktail bitters gives the stew a uniquely authentic flavor.

You can substitute delicata or carnival squash for the butternut squash.

To make this dish spicier, mince the ribs and seeds from the habanero and add them in.

You can use chicken broth instead of vegetable broth, if you like.

You can substitute ¼ teaspoon dried thyme for the fresh thyme.

1 medium (2- to 2½-pound) butternut squash
2 onions
4 garlic cloves
Fresh thyme
1 habanero or Scotch bonnet chile
2 tablespoons vegetable oil
Salt
Pinch cayenne pepper
3½ cups vegetable broth
1 pound Swiss chard
1 cup canned coconut milk
Angostura bitters (optional)

**1 Prep Vegetables** Peel and seed squash, then cut into ½ inch pieces (about 6 cups). Chop onions fine and mince garlic. Mince 1 teaspoon thyme. Stem and seed chile, then mince.

**2 Sauté Aromatics** Heat oil in Dutch oven over medium heat until shimmering. Stir in onions and ½ teaspoon salt and cook until softened, about 5 minutes. Stir in cayenne, garlic, thyme, and habanero and cook until fragrant, about 30 seconds.

**3 Cook Squash** Stir in broth and squash, scraping up any browned bits, and bring to boil. Reduce heat to medium-low and simmer gently for 15 minutes.

**4 Prep and Cook Chard** While squash simmers, stem chard by cutting away leafy green portion from either side of stalk, then chop leaves into 1-inch pieces. Stir chard into pot and continue to simmer until squash and chard are tender, 10 to 15 minutes.

**5 Add Coconut Milk** Stir in coconut milk and bring to brief simmer.

**6 Puree Stew and Finish** Process 2 cups stew in blender until smooth, about 45 seconds; return to pot. Season with bitters, if using, and salt to taste, and serve.

# African Sweet Potato and Peanut Stew

serves 6; total time 1 hour

## notes for the cook

Perhaps unusual to Western palates, this nourishing West African soup featuring sweet potatoes and peanuts has an appealing blend of savory and sweet flavors.

Pureeing only some of the soup while keeping the rest intact gives the broth body while still leaving the soup with a great hearty texture.

You can use chicken broth instead of vegetable broth, if you like.

1 ¼ cups raw peanuts
1 onion
1 red bell pepper
3 garlic cloves
2 pounds sweet potatoes
2 tablespoons unsalted butter
Salt and pepper
½ teaspoon ground coriander
¼ teaspoon cayenne pepper
4 cups vegetable broth
Fresh cilantro

**1 Toast Nuts** Toast peanuts in 10-inch skillet over medium heat, shaking pan occasionally, until golden and fragrant, 3 to 5 minutes. Transfer to bowl to cool, then chop cooled nuts coarse.

**2 Prep Vegetables** While nuts cool, chop onion fine. Stem and seed bell pepper, then chop fine. Mince garlic. Peel sweet potatoes, then cut into ½-inch pieces.

**3 Cook Aromatics** Melt butter in Dutch oven over medium heat. Add onion, bell pepper, and ½ teaspoon salt and cook until softened, about 5 minutes. Stir in coriander, cayenne, and garlic and cook until fragrant, about 30 seconds.

**4** **Add Broth, Peanuts, and Potatoes** Stir in broth, 1 cup chopped peanuts, and sweet potatoes and bring to boil. Reduce heat to low and simmer, partially covered, until sweet potatoes are tender, 15 to 20 minutes.

**5** **Puree Soup** While soup cooks, mince ¼ cup cilantro. Measure out 3 cups solids and 1 cup liquid from soup and transfer to blender. Process in blender until completely smooth, about 30 seconds. Return to pot with remaining soup and stir to combine.

**6** **Finish Soup** Stir in cilantro and season with salt and pepper to taste. Serve, sprinkling individual portions with remaining chopped peanuts.

# Black Bean Soup

serves 4 to 6; total time 45 minutes

## notes for the cook

To develop deep flavor in this quick-cooking soup, we add meaty dried porcini mushrooms and a hearty base of aromatics.

Pureeing a portion of the beans gives our soup body and silky richness.

To rinse the dried porcini, place the mushrooms in a fine-mesh strainer and run them under water, using your fingers as needed to rub dirt and grit out of the crevices.

Note that you'll need ½ cup of cilantro, so shop accordingly.

You can use chicken broth instead of vegetable broth, if you like.

4 (15-ounce) cans black beans

3 cups vegetable broth

1 onion

1 red bell pepper

6 garlic cloves

¼ ounce dried porcini mushrooms

2 tablespoons vegetable oil

1 teaspoon dried oregano

½ teaspoon ground cumin

½ teaspoon chili powder

Fresh cilantro

1 lime

Salt and pepper

**1 Puree Portion of Beans** Drain and rinse black beans. Process 2 cups of beans and 1 cup broth in blender until smooth, about 10 seconds; set aside.

**2 Prep Vegetables** Chop onion fine. Stem and seed bell pepper, then chop fine. Mince garlic. Rinse and mince mushrooms.

**3 Sauté Vegetables** Heat oil in Dutch oven over medium heat until shimmering. Add onion and bell pepper and cook until vegetables are softened and lightly browned, 5 to 7 minutes.

**4** **Sauté Aromatics and Broth** Stir in oregano, cumin, chili powder, garlic, and mushrooms and cook until fragrant, about 30 seconds. Stir in remaining 2 cups broth, scraping up any browned bits.

**5** **Add Bean Puree and Beans** Stir in pureed beans and remaining whole beans and bring to boil. Reduce heat to medium-low and simmer until flavors meld, about 15 minutes.

**6** **Prep Cilantro and Finish Soup** While soup simmers, mince ½ cup cilantro and cut lime into wedges. Stir cilantro into soup and season with salt and pepper to taste. Serve with lime wedges.

Beef, Pork & Lamb

# Sichuan-Style Orange Beef with Sugar Snap Peas and Rice

serves 4; total time 45 minutes

## notes for the cook

An appealing combination of hot and sweet flavors makes this bright and citrusy stir-fry a new weeknight favorite.

Flank steak is a cut that has it all: rich, beefy flavor; lean meat; and a reasonable price tag. Cooking it in thin slices helps keep the texture from getting too chewy.

Cooking the beef right in the sauce gives the meat great flavor, and the honey in the sauce aids in browning and caramelization.

1½ cups long-grain white rice
Salt
2 garlic cloves
1 orange
8 ounces sugar snap peas
2 scallions
1 (1½-pound) flank steak
¼ cup soy sauce
2 tablespoons toasted sesame oil
1 tablespoon honey
¼ teaspoon red pepper flakes

**1 Make Rice** Rinse rice in fine-mesh strainer until water runs clear. Bring rice, 2¼ cups water, and ¼ teaspoon salt to simmer in large saucepan over medium heat. Reduce heat to low, cover, and simmer until rice is tender and liquid is absorbed, 16 to 18 minutes. Remove pot from heat, lay clean folded dish towel underneath lid, and let sit for 10 minutes.

**2 Prep Vegetables** While rice cooks, mince garlic. Grate 2 teaspoons orange zest and squeeze ½ cup juice. Remove strings from snap peas. Slice scallions thin on bias.

**3 Prep Beef** Trim flank steak. Cut steak into thirds with the grain, then slice crosswise ¼ inch thick.

**4** **Cook Beef** Whisk soy sauce, oil, honey, pepper flakes, orange zest and juice, and garlic together in bowl. Combine beef and ⅓ cup orange juice mixture in 12-inch nonstick skillet. Cook over medium-high heat, stirring occasionally, until liquid has evaporated and beef is caramelized, about 15 minutes. Transfer beef to plate and tent with aluminum foil.

**5** **Cook Snap Peas** Add snap peas and remaining orange juice mixture to now-empty skillet and cook, covered, over medium heat until snap peas are bright green, about 2 minutes. Uncover and continue to cook, stirring occasionally, until sauce thickens and snap peas are tender, about 1 minute.

**6** **Finish Dish** Return beef, along with any accumulated juices, to skillet and toss with snap peas to combine. Transfer to platter and sprinkle with scallions. Serve with rice.

# Grilled Cumin-Rubbed Flank Steak with Mexican Street Corn

serves 4; total time 45 minutes

## notes for the cook

Mexican street corn is grilled, slathered with a creamy, chili-spiked sauce, and sprinkled with crumbly cheese. Here, it makes the perfect pairing with a smoky grilled flank steak.

Mayonnaise does double duty in this recipe, first as a flavorful fat for grilling the corn and then as the base of our sauce.

You can remove stubborn threads of corn silk from the cobs with a clean toothbrush.

Slicing flank steak against the grain before serving (that is, perpendicular to the orientation of the muscle fibers) makes this relatively tough cut much more tender.

1 tablespoon ground cumin

¾ teaspoon chili powder

Salt and pepper

1 (1½-pound) flank steak

4 ears corn

Fresh cilantro

1 garlic clove

2 limes

½ ounce Pecorino Romano cheese

¼ cup mayonnaise

**1 Heat Grill** Turn all burners to high, cover, and heat grill until hot, about 15 minutes. Leave primary burner on high and turn other burner(s) to medium.

**2 Season Steak** While grill heats, combine cumin, ½ teaspoon chili powder, 1½ teaspoons salt, and ½ teaspoon pepper in bowl. Trim steak, pat dry with paper towels, and sprinkle evenly with spice mixture.

**3 Prep Corn and Sauce** Remove husks and silk from corn. Mince 2 tablespoons cilantro and mince garlic. Squeeze 1 tablespoon lime juice from 1 lime and cut remaining lime into wedges. Grate Pecorino (¼ cup). Combine mayonnaise, remaining ¼ teaspoon chili powder, cilantro, garlic, lime juice, Pecorino, and ¼ teaspoon salt in small bowl. Brush corn evenly with half of mayonnaise mixture.

**4** **Grill Steak** Clean and oil cooking grate. Grill steak over hotter side of grill, covered, until meat registers 120 to 125 degrees (for medium-rare), 4 to 6 minutes per side. Transfer to carving board, tent with aluminum foil, and let rest.

**5** **Grill Corn** While steak rests, grill corn on hotter side of grill, covered, turning often, until well browned on all sides, about 12 minutes.

**6** **Finish Dish** Transfer corn to cutting board, cut ears in half, and brush with remaining mayonnaise mixture. Slice steak thin against grain. Serve with corn and lime wedges.

# Grilled Flank Steak with Vegetables and Salsa Verde

serves 4; total time 1 hour

## notes for the cook

Rich and beefy flank steak is thin, flat, and quick-cooking, making it ideal for grilling.

We pair our flank steak with a pungent, easy-to-make Italian *salsa verde*. The sauce elevates the simple char-grilled steak and adds a welcome freshness.

Slicing flank steak against the grain before serving (that is, perpendicular to the orientation of the muscle fibers) makes this relatively tough cut much more tender.

A side made with fresh zucchini and earthy eggplant complements the Italian flavors of the sauce. These hearty vegetables are also a perfect match for the high heat of the grill.

Note that you will need 1½ cups of parsley and ½ cup of mint, so shop accordingly.

2 zucchini

1 pound eggplant

5 tablespoons extra-virgin olive oil

Salt and pepper

Fresh parsley

Fresh mint

1 tablespoon capers

2 anchovy fillets

1 garlic clove

1 (1½-pound) flank steak

1½ tablespoons white wine vinegar

---

**1 Heat Grill** Turn all burners to high, cover, and heat grill until hot, about 15 minutes. Leave all burners on high.

**2 Prep Vegetables** While grill heats, slice zucchini lengthwise into ¾-inch-thick planks. Slice eggplant lengthwise into ¾-inch-thick planks. Brush zucchini and eggplant with 1 tablespoon oil and season with salt and pepper. Pick 1½ cups parsley leaves and ½ cup mint leaves. Rinse capers. Rinse anchovies and pat dry. Mince garlic.

**3 Prep Steak** Trim steak, pat dry with paper towels, and season with salt and pepper.

**4** **Grill Vegetables and Steak** Clean and oil cooking grate. Place steak and vegetables on grill. Cover and cook, flipping steak and turning vegetables as needed, until steak is well browned and registers 120 to 125 degrees (for medium-rare) and vegetables are slightly charred and tender, 7 to 12 minutes. Transfer steak and vegetables to carving board as they finish cooking, tent with aluminum foil, and let rest.

**5** **Make Salsa Verde** While steak rests, pulse vinegar, remaining ¼ cup oil, parsley, mint, capers, anchovies, garlic, 1 tablespoon water, and ⅛ teaspoon salt in food processor until finely chopped, about 15 pulses, scraping down sides of bowl as needed. Transfer to bowl.

**6** **Slice Steak and Finish Dish** Cut zucchini and eggplant into 2-inch pieces. Arrange vegetables on serving platter and season with salt and pepper to taste. Slice steak thin against grain and arrange on platter with vegetables. Drizzle steak with ¼ cup salsa verde. Serve, passing remaining salsa verde separately.

# Skirt Steak with Pinto Bean Salad

serves 4; total time 45 minutes

## notes for the cook

Thin slices of skirt steak pair perfectly with a simple arugula and pinto bean salad. A dressing with chipotle chile and lime juice adds subtle spicy and smoky notes as well as a hit of brightness for a satisfying Southwestern flavor profile.

It's fine if the pieces of steak overlap a little when you first put them in the skillet; they will shrink as they cook.

If you can't find skirt steak, you can substitute flank steak, although the meat will be a bit less tender.

Be sure to slice the cooked steak thin against the grain (that is, perpendicular to the orientation of the muscle fibers) or it will be chewy.

2 (15-ounce) cans pinto beans

1 small red onion

Fresh cilantro

Canned chipotle chile in adobo sauce

1 lime

1½ pounds skirt steak

1 teaspoon paprika

Salt and pepper

2 tablespoons vegetable oil

2 ounces (2 cups) baby arugula

**1 Prep Beans** Drain and rinse beans; transfer to large bowl.

**2 Prep Vegetables** Finely chop ½ cup red onion. Chop ¼ cup cilantro. Mince 2 teaspoons chipotle. Squeeze 1 tablespoon lime juice.

**3 Prep Steak** Trim steak. Cover with plastic wrap and pound ¼ inch thick. Cut steak crosswise into thirds with grain. Pat dry with paper towels, sprinkle evenly with paprika, and season with salt and pepper.

**4** **Cook Steak** Heat 1 tablespoon oil in 12-inch skillet over medium-high heat until just smoking. Cook steak until well browned and meat registers 130 degrees (for medium), 2 to 3 minutes per side. Transfer steak to carving board, tent loosely with aluminum foil, and let rest.

**5** **Make Salad** While steak rests, add onion, chipotle, lime juice, remaining 1 tablespoon oil, ½ teaspoon salt and ½ teaspoon pepper to beans in bowl and stir to combine. Add arugula and cilantro and gently toss to combine.

**6** **Finish Dish** Transfer bean salad to platter. Slice steak thin against grain and arrange on top of bean salad. Serve.

# Grilled Skirt Steak and Poblano Tacos with Lime Crema

serves 6; total time 1 hour

## notes for the cook

In this popular north Mexican dish, smoky beef is perfectly complemented by sweet-hot poblano chiles and juicy onions.

Putting the grilled poblanos in a covered bowl when they come off the grill makes the charred skins easier to peel off later.

Our steak actually gets marinated after it's cooked, rather than before; we found that covering the cooked steak with a bright onion-lime puree after grilling infused it with tons of flavor while it rested.

If you can't find skirt steak, you can substitute flank steak, although the meat will be a bit less tender.

Be sure to slice the cooked steak thin against the grain or it will be chewy.

4 onions
3 garlic cloves
5 limes
½ teaspoon ground cumin
Salt and pepper
1½ pounds poblano chiles
1 tablespoon vegetable oil
2 pounds skirt steak
½ cup sour cream
18 (6-inch) corn tortillas

**1 Heat Grill and Make Onion Marinade** Turn all burners to high, cover, and heat grill until hot, about 15 minutes. Leave primary burner on high and turn other burner(s) off. While grill heats, slice 3 onions crosswise into ½-inch-thick rounds. Chop remaining onion. Mince garlic. Squeeze ½ cup lime juice from 4 limes. Cut remaining lime into wedges. Process cumin, chopped onion, garlic, 6 tablespoons lime juice, and 1 teaspoon salt in food processor until smooth.

**2 Season Onions, Poblanos, and Steak and Make Crema** Brush onion rounds and poblanos with oil and season with salt and pepper. Trim steak, pat dry with paper towels, and season with salt and pepper. In small bowl, whisk sour cream and remaining 2 tablespoons lime juice together and season with salt and pepper to taste; set aside.

**3 Grill Poblanos and Onions** Clean and oil cooking grate. Place poblanos on hotter side of grill and onion rounds on cooler side of grill. Grill, covered, turning as needed, until poblanos are blistered and blackened and onions are softened and golden, 6 to 12 minutes. Transfer onions to platter and cover with aluminum foil to keep warm. Transfer peppers to bowl, cover with plastic wrap, and let steam.

**4** **Grill Steak and Marinate** While peppers steam, place steak on hotter side of grill. Grill, covered, turning as needed, until well browned on both sides and meat registers 130 degrees (for medium), 4 to 8 minutes. Transfer steak to 13 by 9-inch dish and poke all over with fork. Pour pureed onion mixture over top, cover with foil, and let marinate while grilling tortillas.

**5** **Grill Tortillas** While steak marinates, grill tortillas in batches, turning as needed, until warm and spotty brown, about 30 seconds; wrap tightly in foil to keep warm.

**6** **Finish Dish** Peel, stem, and seed poblanos, then slice thin. Separate onions into rings and chop coarse, then toss with sliced poblanos. Remove steak from marinade, slice with grain into 4- to 6-inch lengths, then slice thin against grain. Serve with lime wedges, crema, warm tortillas, and poblano-onion mixture.

# Skillet Steak Tips with Roasted Feta Potatoes and Mesclun Salad

serves 4; total time 45 minutes

## notes for the cook

For a fresh take on steak, salad, and potatoes, we add powerhouse, flavor-packed ingredients to this basic combination, including briny feta cheese, tangy-sweet balsamic vinegar, fresh mint, and bright, crunchy radishes.

Lining the rimmed baking sheet with parchment prevents the potatoes from sticking to the pan and makes cleanup easy.

Sirloin steak tips, also known as flap meat, can be sold as whole steaks, cubes, and strips. To ensure uniform pieces, we prefer to purchase whole steaks and cut them ourselves.

1½ pounds Yukon Gold potatoes

4 scallions

2 ounces feta cheese

6 tablespoons extra-virgin olive oil

Salt and pepper

1½ pounds sirloin steak tips

1 tablespoon balsamic vinegar

1 teaspoon Dijon mustard

3 radishes

Fresh mint

5 ounces (5 cups) mesclun

**1** **Prep Vegetables** Adjust oven rack to middle position and heat oven to 475 degrees. Slice potatoes ¼ inch thick. Slice scallion greens thin and mince white parts, keeping them separate. Crumble feta (½ cup).

**2** **Cook Potatoes** Toss potatoes with 2 tablespoons oil, ¼ teaspoon salt, and ¼ teaspoon pepper and arrange in single layer on parchment-lined rimmed baking sheet. Roast potatoes until spotty brown and tender, 15 to 20 minutes. Sprinkle potatoes with scallion greens and crumbled feta and continue to bake until cheese is just melted, about 5 minutes.

**3** **Prep Steak** While potatoes cook, trim steak and cut into 2-inch pieces. Pat steak dry with paper towels and season with salt and pepper.

**4** **Cook Steak** Heat 1 tablespoon oil in 12-inch skillet over medium-high heat until just smoking. Add steak and cook until well browned all over and meat registers 125 degrees (for medium-rare), 7 to 10 minutes. Transfer to plate, tent with aluminum foil, and let rest.

**5** **Make Dressing** While steak cooks, whisk vinegar, mustard, and minced scallion whites together in large bowl. Whisking constantly, slowly drizzle in remaining 3 tablespoons oil until incorporated.

**6** **Finish Dish** While steak rests, trim radishes and slice thin. Chop 2 tablespoons mint. Add mesclun, radishes, and mint to dressing and season with salt and pepper to taste. Serve with steak and potatoes.

# Grilled Beef Skewers with Arugula Salad and Heirloom Tomatoes

serves 4 to 6; total time 45 minutes

## notes for the cook

Richly marbled steak tips have great beefy flavor and tender texture. Grilling them on skewers and pairing them with a supersimple salad plus a tomato side dish makes for a quick, fresh dinner.

We prefer the bright flavor of heirloom tomatoes here, but any ripe in-season tomatoes can be substituted.

You will need four 12-inch metal skewers for this recipe.

Sirloin steak tips, also known as flap meat, can be sold as whole steaks, cubes, and strips. To ensure uniform pieces, we prefer to buy whole steaks and cut them ourselves.

4 garlic cloves

2 pounds sirloin steak tips

½ cup balsamic vinegar

2 tablespoons Dijon mustard

½ teaspoon red pepper flakes

Salt and pepper

6 tablespoons extra-virgin olive oil

1 red onion

1 lemon

1 ounce Parmesan cheese

2 large heirloom tomatoes

8 ounces (8 cups) baby arugula

**1 Heat Grill and Prep Steak** Turn all burners to high, cover, and heat grill until hot, about 15 minutes. Leave all burners on high. While grill heats, mince garlic. Trim steak and cut into 1-inch pieces.

**2 Make Marinade and Marinate Steak** Whisk vinegar, mustard, pepper flakes, garlic, ½ teaspoon salt, and ½ teaspoon pepper together in large bowl. Whisking constantly, slowly drizzle in ¼ cup oil until incorporated. Transfer ½ cup vinegar mixture to small saucepan. Add steak to remaining vinegar mixture, toss to coat, and let marinate for 10 minutes.

**3 Make Basting Sauce and Thread Skewers** While steak marinates, cook reserved ½ cup vinegar mixture over medium heat until slightly thickened, about 2 minutes; set aside basting sauce. Cut onion through root end into 8 equal wedges. Working with 1 skewer at a time, thread 1 onion wedge, followed by one-quarter of marinated steak, then 1 onion wedge onto each skewer.

**4** **Prep Dressing and Tomatoes**
Squeeze 2 tablespoons lemon juice.
Whisk lemon juice, ¼ teaspoon salt,
and ⅛ teaspoon pepper with remaining
2 tablespoons oil in large bowl. Shave
Parmesan into thin strips using vegetable
peeler. Core tomatoes and slice thin.

**5** **Grill Steak and Onion** Grill skewers,
covered, turning every 2 minutes and
basting with sauce until well charred on
all sides and meat registers 125 degrees
(for medium-rare), 10 to 12 minutes. Transfer
to platter, tent with aluminum foil, and let rest.

**6** **Finish Dish** While skewers rest, toss
arugula with dressing in bowl and
sprinkle with Parmesan. Arrange
tomatoes on platter, then drizzle with
extra oil to taste and season with salt and
pepper. Remove steak and onions from
skewers and season with salt and pepper to
taste. Serve.

# Easy Steak Frites

serves 4; total time 1 hour

## notes for the cook

To bring this low-key French bistro classic home, we use a quick and easy frying technique that starts the potatoes in cold oil. For an almost effortless sauce, we make a compound butter that melts into a rich topping for the steaks.

For the best frites, we recommend using large Yukon Gold potatoes (10 to 12 ounces each) that are similar in size.

We prefer peanut oil for frying because of its high smoke point and the clean taste it imparts to fried foods, but you can use vegetable oil, if desired.

Use a Dutch oven that holds 6 quarts or more for this recipe.

4 tablespoons unsalted butter

1 shallot

Fresh parsley

1 garlic clove

Salt and pepper

2½ pounds large Yukon Gold potatoes

6 cups plus 1 tablespoon peanut or vegetable oil

2 (1-pound) boneless strip steaks, 1¼ to 1½ inches thick

**1 Prep Ingredients** Cut butter into pieces and let soften to room temperature. Meanwhile, mince shallot and 1 tablespoon parsley. Mince garlic. Square off potatoes by cutting ¼-inch-thick slice from each of their 4 long sides; discard slices. Cut potatoes lengthwise into ¼-inch-thick planks. Stack 3 or 4 planks and cut into ¼-inch-thick fries. Repeat with remaining planks. (Do not place sliced potatoes in water.)

**2 Make Compound Butter** Mash softened butter, shallot, parsley, garlic, ¼ teaspoon salt, and ¼ teaspoon pepper together in bowl; set compound butter aside.

**3 Make Frites** Line rimmed baking sheet with triple layer of paper towels. Combine potatoes and 6 cups oil in Dutch oven. Cook over high heat until oil is bubbling, about 5 minutes. Continue to cook, without stirring, until potatoes are limp but exteriors are beginning to firm, about 15 minutes. Using tongs, stir potatoes, gently scraping up any that stick, and continue to cook, stirring occasionally, until golden and crispy, 7 to 10 minutes.

4 **Prep Steak** While frites cook, trim steaks and pat dry with paper towels. Cut each steak in half crosswise to create four 8-ounce steaks.

5 **Cook Steak** Heat remaining 1 tablespoon oil in 12-inch skillet over medium-high heat until just smoking. Add steaks and cook until well browned and meat registers 120 to 125 degrees (for medium-rare), 4 to 7 minutes per side. Transfer steaks to platter, top each with compound butter, tent with aluminum foil, and let rest.

6 **Finish Dish** While steaks rest, use spider or slotted spoon to transfer frites to prepared sheet and season with salt. Serve frites with steaks.

# Thick-Cut Steaks with Broiled Asparagus and Brown Butter Sauce

serves 4; total time 1 hour

## notes for the cook

For an upscale but still weeknight-friendly steak dinner, we use a technique called reverse searing: We start thick-cut steaks in a low oven and then finish them with a quick sear on the stovetop. This helps cook the thick steaks evenly all the way through.

We pair the steaks with a rich brown butter sauce and tender asparagus. A quick gremolata adds complexity and freshness.

Be ready to make the sauce as soon as the asparagus goes under the broiler.

Try to find asparagus thicker than ¾ inch thick; these sturdier spears hold up under the direct heat of the broiler.

You can substitute rib eye for the strip steaks in this recipe.

2 (1-pound) boneless strip steaks, 1½ to 1¾ inches thick

Salt and pepper

2 pounds thick asparagus

Fresh parsley

1 lemon

1 garlic clove

3 tablespoons extra-virgin olive oil

4 tablespoons unsalted butter

**1 Start Steak in Oven** Adjust 1 oven rack to middle position and second rack 6 inches from broiler element. Heat oven to 275 degrees. Trim steaks and pat dry with paper towels. Cut each steak in half crosswise to create four 8-ounce steaks. Season steaks with salt and pepper. Place steaks on wire rack set in rimmed baking sheet. Cook until meat registers 90 to 95 degrees (for rare to medium-rare), 20 to 25 minutes.

**2 Prep Asparagus and Make Gremolata** While steak is cooking, trim bottom inch of asparagus spears and discard. Peel bottom halves of spears until white flesh is exposed. Mince ¼ cup parsley. Grate 2 teaspoons lemon zest and squeeze 1½ teaspoons juice. Mince garlic. Combine parsley, lemon zest, garlic, and pinch salt in small bowl.

**3 Sear Steak** Heat broiler. Heat 1 tablespoon oil in 12-inch skillet over high heat until just smoking. Pat steaks dry, place in skillet, and cook, without moving, until well browned, 2 to 2½ minutes. (Reduce heat if fond begins to burn.) Flip steaks and cook until well browned on second side, 2 to 2½ minutes. Transfer steaks to carving board, tent with aluminum foil, and let rest.

4 **Broil Asparagus** While steaks rest, toss asparagus with remaining 2 tablespoons oil, ½ teaspoon salt, and ¼ teaspoon pepper on clean rimmed baking sheet; spread into even layer. Broil asparagus, shaking pan occasionally, until tender and lightly browned, about 10 minutes.

5 **Make Sauce** While asparagus broils, discard fat from pan, wipe skillet clean with paper towels, add butter to skillet, and melt over medium-high heat. Continue to cook, stirring and scraping bottom of pan with spatula until milk solids are browned and butter has nutty aroma, 1 to 2 minutes. Immediately transfer butter to bowl, scraping skillet with spatula. Let stand for 2 minutes, then stir in lemon juice.

6 **Finish Dish** Slice steak crosswise into ½-inch-thick slices. Spoon gremolata onto steak and drizzle butter sauce over steak and asparagus. Serve.

# Perfect Cheeseburgers with Easy Grilled Coleslaw

serves 4; total time 1 hour

## notes for the cook

These perfectly juicy cheeseburgers are the ideal version of this grilled classic. Our grilled coleslaw adds a new twist to a picnic staple for a modern take on dinner off the grill.

Eighty percent lean ground chuck is our favorite for flavor, but 85 percent lean works, too.

Making a slight dimple in the center of each burger patty before grilling helps them cook to a perfectly even thickness.

Do not remove the core from the cabbage; it will keep the leaves intact on the grill.

½ head green cabbage (1 pound)

1 shallot

1 carrot

Fresh cilantro

1½ pounds 80 percent lean ground chuck

Salt and pepper

2 tablespoons extra-virgin olive oil

4 slices American cheese

¼ cup mayonnaise

4 teaspoons cider vinegar

4 hamburger buns

1 large tomato

1 small head green leaf lettuce (8 ounces)

**1 Heat Grill** Turn all burners to high, cover, and heat grill until hot, about 15 minutes. Leave all burners on high.

**2 Prep Vegetables and Aromatics** While grill heats, cut cabbage into 2 wedges. Mince shallot. Peel and shred carrot. Mince 2 tablespoons cilantro.

**3 Shape Burgers** Break meat into small pieces in medium bowl, sprinkle with salt and pepper, and toss lightly to mix. Divide meat into 4 portions. Working with 1 portion at a time, lightly toss from hand to hand to form ball, then gently flatten into ¾-inch-thick patty. Press center of patties down with your fingertips to create ¼-inch-deep depression.

**4 Grill Cabbage** Brush cabbage wedges with oil and season with salt and pepper. Clean and oil cooking grate. Place cabbage on grill and cook, covered, turning as needed, until cabbage is lightly charred on all sides, 8 to 12 minutes. Transfer cabbage to platter and cover with aluminum foil.

**5 Grill Burgers** Place burgers on grill and cook, covered, without pressing, until well browned on first side, 2 to 3 minutes. Flip and continue to cook until burgers register 120 to 125 degrees (for medium-rare) or 130 to 135 degrees (for medium), 2½ to 4 minutes. Place 1 slice of cheese on each burger about 2 minutes before they reach desired doneness. Transfer to platter with cabbage, tent with foil, and let rest.

**6 Finish Dish** While burgers rest, whisk mayonnaise, vinegar, and shallots together in large bowl. Slice cabbage thin, discarding core. Add cabbage, carrot, and cilantro to mayonnaise mixture and toss to combine. Season with salt and pepper to taste. Core tomato then cut into 4 slices and separate lettuce leaves. Place burgers on bottom buns and top with tomato and lettuce. Serve with grilled coleslaw.

# Fennel-Crusted Pork Chops with Apples, Shallots, and Brown Rice

serves 4; total time 1 hour

## notes for the cook

Pork and apples make a classic pairing. For this dinner, we use the same skillet to cook the apples (plus shallots and prunes) as we use for the pork, so the fond from the meat helps flavor the fruit and shallot topping.

A mixture of port, orange juice, and cider vinegar makes an intense braising liquid for the fruit and shallots that then becomes a flavorful sauce for the finished pork.

You will need a 12-inch skillet with a tight-fitting lid for this recipe.

You can substitute a Honeycrisp or Fuji apple for the Braeburn apple, if desired.

Try to avoid using shallots heavier than 1 ounce each as they may not cook through until after the apples turn mushy.

1½ cups long-grain brown rice

Salt and pepper

6 small shallots

1 Braeburn apple

½ cup prunes

1 large orange

Fresh parsley

4 (8- to 10-ounce) bone-in pork rib chops, ¾ to 1 inch thick

1 tablespoon ground fennel

2 tablespoons extra-virgin olive oil

2 tablespoons unsalted butter

1 cup port

½ cup cider vinegar

**1 Cook Rice** Bring 3 quarts water to boil in large saucepan over high heat. Add rice and 1 tablespoon salt and cook, uncovered, stirring occasionally, until tender, 25 to 35 minutes. Drain well, return to pot, and cover to keep warm.

**2 Prep Sauce** While rice cooks, halve shallots lengthwise (or quarter if large) leaving root end intact. Core apple, cut in half, then cut into ¾-inch-thick wedges. Halve prunes. Grate 1 teaspoon orange zest and squeeze ½ cup juice. Chop ¼ cup parsley.

**3 Prep and Cook Pork** Trim pork, pat dry with paper towels, and season with salt, pepper, and 2 teaspoons fennel. Heat 1 tablespoon oil in 12-inch skillet over medium-high heat until just smoking. Add pork and cook until well browned and meat registers 145 degrees, 3 to 5 minutes per side; transfer to platter, tent with aluminum foil, and let rest.

**4 Sear Shallots and Apple**
While pork rests, melt butter in now-empty skillet over medium-high heat. Add shallots and apple, cut side down and cook, without moving, until well browned, 2 to 4 minutes.

**5 Make Sauce** Off heat, slowly stir in port, vinegar, prunes, orange zest and juice, remaining 1 teaspoon fennel, and ¼ teaspoon salt and bring to boil. Cover, reduce heat to medium, and cook for 5 minutes. Uncover and continue to cook until shallots are tender and sauce is thickened, 7 to 10 minutes. Stir any accumulated juices from pork into sauce.

**6 Finish Dish** Stir 2 tablespoons parsley and remaining 1 tablespoon oil into rice and season with salt and pepper to taste. Pour apple and prune compote over pork and sprinkle with remaining 2 tablespoons parsley. Serve over rice.

# Roasted Pork Chops and Vegetables with Parsley Vinaigrette

serves 4; total time 1 hour

## notes for the cook

Thick-cut bone-in pork chops deliver the succulence of a larger roast but cook in just 10 to 15 minutes, making them the perfect weeknight treat.

These pork chops also stand up great to high heat and assertive flavors, so they're a natural pairing with hearty root vegetables and a bold vinaigrette.

Be sure to use pork chops that measure between 1 and 1½ inches thick for this recipe.

1 pound Yukon Gold potatoes

1 pound carrots

1 fennel bulb

10 garlic cloves

⅓ cup extra-virgin olive oil

½ teaspoon dried rosemary

Salt and pepper

1 teaspoon paprika

1 teaspoon ground coriander

4 (12-ounce) bone-in center-cut pork chops,
   1 to 1½ inches thick

1 small shallot

Fresh parsley

4 teaspoons red wine vinegar

⅛ teaspoon sugar

**1 Prep Vegetables and Aromatics** Adjust oven rack to upper-middle position and heat oven to 450 degrees. Cut potatoes in half lengthwise, then cut crosswise into ½-inch-thick slices. Peel carrots and cut into 3-inch lengths, quartering thick ends lengthwise. Discard fennel stalks, halve bulb, and cut into ½-thick-wedges. Peel garlic.

**2 Roast Vegetables** Toss 1 tablespoon oil, rosemary, potatoes, carrots, fennel, garlic, ¾ teaspoon salt, and ¼ teaspoon pepper together in bowl. Spread vegetables in single layer on rimmed baking sheet. Roast until beginning to soften, about 25 minutes.

**3 Prep Pork** While vegetables roast, combine paprika, coriander, 1 teaspoon salt, and 1 teaspoon pepper in bowl. Trim pork and pat dry with paper towels. Cut 2 slits, about 2 inches apart, through fat on edges of each chop. Rub chops with 1 teaspoon oil, then season thoroughly with spice mixture.

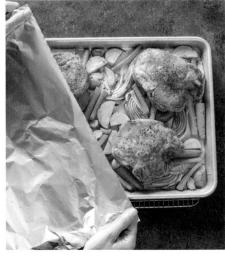

4 **Roast Pork** Lay chops on top of vegetables and continue to roast until chops register 145 degrees and vegetables are tender, 10 to 15 minutes, rotating sheet halfway through roasting.

5 **Make Vinaigrette** While pork cooks, mince shallot. Mince 2 tablespoons parsley. Whisk vinegar, sugar, remaining ¼ cup oil, shallot, parsley, ¼ teaspoon salt, and ¼ teaspoon pepper together in bowl.

6 **Finish Dish** When pork is cooked, remove sheet from oven, tent with aluminum foil, and let rest for 5 to 10 minutes. Drizzle vinaigrette over pork and serve.

# Pan-Seared Thick-Cut Boneless Pork Chops with Peaches and Spinach

serves 4; total time 1 hour

## notes for the cook

For perfectly even thick-cut pork chops, we prefer to buy a whole center-cut pork loin roast and cut it into chops ourselves.

To get a deep sear and a juicy, tender interior on these meaty chops, we use a screaming-hot cast-iron pan.

The fond left by the pork contributes deep flavor to the peaches, onion, and wilted spinach that complete the dish.

Look for a pork loin that is 7 to 8 inches long and 3 to 3½ inches in diameter.

We strongly prefer using natural pork here. Using pork that is enhanced (injected with a salt solution) will inhibit browning.

This recipe works best in a cast-iron skillet, but a 12-inch stainless-steel skillet will work.

2 ripe peaches

1 red onion

Fresh tarragon

2 teaspoons ground coriander

Salt and pepper

1 (2½- to 3-pound) boneless center-cut pork loin roast

3 tablespoons vegetable oil

12 ounces (12 cups) baby spinach

**1 Prep Peaches and Onion** Halve and pit peaches, then cut into 1-inch wedges. Chop onion. Mince 1 tablespoon tarragon.

**2 Prep Pork** Combine coriander, ½ teaspoon salt, and ¼ teaspoon pepper in small bowl. Trim pork, then cut roast crosswise into 4 chops of equal thickness. Pat chops dry with paper towels then season with coriander mixture.

**3 Cook Pork** Heat 12-inch cast-iron skillet over medium heat for 5 minutes. Add 1 tablespoon oil and heat until just smoking. Add chops and cook, without moving, until lightly browned on both sides, about 2 minutes per side. Flip chops and continue to cook, flipping every 2 minutes, until well browned and meat registers 140 degrees, 12 to 14 minutes. Transfer chops to cutting board, tent with aluminum foil, and let rest.

**4 Cook Peaches** While pork rests, add 1 tablespoon oil to now-empty skillet and heat over medium-low heat until shimmering. Add peaches, cut side down, and cook until caramelized on first side, about 2 minutes. Flip and continue to cook until caramelized on second side and tender, about 2 minutes. Transfer to serving bowl.

**5 Cook Onion** Add remaining 1 tablespoon oil to now-empty skillet and heat over medium heat until shimmering. Add onion and 1/4 teaspoon salt and cook, stirring occasionally, until softened and lightly browned, 2 to 4 minutes.

**6 Cook Spinach and Finish Dish** Add spinach to skillet 1 handful at a time and cook until wilted and tender, about 2 minutes. Off heat, season with salt and pepper to taste. Sprinkle peaches with tarragon and serve alongside pork and spinach.

# Sesame Pork Cutlets with Wilted Napa Cabbage Salad

serves 4 to 6; total time 45 minutes

## notes for the cook

Adding sesame seeds to a traditional egg, flour, and panko breading not only contributes great nutty flavor but also makes these pan-fried pork chops extra-crisp.

A warm Asian-style salad with wilted cabbage, shredded carrots, and matchsticks of crisp, crunchy Asian pear complements the rich nuttiness of the chops.

We like using Asian pear in this recipe for its bright crispness, but Bosc or Anjou pears will also work.

You will need a 12-inch nonstick skillet with a tight-fitting lid for this recipe.

2 garlic cloves
Fresh ginger
1 small head napa cabbage (1½ pounds)
1 carrot
1 Asian pear
Fresh cilantro
8 (4-ounce) boneless pork chops
Salt and pepper
⅔ cup all-purpose flour
2 large eggs
1 cup panko bread crumbs
⅔ cup sesame seeds
⅓ cup plus 1 tablespoon vegetable oil
1½ teaspoons toasted sesame oil
3 tablespoons rice vinegar

**1 Prep Vegetables** Mince garlic. Peel and grate 1 teaspoon ginger. Remove core from cabbage, then slice thin. Peel carrot and shred. Peel, halve, and core pear, then slice into 2-inch matchsticks. Mince ¼ cup cilantro.

**2 Pound and Season Pork** Trim pork chops. Cover with plastic wrap and pound each chop to ½-inch thickness. Pat pork dry with paper towels and season with salt and pepper.

**3 Dredge Pork** Spread flour in shallow dish. Beat eggs in second shallow dish. Combine panko and sesame seeds in third shallow dish. Working with 1 cutlet at a time, dredge cutlets in flour, shaking off excess; dip in egg, allowing excess to drip off; then coat with sesame-panko mixture, pressing gently to adhere. Transfer to large plate.

4 **Fry Pork** Line separate large plate with triple layer of paper towels. Heat ⅓ cup vegetable oil in 12-inch nonstick skillet over medium-high heat until shimmering. Carefully place 4 cutlets in skillet and cook until golden brown and crisp, 2 to 3 minutes per side. Transfer to prepared plate and repeat with remaining 4 cutlets.

5 **Wilt Cabbage** Wipe skillet clean with paper towels. Add sesame oil and remaining 1 tablespoon vegetable oil to now-empty skillet and heat over medium heat until shimmering. Add garlic and ginger and cook until fragrant, about 30 seconds. Add cabbage and carrot, cover, and cook until just wilted, stirring occasionally, about 5 minutes.

6 **Finish Dish** Off heat, add vinegar, pear, and cilantro to skillet and toss to combine. Season with salt and pepper to taste, and serve with pork.

# Stir-Fried Pork with Green Beans and Cashews

serves 4; total time 45 minutes

## notes for the cook

Quick-cooking, flavorful stir-fries like this one are ideal weeknight fare.

"Velveting" the sliced pork with oil and cornstarch before browning it helps the meat retain moisture as it cooks and encourages the stir-fry sauce to cling.

Adding the aromatics (ginger and garlic) at the end of cooking gives them just enough time to develop flavor without burning or becoming bitter.

Chicken broth gives our sauce some backbone and cornstarch thickens it slightly so that it perfectly coats the meat and green beans.

If you can't find mirin, use dry sherry.

1½ cups long-grain white rice

Salt

¼ cup cashews

8 ounces green beans

6 garlic cloves

Fresh ginger

1 cup chicken broth

¼ cup mirin

¼ cup soy sauce

3 tablespoons cornstarch

1 (1-pound) pork tenderloin

3 tablespoons vegetable oil

**1** **Make Rice** Rinse rice in fine-mesh strainer until water runs clear. Bring rice, 2¼ cups water, and ¼ teaspoon salt to simmer in large saucepan over medium heat. Reduce heat to low, cover, and simmer until rice is tender and liquid is absorbed, 16 to 18 minutes. Remove pot from heat, lay clean folded dish towel underneath lid, and let sit for 10 minutes.

**2** **Toast Nuts and Prep Vegetables** While rice cooks, toast cashews in 12-inch nonstick skillet over medium heat, shaking occasionally, until golden and fragrant, 3 to 5 minutes; transfer to small bowl to cool. Trim green beans and cut into 2-inch pieces. Mince garlic. Peel and grate 1 tablespoon ginger. Chop cooled cashews coarse.

**3** **Make Sauce and Velvet Pork** Whisk broth, mirin, soy sauce, and 1 tablespoon cornstarch together in bowl; set aside. Trim pork. Cut pork in half lengthwise, then slice crosswise into thin pieces. Toss pork, 1 tablespoon oil, and remaining 2 tablespoons cornstarch together in large bowl.

**4** **Stir-Fry Pork** Heat 2 teaspoons oil in now-empty skillet over medium-high heat until just smoking. Brown half of pork, 3 to 5 minutes; transfer to plate. Repeat with 2 teaspoons oil and remaining pork.

**5** **Add Green Beans and Aromatics** Add green beans and remaining 2 teaspoons oil to now-empty skillet and cook until bright green, about 1 minute. Add garlic and ginger and cook until fragrant, about 30 seconds.

**6** **Add Sauce and Finish Dish** Whisk broth mixture to recombine and add to skillet. Cook until thickened, about 2 minutes. Return pork and any accumulated juices to skillet and cook until heated through, about 1 minute. Sprinkle with cashews and serve with rice.

# Grilled Pork Tenderloin with Tomato-Onion Salad

serves 4; total time 45 minutes

## notes for the cook

We use a quick and easy spice rub with salt, pepper, and fennel to add texture and flavor to lean, mild pork tenderloin before throwing it on the grill in this recipe. Ground fennel adheres well to the pork and imparts more flavor than whole fennel seeds.

A bright salad of grilled onions and fresh tomatoes with capers, basil, and red wine vinaigrette livens up this dinner with sweetness and a bit of acidity.

You can substitute vine-ripened or heirloom tomatoes for the plum tomatoes.

Buy tenderloins that are of equal size and weight so they cook at the same rate.

1 red onion

4 plum tomatoes

3 tablespoons extra-virgin olive oil

Salt and pepper

Fresh basil

2 tablespoons capers

1 tablespoon ground fennel

2 (12- to 16-ounce) pork tenderloins

2 tablespoons red wine vinegar

1 **Heat Grill** Turn all burners to high, cover, and heat grill until hot, about 15 minutes. Leave all burners on high.

2 **Prep Onion and Tomatoes** While grill heats, slice onion into ¼-inch-thick rounds. Core tomatoes and slice into ¼-inch-thick-rounds; set aside. Brush onion with 1 tablespoon oil and sprinkle with ¼ teaspoon salt and ¼ teaspoon pepper. Chop ¼ cup basil and rinse capers.

3 **Prep Pork** Combine fennel, 1 teaspoon salt, and 1 teaspoon pepper in bowl. Trim pork, pat dry with paper towels, and sprinkle with fennel mixture.

**4** **Grill Pork** Clean and oil cooking grate. Grill pork, covered, turning occasionally, until well browned and meat registers 145 degrees, 12 to 15 minutes. Transfer to carving board, tent with aluminum foil, and let rest.

**5** **Grill Onion** While pork rests, grill onion rounds until lightly charred, about 2 minutes per side; transfer to large bowl and separate rings.

**6** **Finish Dish** Add vinegar, tomatoes, basil, capers, and remaining 2 tablespoons oil to bowl with onion and toss to combine. Season with salt and pepper to taste. Cut pork into ½-inch-thick slices and serve with salad.

# Roasted Pork Tenderloin with Green Beans and Potatoes

serves 4; total time 1 hour

## notes for the cook

To create a satisfying one-pan meal we pair quick-cooking pork tenderloin with green beans and fingerling potatoes, all on a single baking sheet. Placing the meat on the beans helps protect the lean pork from the hot pan, preventing overcooking.

Brushing a layer of sweet-savory hoisin sauce over the meat gives it a flavor boost and an appealing caramelized sheen.

An easy garlic-chive butter, melted over the resting pork and tossed with the vegetables, makes for a rich, flavorful finish.

Buy tenderloins that are of equal size and weight so they cook at the same rate.

A rasp-style grater makes quick work of turning the garlic into a paste.

1 pound green beans

1½ pounds fingerling potatoes

4 tablespoons unsalted butter

3 tablespoons extra-virgin olive oil

Salt and pepper

2 (12- to 16-ounce) pork tenderloins

¼ cup hoisin sauce

Fresh chives

1 garlic clove

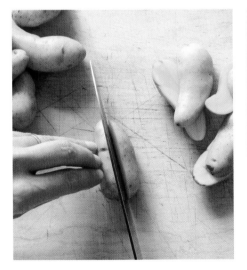

**1 Heat Oven and Prep Vegetables** Adjust oven rack to lower-middle position and heat oven to 450 degrees. Trim green beans. Cut potatoes in half lengthwise. Cut butter into 4 pieces and let soften at room temperature.

**2 Arrange Vegetables for Oven** Toss green beans with 1 tablespoon oil, ¼ teaspoon salt, and ¼ teaspoon pepper in bowl. Arrange beans crosswise down center of rimmed baking sheet, leaving room on both sides for potatoes. Toss potatoes with remaining 2 tablespoons oil, ¼ teaspoon salt, and ¼ teaspoon pepper in now-empty bowl. Place potatoes, cut side down, on either side of green beans.

**3 Prep Pork** Trim pork and pat dry with paper towels. Brush all over with hoisin sauce and season with pepper. Lay tenderloins on top of green beans. Roast until pork registers 145 degrees, 20 to 25 minutes.

4 **Make Compound Butter** While pork cooks, mince 2 tablespoons chives. Mince garlic to paste. Mash softened butter, chives, garlic, ¼ teaspoon salt, and ¼ teaspoon pepper together in bowl.

5 **Remove Pork from Oven and Continue to Roast Vegetables** Remove sheet from oven and transfer tenderloins to cutting board. Dot each tenderloin with 1 tablespoon chive butter, tent with aluminum foil, and let rest while vegetables finish cooking. Gently stir vegetables on sheet to combine and continue to roast until tender and golden, 5 to 10 minutes.

6 **Finish Dish** Remove sheet from oven, add remaining 2 tablespoons chive butter to vegetables, and toss to coat. Cut pork into ½-inch-thick slices and serve with vegetables.

# Pork Milanese with Arugula, Parsley, and Parmesan Salad

serves 4; total time 45 minutes

## notes for the cook

Milanese is a style of pan-fried breaded cutlet that includes Parmesan and lemon in the breading for great savory Italian flavor.

For tender, crispy cutlets, we cut a pork tenderloin into four equal pieces and pound them thin. Making your own cutlets rather than buying them ensures they'll be evenly sized.

We pair the cutlets with traditional peppery arugula salad dressed with a tangy lemon vinaigrette and sprinkled with shaved Parmesan cheese. The flavors in the salad echo and accentuate the flavors in the breading to tie the whole meal together.

2 lemons

1 tablespoon plus 1 cup extra-virgin olive oil

Salt and pepper

1½ ounces Parmesan cheese

Fresh parsley

1 (16-ounce) pork tenderloin

½ cup all-purpose flour

2 large eggs

1 cup panko bread crumbs

4 ounces (4 cups) baby arugula

**1 Make Dressing** Grate ½ teaspoon lemon zest and squeeze 2 teaspoons juice from 1 lemon. Cut remaining lemon into wedges. Whisk 1 tablespoon oil, lemon juice, ¼ teaspoon salt, and ¼ teaspoon pepper together in large bowl; set dressing aside. Grate ¼ cup Parmesan cheese then shave remaining Parmesan into thin strips using vegetable peeler. Mince 2 tablespoons parsley.

**2 Prep Pork** Trim tenderloin and cut crosswise into 4 equal lengths. Stand pieces cut side up on cutting board, cover with plastic wrap, and pound with meat pounder to even ¼-inch thickness. Pat cutlets dry with paper towels and season with pepper.

**3 Dredge Pork** Spread flour in shallow dish. Beat eggs in second shallow dish. Combine panko, lemon zest, grated Parmesan, parsley, ½ teaspoon salt, and ½ teaspoon pepper in third shallow dish. Working with 1 cutlet at a time, dredge cutlets in flour, shaking off excess; dip in eggs, allowing excess to drip off; and coat with panko mixture, pressing gently to adhere. Transfer to large plate.

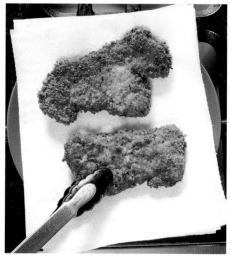

**4 Fry Pork** Line separate large plate with triple layer of paper towels. Heat remaining 1 cup oil in 12-inch nonstick skillet over medium-high heat until shimmering. Place 2 cutlets in skillet and cook until deep golden brown and pork is cooked through, 2 to 3 minutes per side, gently pressing on cutlets with spatula to ensure even browning.

**5 Drain Pork and Finish Cooking** Transfer cutlets to prepared plate and let drain. Repeat with remaining 2 cutlets.

**6 Finish Dish** Add arugula and shaved Parmesan to bowl with dressing and toss gently to combine. Serve pork with salad, passing lemon wedges separately.

# Sausage and White Beans with Mustard Greens

serves 4; total time 1 hour

## notes for the cook

This rich, stew-like dish combines meaty sausage, creamy white beans, and hearty greens.

Browning the sausage deepens its flavor and renders the fat, which is then used to sauté onion, garlic, and thyme, building a base of deep savory flavor.

You can use 2 teaspoons of dried thyme in place of the fresh thyme if you want.

For the greens, we enjoy the peppery spice of mustard greens, which we gently wilt before braising them. You can substitute kale for the mustard greens.

1 pound hot or sweet Italian sausages
2 tablespoons extra-virgin olive oil
1 onion
6 garlic cloves
Fresh thyme
Salt and pepper
1 (14.5-ounce) can diced tomatoes
1 (15-ounce) can cannellini beans
½ cup dry white wine
1½ cups chicken broth
12 ounces mustard greens
Fresh parsley

1 **Brown Sausages** Prick sausages with fork in several places. Heat 1 tablespoon oil in Dutch oven over medium-high heat until just smoking. Brown sausages well on all sides, about 8 minutes; transfer to plate. While sausages brown, chop onion fine. Mince garlic and 2 teaspoons thyme.

2 **Sauté Aromatics** Heat remaining 1 tablespoon oil in now-empty pot over medium heat until shimmering. Add onion and ¼ teaspoon salt and cook until softened and lightly browned, 5 to 7 minutes. Stir in garlic and thyme and cook until fragrant, about 30 seconds.

3 **Add Liquids** While aromatics cook, drain tomatoes, reserving juice. Drain and rinse beans. Stir wine and reserved tomato juice into pot, scraping up any browned bits, and cook until nearly evaporated, about 5 minutes. Stir in broth, tomatoes, and beans and bring to simmer.

**4 Stem Mustard Greens and Add to Pot** While mixture comes to simmer, stem mustard greens by cutting away leafy green portion from either side of stalk, then chop leaves into 2-inch pieces. Stir greens into pot and cook until slightly wilted, about 1 minute.

**5 Simmer Sausages** Place sausages on top of greens. Reduce heat to low, cover, and cook until greens are wilted and reduced in volume by about half, about 10 minutes. Uncover, increase heat to medium-low, and continue to cook, stirring occasionally, until sausages are cooked through and greens are tender, about 15 minutes.

**6 Finish Dish** While sausages cook, mince 2 tablespoons parsley. Off heat, use back of spoon to mash portion of beans against side of pot to thicken sauce. Serve, sprinkling individual portions with parsley.

# Polenta with Sausage, Peppers, and Olives

serves 4; total time 45 minutes

## notes for the cook

Creamy polenta is classically served with a deeply flavored Italian ragu, but making a long-simmered sauce in addition to making polenta from scratch takes more time and effort than we typically have on a busy weeknight. For a quicker dish that still had tons of complex flavor, we turned to Italian sausages.

Browning the sausages on all sides provides a flavorful fond that then becomes the base for the sauce. We sauté peppers and onions with the sausages and then add crushed tomatoes, olives, and red pepper flakes to finish the topping.

For a spicy kick, use hot Italian sausages.

Pinch baking soda

Salt and pepper

1 cup coarse-ground cornmeal

1 red bell pepper

1 small onion

½ cup pitted kalamata olives

1½ pounds hot or sweet Italian sausage

1 (14.5-ounce) can crushed tomatoes

¼ teaspoon red pepper flakes

2 tablespoons unsalted butter

**1 Cook Polenta** Bring 5 cups water to boil in large saucepan over medium-high heat. Stir in baking soda and 1 teaspoon salt. Slowly pour cornmeal into water in steady stream while whisking constantly and bring to boil. Reduce heat to lowest possible setting, cover, and cook, stirring often, until grains of cornmeal are tender, about 30 minutes.

**2 Prep Vegetables** While polenta cooks, stem and seed bell pepper, then slice into thin strips. Halve onion and slice thin. Halve oilves.

**3 Brown Sausages** Cook sausage in 12-inch nonstick skillet over medium heat until browned on all sides, about 6 minutes.

**4 Cook Pepper and Onion** Increase heat to medium-high, add bell pepper and onion, and cook until vegetables are softened, 4 to 6 minutes.

**5 Build Sauce** Add tomatoes and pepper flakes. Cook until sauce has thickened slightly, about 3 minutes. Remove from heat, stir in olives, and season with salt and pepper to taste; cover to keep warm.

**6 Finish Dish** When polenta is tender, remove pot from heat and stir in butter. Season with salt and pepper to taste. Divide polenta among individual serving dishes and top with sausage and sauce. Serve.

# Bratwurst Sandwiches with Red Potato and Kale Salad

serves 4; total time 45 minutes

## notes for the cook

Bratwurst sandwiches are a simple dinner solution but that doesn't mean they have to be boring. We pair them with a mustardy roasted potato and baby kale salad and use a sheet pan to make the whole cooking process a breeze.

While the sausages and vegetables are cooking, there's time to whisk together a flavorful vinaigrette of whole-grain mustard, red wine vinegar, and olive oil. Using the same whole-grain mustard on the buns reinforces the vinaigrette's flavor profile.

Toasting the buns on the rack means one less dirty pan and also helps mimic the feel and taste of grilled buns.

Use small red potatoes measuring 1 to 2 inches in diameter.

1 pound small red potatoes

2 red onions

7 tablespoons extra-virgin olive oil

Salt and pepper

1 pound bratwurst (4 sausages)

2 tablespoons red wine vinegar

¼ cup whole-grain mustard

4 radishes

4 hot dog buns

5 ounces (5 cups) baby kale

**1 Prep Potatoes and Onions** Adjust oven rack to middle position, place rimmed baking sheet on rack, and heat oven to 425 degrees. Cut potatoes in half. Cut onions in half and slice ¼ inch thick. Toss potatoes with 2 tablespoons oil, ¼ teaspoon salt, and ¼ teaspoon pepper in bowl. In separate bowl, toss onions with 1 tablespoon oil.

**2 Cook Sausages, Onions, and Potatoes** Place bratwurst on 1 side of hot sheet and spread potatoes, cut side down, on other side. Scatter onions around bratwurst on sheet. Roast until sausages register 160 degrees and potatoes are tender, 25 to 30 minutes, flipping bratwurst halfway through roasting.

**3 Make Dressing and Slice Radishes** While bratwurst and vegetables cook, whisk vinegar and 2 tablespoons mustard together in large bowl. Whisking constantly, slowly drizzle in remaining ¼ cup oil until incorporated. Trim radishes and slice thin.

**4 Dress Potatoes** Remove sheet from oven. Transfer potatoes to bowl with dressing and toss to coat; cover with aluminum foil to keep warm. Tent sheet with aluminum foil to keep warm.

**5 Toast Buns** Place hot dog buns directly on rack and toast until lightly browned, about 5 minutes.

**6 Finish Dish** Remove buns from oven. Spread remaining 2 tablespoons mustard evenly into buns, then top with onions and bratwurst. Add kale and radishes to potatoes and toss gently to combine. Season with salt and pepper to taste and serve immediately with sandwiches.

# Thai-Style Pork Burgers with Sesame Green Beans

serves 4; total time 1 hour

## notes for the cook

Burgers made from ground pork are notoriously dry and crumbly, so we add a panade (a mixture of bread and milk) to keep the burgers moist and cohesive.

We give the mild pork a seasoning boost and Thai flavor profile with fish sauce, cilantro, lime, and Sriracha sauce.

A simple green bean side pairs perfectly with these flavorful burgers. Shocking the cooked beans in ice water ensures they keep their vibrant color and crisp bite.

Note that you will need a total of about ¾ cup of cilantro, so shop accordingly.

1 pound green beans
Salt and pepper
1 lime
¼ cup mayonnaise
4 teaspoons Sriracha sauce
1 tablespoon toasted sesame oil
1 tablespoon sesame seeds
Fresh cilantro
1 slice hearty white sandwich bread
3 tablespoons milk
1 teaspoon fish sauce
1½ pounds 80 to 85 percent lean ground pork
1 tablespoon vegetable oil
4 hamburger buns

**1 Cook and Blanch Green Beans** Bring 2 quarts water to boil in large saucepan. Fill large bowl halfway with ice and water. Trim ends of green beans. Add green beans and 1 tablespoon salt to boiling water and cook until crisp-tender, about 6 minutes. Drain green beans and place in ice bath to cool. Drain again, transfer to salad spinner, and spin dry.

**2 Make Sriracha Mayo and Dress Beans** While beans are cooking, grate 1½ teaspoons lime zest and squeeze 1 tablespoon juice. Whisk mayonnaise, 2 teaspoons Sriracha, and ½ teaspoon lime zest together in small bowl. Season with salt to taste; set aside. Transfer drained beans to serving bowl and toss with sesame oil, sesame seeds, and lime juice. Season with salt and pepper to taste; set aside.

**3 Make Panade** Mince 3 tablespoons cilantro. Tear bread into rough 1-inch pieces. Combine milk, fish sauce, remaining 1 teaspoon lime zest, remaining 2 teaspoons Sriracha, cilantro, bread, and 1 teaspoon pepper in large bowl. Mash to paste with fork. Using your hands, add pork and mix until well combined.

**4** **Form Patties** Divide pork mixture into 4 equal balls, then flatten into ¾-inch-thick patties, about 4 inches wide.

**5** **Cook Burgers** Heat vegetable oil in 12-inch nonstick skillet over medium-low heat until shimmering. Add patties and cook until well browned on first side, 6 to 8 minutes. Flip burgers and continue to cook until second side is well browned and meat registers 150 degrees, 7 to 9 minutes, flipping as needed to ensure even browning. Transfer burgers to wire rack set in rimmed baking sheet and let rest.

**6** **Finish Dish** While burgers rest, pick ½ cup cilantro leaves. Spread layer of Sriracha mayo onto bottom buns. Top with burgers and cilantro leaves. Serve with green beans.

# Spicy Korean-Style Pork Tacos with Red Cabbage Slaw

serves 4; total time 45 minutes

## notes for the cook

These tacos get bold flavor from the Korean chile paste *gochujang*.

A light, fresh slaw made from cabbage, snow peas, and scallions is the perfect complement to the saucy, meaty pork.

You can find gochujang in Asian markets and some well-stocked supermarkets.

If you have a few extra minutes, try our preferred tortilla-warming method: Using a dry skillet over medium-high heat, warm the tortillas one at a time until softened and speckled brown, 20 to 30 seconds per side.

You can also use the shredding disk of a food processor to prepare the cabbage.

5 scallions
4 garlic cloves
Fresh ginger
1 small head red cabbage (1¼ pounds)
4 ounces snow peas
1½ pounds boneless country-style pork ribs
Salt and pepper
1 cup chicken broth
1 teaspoon cornstarch
2 tablespoons vegetable oil
3 tablespoons gochujang
2 tablespoons rice vinegar
1 teaspoon sugar
12 (6-inch) corn tortillas

**1 Prep Vegetables** Slice scallion whites thin and slice scallion greens thin on bias, keeping whites and greens separate. Slice greens thin on bias. Mince garlic. Peel and grate 1 tablespoon ginger. Quarter and core cabbage, then slice 3 cups thin. Remove strings from snow peas and halve lengthwise.

**2 Prep Pork** Trim pork and cut crosswise into ¼-inch-thick slices. Pat dry with paper towels and season with salt and pepper.

**3 Build Sauce** Whisk 2 tablespoons broth and cornstarch together in small bowl; set aside. Heat 1 tablespoon oil in 12-inch nonstick skillet over medium heat until shimmering. Add scallion whites and cook until softened, about 2 minutes. Add garlic and ginger and cook until fragrant, about 30 seconds. Stir in gochujang and remaining broth, bring to simmer, and cook, stirring occasionally, until sauce has reduced to glaze, 5 to 7 minutes.

4 **Cook Pork** Whisk reserved cornstarch mixture to recombine then whisk into sauce. Cook until slightly thickened, about 30 seconds. Add pork to skillet, stir to coat, and cook, stirring occasionally, until pork is cooked through, 5 to 7 minutes. Remove from heat and cover to keep warm.

5 **Make Slaw** Whisk vinegar, sugar, remaining 1 tablespoon oil, ½ teaspoon salt, and ⅛ teaspoon pepper together in large bowl until sugar has dissolved. Add cabbage, snow peas, and ¼ cup scallion greens to bowl and toss well. Season with salt and pepper to taste.

6 **Finish Dish** Place tortillas on plate, cover with damp dish towel, and microwave for 60 to 90 seconds until warm. Sprinkle remaining scallion greens over pork mixture. Serve with warm tortillas and slaw.

# Chorizo, Corn, and Tomato Tostadas with Lime Crema

serves 4; total time 45 minutes

## notes for the cook

Tostadas are flat, crisped tortillas that serve as a crunchy base for flavorful toppings. To make them hearty enough for a meal, we top ours with chorizo sausage, black beans, corn, tomatoes, and cabbage slaw.

To simplify this multi-component meal, we use a sheet pan to brown the chorizo and corn, and warm the tostadas—spread with a flavorful black bean–jalapeño mixture—on another baking sheet at the same time.

The brine from the jarred jalapeños adds zingy flavor to our quick cabbage slaw.

Another hard, cured sausage (such as linguiça) can be substituted for the chorizo.

Look for tostadas next to the taco kits at most supermarkets.

8 ounces Spanish-style chorizo sausage

4 ears corn

Jarred jalapeños with their brine

2 limes

1 (14-ounce) bag green coleslaw mix

Salt and pepper

½ cup sour cream

1 tablespoon vegetable oil

1 (15-ounce) can black beans

¼ cup chicken or vegetable broth

12 (6-inch) corn tostadas

6 ounces cherry tomatoes

Fresh cilantro

4 ounces queso fresco or feta cheese

**1 Heat Oven and Prep Ingredients** Adjust oven racks to upper-middle and lower-middle positions, place rimmed baking sheet on upper rack, and heat oven to 450 degrees. Meanwhile, cut chorizo in half lengthwise, then slice crosswise into ¼-inch-thick pieces. Remove husks and silk from corn and cut kernels from cobs. Chop 1 tablespoon jalapeño fine and measure out ¼ cup brine.

**2 Make Slaw and Crema** Squeeze 3 tablespoons lime juice. Toss coleslaw mix with 3 tablespoons jalapeño brine in bowl and season with salt and pepper to taste. In second bowl, whisk sour cream and 2 tablespoons lime juice together, and season with salt and pepper to taste; set slaw and crema aside for serving.

**3 Roast Chorizo and Corn** Combine oil, chorizo, and corn in bowl. Remove sheet from oven and spread chorizo and corn in single layer on hot sheet. Cook until browned, about 15 minutes.

4 **Heat and Mash Beans** While chorizo and corn cook, drain and rinse beans. Combine broth, chopped jalapeños, remaining 1 tablespoon brine, and beans in clean bowl and microwave until warm, about 2 minutes. Mash beans with potato masher until spreadable, season with salt and pepper to taste, and spread evenly over tostadas. Arrange on clean rimmed baking sheet, overlapping as needed.

5 **Prep Toppings and Heat Tostadas** Quarter tomatoes. Pick ¼ cup cilantro leaves. During final 5 minutes of roasting chorizo, transfer sheet with tostadas to lower oven rack to warm through.

6 **Finish Dish** Remove tostadas from oven. Transfer chorizo-corn mixture to large bowl, and stir in remaining 1 tablespoon lime juice and tomatoes. Divide mixture evenly among tostadas. Top tostadas with slaw and crema. Crumble queso fresco (1 cup) over top and sprinkle with cilantro. Serve.

# Lamb Meatballs with Couscous and Yogurt Sauce

serves 4; total time 1 hour

## notes for the cook

Lamb meatballs are a staple in Mediterranean cooking. Our weeknight-friendly version pairs tender, spiced lamb with a light, lemony couscous salad enhanced with chopped mint and radicchio, plus a creamy yogurt sauce.

A quick panade made from bread crumbs and Greek yogurt plus an egg yolk not only binds our meatballs together but also keeps them from drying out.

You can brown the meatballs in just one batch; it takes only a few minutes in the hot skillet to create a perfectly seared exterior.

2 lemons

Fresh mint

2 garlic cloves

1 cup plain Greek yogurt

3 tablespoons extra-virgin olive oil

Salt and pepper

1½ cups couscous

1 small head radicchio (6 ounces)

1 large egg

3 tablespoons panko bread crumbs

1 pound ground lamb

1 teaspoon ground cumin

¾ teaspoon ground cinnamon

**1 Make Sauce** Grate ½ teaspoon lemon zest and squeeze 3 tablespoons juice from 1 lemon. Cut remaining lemon into wedges. Mince 6 tablespoons mint. Mince garlic. Combine ⅔ cup yogurt, 2 tablespoons water, 1 tablespoon oil, lemon zest and ½ teaspoon juice, 1 tablespoon mint, half of garlic, and ¼ teaspoon salt in bowl. Season with salt and pepper to taste. Cover and refrigerate until ready to serve.

**2 Make Couscous and Prep Radicchio** Heat 1 tablespoon oil in medium saucepan over medium-high heat until shimmering. Add couscous and cook, stirring frequently, until grains are just beginning to brown, 3 to 5 minutes. Stir in 1½ cups water and ¼ teaspoon salt. Cover, remove saucepan from heat, and let sit until couscous is tender, about 7 minutes. Meanwhile, halve and core radicchio and slice thin; set aside.

**3 Form Meatballs** Separate egg and discard white. Using fork, mash panko, 2 tablespoons water, and remaining ⅓ cup yogurt in large bowl to form paste. Add ground lamb, cumin, cinnamon, 2 tablespoons mint, remaining garlic, egg yolk, ¼ teaspoon salt, and ⅛ teaspoon pepper and knead with your hands until thoroughly combined. Pinch off and roll mixture into 20 tightly packed 1½-inch meatballs.

4 **Cook Meatballs** Heat remaining 1 tablespoon oil in 12-inch nonstick skillet over medium-high heat until just smoking. Brown meatballs well on all sides, 6 to 8 minutes; transfer to serving platter and tent with aluminum foil.

5 **Sauté Radicchio** Pour off all but 1 tablespoon fat from skillet. Add radicchio and cook over medium heat, stirring occasionally, until wilted and beginning to brown, about 1 minute. Transfer to serving bowl.

6 **Finish Dish** Uncover couscous and fluff with fork. Stir couscous into bowl with radicchio, along with remaining lemon juice and 2 tablespoons mint until well combined. Season with salt and pepper and drizzle with extra oil to taste. Sprinkle meatballs with remaining 1 tablespoon mint. Serve with yogurt sauce, couscous, and lemon wedges.

# Lamb and Summer Vegetable Kebabs with Grilled Focaccia

serves 4 to 6; total time 1 hour

## notes for the cook

These smoky lamb kebabs pair well-browned, tender meat with crisp vegetables.

Boneless leg of lamb is inexpensive and easy to work with.

We prefer the lamb cooked to medium in this recipe.

Since the grill is already in use, it's a cinch to grill store-bought focaccia bread for a simple, flavorful accompaniment that makes the perfect vehicle for savoring every bit of juicy lamb and herb oil.

You will need six 12-inch metal skewers for this recipe. If you have long, thin pieces of meat, roll or fold them into approximate 1½-inch cubes before skewering.

Fresh mint

Fresh rosemary

2 pounds boneless leg of lamb

Salt and pepper

1 small loaf focaccia bread

5 tablespoons extra-virgin olive oil

2 garlic cloves

1 lemon

2 small yellow summer squash (12 ounces)

2 red bell peppers

2 red onions

**1 Heat Grill** Turn all burners to high, cover, and heat grill until hot, about 15 minutes. Leave primary burner on high and turn other burner(s) to medium.

**2 Prep Lamb Skewers** While grill heats, mince ¼ cup mint. Mince 2 teaspoons rosemary. Pull lamb apart at seams, trim, then cut into 1½-inch pieces. Combine lamb, 2 tablespoons mint, 1 teaspoon rosemary, ½ teaspoon salt, and ¼ teaspoon pepper in large bowl and toss to coat. Thread lamb tightly onto two 12-inch metal skewers; set aside.

**3 Prep Bread and Make Dressing** Cut focaccia in half, then cut crosswise into 1-inch-thick slices. Brush with 2 tablespoons oil. Mince garlic. Whisk remaining 2 tablespoons mint, remaining 1 teaspoon rosemary, remaining 3 tablespoons oil, garlic, ¼ teaspoon salt, and ¼ teaspoon pepper in large bowl.

**4 Prep Vegetables** Halve lemon. Halve squash lengthwise, then slice crosswise into 1-inch-thick half-moons. Stem and seed bell peppers, then cut into 1½-inch pieces. Chop onions into 1-inch pieces. Add vegetables to bowl with dressing and toss to coat. In alternating pattern of squash, bell pepper, and 3 pieces onion, thread vegetables onto four 12-inch metal skewers.

**5 Grill Kebabs** Clean and oil cooking grate. Place lamb skewers on hotter side of grill and place vegetable skewers and lemon halves on cooler side of grill. Cook, covered, turning skewers every 3 to 4 minutes, until lamb is well browned and registers 130 to 135 degrees (for medium) 8 to 12 minutes. Transfer lamb and lemon halves to serving platter, tent with aluminum foil, and let rest.

**6 Finish Vegetables and Grill Bread** While lamb rests, continue to cook vegetable skewers until tender and lightly charred, 6 to 8 minutes, turning as needed; transfer to platter with lamb. Meanwhile, grill focaccia on hotter side of grill until lightly browned, 1 to 2 minutes per side. Transfer to second platter and drizzle with extra oil to taste. Slide lamb and vegetables off skewers onto plates and cut grilled lemon halves into wedges. Serve.

# Grilled Harissa Lamb Burgers with Cucumber and Olive Salad

serves 4; total time 1 hour

## notes for the cook

Our rich, spiced lamb burgers are a welcome break from traditional beef versions, and a cool, salty cucumber and olive salad is the perfect partner.

Look for harissa chile paste in the international aisle at the supermarket with the Middle Eastern or Indian ingredients.

If you can't find harissa, you can make your own (see page 7).

The red color of the harissa makes these burgers look more rare than they actually are—use an instant-read thermometer to accurately check doneness. We prefer these burgers cooked to 140 to 145 degrees.

If your grill only has two burners, turn the secondary burner off at the end of step 1.

3 cucumbers
¼ cup pitted kalamata olives
1 red onion
2 tablespoons extra-virgin olive oil
Salt and pepper
1 lemon
Fresh mint
3 tablespoons mayonnaise
2 tablespoons harissa
1 pound ground lamb
4 hamburger buns
1 cup baby arugula

**1** **Heat Grill** Turn all burners to high, cover, and heat grill until hot, about 15 minutes. Turn primary burner and secondary burner to medium-high and turn off other burner(s).

**2** **Prep Vegetables** While grill heats, peel cucumbers and halve lengthwise. Scoop out seeds with spoon and slice thin. Evenly spread cucumber slices on paper towel–lined baking sheet and refrigerate. Chop olives coarse. Slice onion into ½-inch-thick rounds. Brush with 2 teaspoons oil and season with salt and pepper.

**3** **Make Harissa Mayo and Dressing** Grate 1½ teaspoons lemon zest and squeeze 2 tablespoons juice. Mince ¼ cup mint. In a small bowl, whisk together mayonnaise, 1 tablespoon harissa, ½ teaspoon lemon zest, and 1 tablespoon mint. Season with salt and pepper to taste. Whisk together remaining 4 teaspoons oil, lemon juice, remaining 3 tablespoons mint, ½ teaspoon salt, and ¼ teaspoon pepper in medium serving bowl.

**4** **Make Lamb Patties** Place lamb, remaining 1 teaspoon lemon zest, remaining 1 tablespoon harissa, ¼ teaspoon salt, and ¼ teaspoon pepper in large bowl and knead gently with your hands until thoroughly combined. Divide lamb mixture into 4 equal balls, then flatten into ¾-inch-thick patties, about 3½ inches wide. Press center of patties down with your fingertips to create ¼-inch-deep depression.

**5** **Grill Burgers and Onion** Clean and oil cooking grate. Grill onion over hotter side of grill, covered, until beginning to brown, about 5 minutes. Flip onions. Add burgers to hotter side of grill. Grill until meat is browned, 4 to 6 minutes, moving to cooler side of grill if flare-ups occur. Flip onions and burgers. Continue to grill until burgers register 140 to 145 degrees, 4 to 6 minutes. Transfer onions and burgers to plate. Toast buns on grill, 1 to 2 minutes.

**6** **Finish Dish** Add chilled cucumbers and olives to bowl with dressing and toss to combine. Season with salt and pepper to taste. Spread layer of harissa mayo onto bottom buns and top with burgers, onion, and arugula. Serve with cucumber salad.

# Sumac Lamb Loin Chops with Carrots, Mint, and Paprika

serves 4; total time 1 hour

## notes for the cook

Lamb is a natural pairing with Mediterranean flavors, so we use a combination of fresh mint, sweet paprika, and the bright, citrusy Middle Eastern spice sumac to amp up mild lamb chops.

The sweetness of cooked carrots complements the lamb and our cooling, nutty tahini sauce tastes great over both elements, tying the whole meal together.

If you can't find tahini, you can make your own (see page 7).

1 small garlic clove

1 lemon

3 tablespoons tahini

3 tablespoons plain Greek yogurt

Salt and pepper

1 pound carrots

8 (4-ounce) lamb loin or rib chops, ¾ to 1 inch thick

1 tablespoon ground sumac

2 tablespoons extra-virgin olive oil

Fresh mint

½ teaspoon paprika

**1 Make Sauce** Mince garlic and squeeze 2 tablespoons lemon juice. Whisk tahini, yogurt, 2 tablespoons water, garlic, 1 tablespoon lemon juice and ¼ teaspoon salt together in bowl until combined.

**2 Prep Carrots** Peel carrots and cut into 1½- to 2-inch lengths. Leave thin pieces whole, halve medium pieces lengthwise, and quarter thick pieces lengthwise.

**3 Cook Lamb** Trim lamb and pat dry with paper towels. Sprinkle sumac evenly over lamb and season with salt and pepper. Heat 1 tablespoon oil in 12-inch skillet over medium-high heat until just smoking. Cook chops until well browned and meat registers 120 to 125 degrees (for medium-rare), 4 to 6 minutes per side. Transfer chops to platter, tent with aluminum foil, and let rest.

4 **Cook Carrots** While lamb is cooking, bring 2 cups water to boil in medium saucepan over high heat. Add carrots and 2 teaspoons salt, cover, and cook until tender throughout, about 6 minutes (start timer as soon as carrots go into water). Drain carrots and return to now-empty pan.

5 **Chop Mint** While carrots cook, chop 2 tablespoons mint.

6 **Finish Dish** Add paprika, remaining 1 tablespoon oil, and 1 teaspoon lemon juice to carrots and stir until combined. Stir in 1 tablespoon chopped mint. Season with salt, pepper, and remaining 2 teaspoons lemon juice to taste. Sprinkle remaining 1 tablespoon mint over lamb, drizzle with extra oil to taste, and season with extra sumac to taste. Serve chops with carrots and sauce.

# Grilled Lamb Shoulder Chops with Zucchini and Corn Salad

serves 4; total time 1 hour

## notes for the cook

Inexpensive lamb shoulder chops are a great match with the grill because their distinctive gutsy flavor holds up well to the smoke.

Grill-charred corn and zucchini brushed with a simple marinade of oil, garlic, and red pepper flakes give our summery salad tons of flavor.

Look for zucchini that are 8 ounces or less.

Try to purchase chops that are at least ¾ inch thick, as they are less likely to overcook.

We like our lamb shoulder chops cooked to medium as this cut can be tough if cooked any less than that.

3 garlic cloves

½ cup extra-virgin olive oil

Salt and pepper

4 (8- to 12-ounce) lamb shoulder chops (blade or round bone), ¾ to 1 inch thick

2 ears corn

1½ pounds zucchini

⅛ teaspoon red pepper flakes

Fresh basil

1 lemon

2 ounces feta cheese

**1 Heat Grill** Turn all burners to high, cover, and heat grill until hot, about 15 minutes. Turn all burners to medium-high.

**2 Marinate Lamb** While grill heats, mince garlic. Whisk one-third of garlic, 3 tablespoons oil, ¾ teaspoon salt, and ½ teaspoon pepper together in baking dish. Trim chops, add to marinade, and turn to coat.

**3 Prep Vegetables and Dressing** Remove husks and silk from corn. Slice zucchini lengthwise into ½-inch-thick planks. Whisk pepper flakes, remaining 5 tablespoons oil, remaining garlic, ½ teaspoon salt, and ¼ teaspoon pepper together in large bowl. Brush corn with 1 tablespoon oil mixture. Add zucchini to remaining oil mixture in bowl and toss to coat.

4 **Grill Vegetables** Clean and oil cooking grate. Place corn and zucchini on grill; do not wash bowl, reserving any oil mixture remaining. Grill, uncovered, turning corn every 2 to 3 minutes until kernels are lightly charred all over, 10 to 15 minutes total, and zucchini is well-browned and tender (not mushy), 5 to 7 minutes per side; transfer to plate. Turn all burners to high.

5 **Grill Lamb** Place chops on grill and cook, covered, until browned and meat registers 130 to 135 degrees (for medium), 4 to 6 minutes per side. Transfer chops to serving platter, tent with aluminum foil, and let rest.

6 **Finish Dish** While lamb rests, cut kernels from cobs. Cut zucchini on bias into ½-inch-thick slices. Chop 2 tablespoons basil. Squeeze 4 teaspoons lemon juice. Add vegetables to bowl with reserved oil mixture. Add basil and lemon juice to vegetables and toss to combine. Season with salt and pepper to taste. Transfer salad to platter and crumble feta (½ cup) over top. Serve with lamb chops.

# Spicy Lamb with Lentils and Yogurt

serves 4; total time 1 hour

## notes for the cook

This skillet recipe combines earthy lentils with warm-spiced ground lamb for a hearty but not fussy meal. Cilantro and tomatoes add freshness, while Greek yogurt stirred in at the end brings the dish together.

We create a full-flavored fond by sautéing our aromatics and then deglazing the pan to dissolve all that complex flavor into the dish.

Adding a tiny amount of baking soda helps tenderize the ground lamb by raising its pH.

Note that you will need ¾ cup of cilantro, so shop accordingly.

We prefer how small green *lentilles du Puy*, or French lentils, hold their shape in this recipe; we do not recommend substituting other types.

1 pound ground lamb
¼ teaspoon baking soda
Salt and pepper
1 cup lentilles du Puy
3 garlic cloves
Fresh ginger
1 tablespoon tomato paste
2 teaspoons garam masala
1 teaspoon red pepper flakes
1 onion
2 tomatoes
Fresh cilantro
1 tablespoon vegetable oil
2 naan breads
¾ cup plain Greek yogurt

**1** **Season Lamb** Toss lamb with baking soda, 2 tablespoons water, and ½ teaspoon salt in bowl until thoroughly combined; set aside for 20 minutes.

**2** **Cook Lentils** While lamb sits, pick over lentils and rinse. Bring lentils, 4 cups water, and 1 teaspoon salt to boil in medium saucepan over high heat. Reduce heat to low and simmer until lentils are just tender, 18 to 22 minutes. Drain well.

**3** **Prep Vegetables** While lentils cook, mince garlic. Peel and grate 1 teaspoon ginger. Combine tomato paste, garam masala, pepper flakes, garlic, and ginger in small bowl. Chop onion. Core tomatoes and cut into ½-inch pieces. Chop ¾ cup cilantro.

**4** **Cook Aromatics** Adjust oven rack to middle position and heat oven to 400 degrees. Heat oil in 12-inch skillet over medium heat until shimmering. Add onion and ¼ teaspoon salt and cook until softened and lightly browned, 5 to 7 minutes. Stir in garlic mixture and cook, stirring constantly until bottom of skillet is dark brown, 1 to 2 minutes.

**5** **Cook Lamb and Finish Lentils** Add 1 cup water and bring to boil, scraping up any browned bits. Reduce heat to medium-low, add lamb in 2-inch chunks to skillet, and bring to gentle simmer. Cover and cook until lamb is cooked through, 10 to 12 minutes, stirring and breaking up lamb chunks with 2 forks halfway through. Uncover skillet, increase heat to medium, stir in drained lentils, and cook until liquid is mostly absorbed, 3 to 5 minutes.

**6** **Finish Dish** While lamb cooks, place naan on rimmed baking sheet and bake until warmed through, about 5 minutes. Off heat, stir chopped tomatoes, ½ cup chopped cilantro, and 2 tablespoons yogurt into lentils and season with salt and pepper to taste. Sprinkle with remaining ¼ cup cilantro. Serve with naan and remaining yogurt.

# Poached Chicken with Quinoa and Warm Tomato-Ginger Vinaigrette

serves 4; total time 1 hour

## notes for the cook

Poached chicken can be much more than bland health food; ours starts with a flavorful poaching liquid that adds juiciness.

Poaching the chicken in a steamer basket keeps it from coming into contact with the hot pot bottom and ensures even cooking.

While the chicken poaches, there's plenty of time to cook a side of quinoa pilaf and prep the ingredients for a warm vinaigrette that flavors the quinoa and sauces the chicken.

We like the convenience of prewashed quinoa; rinsing removes the quinoa's bitter protective coating (called saponin). If you buy unwashed quinoa, rinse it and then spread it out on a clean dish towel to dry for 15 minutes.

8 garlic cloves
1 shallot
½ cup soy sauce
Salt and pepper
4 (6- to 8-ounce) boneless, skinless chicken breasts
3 tablespoons extra-virgin olive oil
1½ cups prewashed white quinoa
Fresh ginger
12 ounces cherry tomatoes
Fresh parsley
⅛ teaspoon ground cumin
⅛ teaspoon ground fennel
2 teaspoons red wine vinegar

1 **Make Poaching Liquid** Peel and smash 6 garlic cloves and mince remaining 2 cloves. Mince shallot. Whisk 4 quarts water, soy sauce, smashed garlic cloves, and ¼ cup salt in Dutch oven until salt is dissolved. Trim chicken, cover with plastic wrap, and pound thick ends until ¾ inch thick.

2 **Poach Chicken** Arrange breasts in steamer basket, then submerge in water. Heat pot over medium heat until water registers 175 degrees, 15 to 20 minutes. Turn off heat, cover pot, and let sit until chicken registers 160 degrees, 15 to 20 minutes. Transfer chicken to cutting board, tent with aluminum foil, and let rest.

3 **Cook Quinoa** Meanwhile, heat 1 tablespoon oil in large saucepan over medium heat until shimmering. Add quinoa, minced garlic, half of shallot, and ½ teaspoon salt and cook until fragrant, about 3 minutes. Stir in 1¾ cups water and bring to simmer. Reduce heat to low, cover, and simmer until quinoa is tender and water is absorbed, 18 to 22 minutes, stirring once halfway through cooking. Remove pot from heat and let sit, covered, for 10 minutes.

**4** **Prep Vegetables** While quinoa cooks, peel and grate 2 teaspoons ginger. Halve tomatoes. Chop ¼ cup parsley.

**5** **Make Tomato Vinaigrette** Heat 1 tablespoon oil in 10-inch nonstick skillet over medium heat until shimmering. Add cumin, fennel, remaining shallot, and ginger and cook until fragrant, about 30 seconds. Stir in tomatoes and ¼ teaspoon salt and cook, stirring frequently, until tomatoes have softened, 3 to 5 minutes. Off heat, stir in vinegar, remaining 1 tablespoon oil, and parsley and season with salt and pepper to taste.

**6** **Finish Dish** Add half of tomato-ginger vinaigrette to quinoa and stir to combine. Season with salt and pepper and drizzle with extra oil to taste. Slice each chicken breast on bias into ¼-inch-thick slices and transfer to serving platter or individual plates. Serve with remaining warm vinaigrette and quinoa.

# Parmesan Chicken with Wilted Radicchio Salad

serves 4; total time 1 hour

## notes for the cook

With its crisp coating and juicy, tender meat, Parmesan chicken is a surefire crowd-pleaser. A vegetable-heavy side dish brightens up the meal.

Use the large holes of a box grater to shred the Parmesan. Don't use preshredded cheese; most of it has bland flavor and a stiff, fibrous texture.

Shred a little extra Parmesan to sprinkle on the chicken before serving, if desired.

Use tongs to dredge and coat the chicken to avoid battering your hands.

The first batch of cutlets can be kept warm in a 200-degree oven while you cook the second batch.

½ cup all-purpose flour

2 large eggs

3 ounces Parmesan cheese

1 cup panko bread crumbs

6 (4-ounce) chicken cutlets, ½ inch thick

Salt and pepper

1 fennel bulb

12 ounces cherry tomatoes

½ head radicchio (5 ounces)

1 small shallot

1 tablespoon white wine vinegar

½ teaspoon Dijon mustard

10 tablespoons extra-virgin olive oil

2 ounces (2 cups) baby arugula

**1 Dredge Chicken** Spread flour in shallow dish. Beat eggs in second shallow dish. Shred Parmesan (1 cup) and combine with panko in third shallow dish. Trim cutlets, pat dry with paper towels, and season with salt and pepper. Working with 1 cutlet at a time, dredge in flour, shaking off excess; dip in egg, allowing excess to drip off; and coat with panko mixture, pressing gently to adhere. Transfer to large plate.

**2 Prep Vegetables** Discard fennel stalks, halve bulb, core, and slice thin. Halve tomatoes. Remove core from radicchio, then slice leaves thin.

**3 Make Vinaigrette** Mince shallot and transfer to large bowl. Whisk in vinegar, mustard, ¼ teaspoon salt, and pinch pepper. Whisking constantly, slowly drizzle in 3 tablespoons oil until emulsified.

**4** **Pan-Fry Chicken** Place wire rack in rimmed baking sheet and line rack with paper towels. Heat 3 tablespoons oil in 12-inch nonstick skillet over medium heat until shimmering. Add 3 cutlets and cook until chicken is tender, golden brown, and crisp, about 4 minutes per side. Transfer cutlets to prepared rack and tent loosely with aluminum foil. Wipe out skillet and repeat with additional 3 tablespoons oil and remaining 3 cutlets.

**5** **Sauté Fennel** Wipe out skillet with paper towels. Heat remaining 1 tablespoon oil in skillet over medium heat until shimmering. Add fennel and cook until softened and just beginning to brown, about 5 minutes; transfer to bowl with vinaigrette.

**6** **Finish Dish** Add tomatoes to now-empty skillet and cook until softened, about 2 minutes; transfer to bowl with vinaigrette. Add radicchio and arugula and gently toss to combine. Season with salt and pepper to taste and serve with chicken.

# Chicken Katsu with Tonkatsu Sauce, Cabbage Salad, and Rice

serves 4 to 6; total time 1 hour

## notes for the cook

This simple pan-fried chicken with Japanese-style barbecue sauce, crunchy cabbage salad, and rice is quick and easy to prepare, and satisfies palates of all ages.

The first batch of cutlets can be kept warm in a 200-degree oven while you cook the second batch.

If you can't find sushi rice, another short-grain white rice, such as Arborio, can be substituted.

Use tongs to dredge and coat the chicken to avoid battering your hands.

1½ cups sushi rice

1 lemon

1 tablespoon soy sauce

1 teaspoon toasted sesame oil

¼ small head green cabbage (5 ounces)

4 scallions

Salt and pepper

¼ cup ketchup

2 tablespoons Worcestershire sauce

1 teaspoon Dijon mustard

2 cups panko bread crumbs

2 large eggs

8 (4-ounce) chicken cutlets, ½ inch thick

½ cup vegetable oil

**1** **Make Rice** Rinse rice in fine-mesh strainer until water runs clear. Bring rice and 1¾ cups plus 2 tablespoons water to boil in large saucepan over high heat. Cover, reduce heat to low, and cook until liquid is absorbed, about 10 minutes. Remove pot from heat and let sit, covered, until tender, about 15 minutes. Fluff rice with fork and cover to keep warm.

**2** **Make Salad** While rice cooks, squeeze 2 teaspoons lemon juice. Whisk 1 teaspoon soy sauce, sesame oil, and lemon juice together in medium bowl. Remove core from cabbage and slice thin. Slice scallions thin on bias. Add cabbage and scallions to dressing and toss to combine. Season with salt and pepper to taste, and refrigerate until ready to serve.

**3** **Make Sauce, Crush Panko, and Prepare Egg Mixture** Whisk ketchup, Worcestershire, mustard, and remaining 2 teaspoons soy sauce together in small bowl; set aside. Place panko in large zipper-lock bag and lightly crush with rolling pin. Transfer crumbs to shallow dish. Beat eggs with ½ teaspoon salt in second shallow dish.

**4** **Dredge Chicken** Trim chicken. Working with 1 cutlet at a time, dredge cutlets in egg mixture, allowing excess to drip off, then coat all sides with panko, pressing gently to adhere. Transfer to large plate. Place wire rack in rimmed baking sheet and line rack with paper towels.

**5** **Pan-Fry Cutlets** Heat ¼ cup oil in 12-inch skillet over medium-high heat until shimmering. Add 4 cutlets and cook until deep golden brown, 2 to 3 minutes per side. Transfer cutlets to prepared rack, season with salt to taste, and tent loosely with aluminum foil. Wipe skillet clean with paper towels. Repeat with remaining ¼ cup oil and remaining 4 cutlets.

**6** **Finish Dish** Slice fried cutlets into ½-inch-wide strips. Drizzle chicken with sauce and serve over rice with cabbage salad.

# Pan-Seared Chicken with Warm Mediterranean Bulgur Pilaf

serves 4; total time 45 minutes

## notes for the cook

Rich, nutty bulgur goes well with simple pan-seared chicken breasts in this Mediterranean-inspired dinner.

Stirring a few easy-to-prep ingredients such as cherry tomatoes, prepitted olives, and crumbled feta into the bulgur creates a hearty, fresh pilaf with tons of flavor.

Note that you'll need ¾ cup of parsley, so shop accordingly.

When shopping, don't confuse bulgur with cracked wheat, which has a much longer cooking time and will not work in this recipe.

1½ cups medium-grind bulgur

Salt and pepper

10 ounces cherry tomatoes

½ cup pitted kalamata olives

4 ounces feta cheese

1 lemon

4 (6- to 8-ounce) boneless, skinless chicken breasts

3 tablespoons extra-virgin olive oil

Fresh parsley

**1 Make Bulgur** Bring 2¼ cups water, bulgur, and ¼ teaspoon salt to boil in large saucepan over medium-high heat. Reduce heat to low, cover, and simmer gently until bulgur is tender, 16 to 18 minutes. Remove pot from heat and let sit, covered, for 10 minutes.

**2 Prep Vegetables** While bulgur cooks, halve tomatoes and halve olives. Crumble feta (1 cup). Squeeze 1 tablespoon lemon juice from half of lemon, and cut remainder into wedges.

**3 Prep and Season Chicken** Trim chicken. Pat dry with paper towels and season with salt and pepper.

4 **Cook Chicken** Heat 1 tablespoon oil in 12-inch skillet over medium-high heat until just smoking. Cook chicken until golden brown and meat registers 160 degrees, 6 to 8 minutes per side. Transfer to cutting board, tent with aluminum foil, and let rest.

5 **Finish Bulgur** While chicken rests, mince ¾ cup parsley. Fluff bulgur with fork, add tomatoes, olives, feta, lemon juice, remaining 2 tablespoons oil, and parsley and gently stir to combine. Season with salt and pepper to taste.

6 **Finish Dish** Slice each chicken breast on bias into ¼-inch-thick slices. Serve with bulgur pilaf and lemon wedges, and drizzle with extra oil to taste.

# Stir-Fried Chicken and Broccoli with Herbs and Scallion Rice

serves 4; total time 45 minutes

## notes for the cook

Quick-cooking stir-fries are a natural choice for weeknight dinners. This one combines easy-prep ingredients with a leveled-up sauce made from Asian pantry staples.

To save on time, use precut broccoli florets rather than fussing with a whole head of broccoli. For a crisp-tender texture and bright green color, we steam the broccoli slightly in the skillet before sautéing it.

You will need a 12-inch nonstick skillet with a tight-fitting lid for this recipe.

Note that you'll need ½ cup of basil, so shop accordingly.

Long-grain white, basmati, or Texmati rice can be substituted for the jasmine rice.

1½ cups jasmine rice

Salt and pepper

¼ cup oyster sauce

1 tablespoon rice vinegar

1 tablespoon Asian chili-garlic sauce

Fresh ginger

Fresh basil

Fresh mint

4 scallions

12 ounces broccoli florets

1 red bell pepper

1 pound boneless, skinless chicken breasts

2 tablespoons plus 1 teaspoon vegetable oil

1 **Make Rice** Rinse rice in fine-mesh strainer until water runs clear. Bring rice, 2¼ cups water, and ¼ teaspoon salt to simmer in large saucepan over medium heat. Reduce heat to low, cover, and simmer until rice is tender and liquid is absorbed, 16 to 18 minutes. Remove pot from heat, lay clean folded dish towel underneath lid, and let sit for 10 minutes.

2 **Make Stir-Fry Sauce and Prep Aromatics** While rice cooks, whisk 2 tablespoons water, oyster sauce, vinegar, and chili-garlic sauce together in small bowl; set aside. Peel and grate 1 tablespoon ginger. Chop ½ cup basil and ¼ cup mint. Slice scallions thin.

3 **Prep Broccoli, Bell Pepper, and Chicken** Cut broccoli florets into 1-inch pieces. Stem and seed bell pepper, then slice thin. Trim chicken, slice each breast in half lengthwise, then slice crosswise ¼ inch thick.

**4** **Cook Chicken and Broccoli** Heat 1 tablespoon oil in 12-inch nonstick skillet over medium-high heat until shimmering. Cook chicken until no longer pink, 1 to 2 minutes per side. Transfer to plate. Add 1 tablespoon oil to now-empty skillet and increase heat to high. Add broccoli and cook for 30 seconds. Add ⅓ cup water, cover, and reduce heat to medium. Steam broccoli until just tender, about 2 minutes.

**5** **Cook Bell Pepper and Ginger** Uncover broccoli, stir in bell pepper, and cook until vegetables are tender and most of liquid has evaporated, about 3 minutes. Push vegetables to sides of skillet. Add remaining 1 teaspoon oil and ginger to center and cook, mashing ginger into pan, until fragrant, about 30 seconds.

**6** **Finish Dish** Return cooked chicken, with any accumulated juices, to skillet and toss to combine. Stir in oyster sauce mixture and simmer until slightly thickened, about 1 minute. Off heat, stir in basil and mint. Fluff rice with fork and stir in scallions. Serve stir-fry over rice.

# Easy Chipotle-Orange Chicken Tacos with Radish-Cilantro Salad

serves 4; total time 45 minutes

## notes for the cook

Chicken breasts braised in a flavorful liquid make the perfect base for quick tacos.

If you have a few extra minutes, try our preferred tortilla-warming method: Using a dry skillet over medium-high heat, warm the tortillas one at a time until softened and speckled brown, 20 to 30 seconds per side.

Note that you'll need 1½ cups of cilantro, so shop accordingly.

If you can't find Cotija cheese, feta cheese can be used in its place.

You will need a 12-inch skillet with a tight-fitting lid for this recipe.

4 garlic cloves
Canned chipotle chile in adobo sauce
1 orange
Fresh cilantro
1½ pounds boneless, skinless chicken breasts
2 tablespoons vegetable oil
1 tablespoon Worcestershire sauce
3 limes
10 ounces radishes
Salt and pepper
1 teaspoon yellow mustard
2 ounces Cotija cheese
12 (6-inch) corn tortillas

**1 Prep Aromatics** Mince garlic and mince 2 teaspoons chipotle chile. Squeeze ½ cup orange juice. Chop ½ cup cilantro and pick 1 cup cilantro leaves; reserve chopped cilantro and cilantro leaves separately.

**2 Poach Chicken** Trim chicken. Heat 1 tablespoon oil in 12-inch skillet over medium-high heat until shimmering. Add garlic and chipotle and cook until fragrant, about 30 seconds. Stir in Worcestershire, orange juice, and chopped cilantro and bring to simmer. Nestle chicken into sauce. Cover, reduce heat to medium-low, and cook until chicken registers 160 degrees, 12 to 18 minutes.

**3 Make Radish Salad** While chicken cooks, squeeze 1 tablespoon lime juice from 1 lime and cut remaining 2 limes into wedges. Trim radishes, halve, and slice thin. Whisk remaining 1 tablespoon oil, lime juice, ⅛ teaspoon salt, and ⅛ teaspoon pepper together in medium bowl. Add radishes and toss to combine; season with salt and pepper to taste and refrigerate until ready to serve.

**4** **Reduce Pan Juices** When chicken is finished cooking, transfer to plate, reserving liquid in skillet. Increase heat to medium-high and cook liquid left in skillet until reduced to ¼ cup, about 5 minutes. Off heat, whisk in mustard, and cover to keep warm.

**5** **Shred Chicken** While sauce reduces, use 2 forks to shred chicken into bite-size pieces. Return chicken to skillet, toss until well coated, and season with salt and pepper to taste. Cover to keep warm.

**6** **Warm Tortillas and Finish Dish** Stir cilantro leaves into radish mixture. Crumble Cotija cheese (½ cup) into small pieces in bowl. Place tortillas on plate, cover with damp dish towel, and microwave for 60 to 90 seconds until warm. Serve chicken in warmed tortillas. Top with radish-cilantro salad and Cotija and serve with lime wedges.

# Chicken and Cauliflower Tikka Masala with Basmati Rice

serves 4; total time 1 hour

## notes for the cook

To make this takeout favorite approachable for a homemade weeknight dinner, we saved time (and dishes) by poaching the chicken directly in the flavorful sauce.

A combination of garlic, ginger, and garam masala bring depth of flavor to our sauce without the usual laundry list of spices.

Adding the cauliflower to the pot at the beginning of the cooking process with the onion ensures it will be tender by the time the chicken is cooked through.

Long-grain white, jasmine, or Texmati rice can be substituted for the basmati rice.

1½ cups basmati rice

Salt and pepper

½ head cauliflower (1 pound)

1 onion

Fresh ginger

3 garlic cloves

1 tablespoon garam masala

4 (6- to 8-ounce) boneless, skinless chicken breasts

2 tablespoons vegetable oil

1 (28-ounce) can crushed tomatoes

Fresh cilantro

¼ cup heavy cream

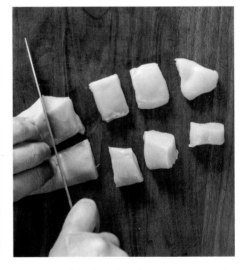

**1 Make Rice** Rinse rice in fine-mesh strainer until water runs clear. Bring rice, 2¼ cups water, and ¼ teaspoon salt to simmer in large saucepan over medium heat. Reduce heat to low, cover, and simmer until rice is tender and liquid is absorbed, 16 to 18 minutes. Remove pot from heat, lay clean folded dish towel underneath lid, and let sit for 10 minutes.

**2 Prep Vegetables** While rice cooks, core cauliflower, then cut florets into ½-inch pieces. Chop onion fine. Peel and grate 2 tablespoons ginger and mince garlic.

**3 Prep Chicken** Combine garam masala, ¾ teaspoon salt, and ½ teaspoon pepper in small bowl. Trim chicken. Cut chicken lengthwise into 1-inch strips, then cut strips crosswise to create 1-inch pieces. In medium bowl, toss chicken with 1 tablespoon oil and 1 tablespoon spice mixture.

4 **Cook Aromatics and Vegetables** Heat remaining 1 tablespoon oil in Dutch oven over medium-high heat until shimmering. Add cauliflower and onion and cook until onions are softened, about 5 minutes. Stir in ginger, garlic, and remaining spice mixture and cook until fragrant, about 30 seconds.

5 **Add Tomatoes and Chicken** Add tomatoes and chicken to pot, bring to simmer, and cook until chicken is cooked through and cauliflower is tender, 10 to 12 minutes.

6 **Finish Dish** While chicken and cauliflower cook, pick ¼ cup cilantro leaves. Off heat, stir in cream. Season with salt and pepper to taste, and sprinkle with cilantro. Serve with rice.

# Crispy Chicken with Moroccan Carrot Salad

serves 4; total time 45 minutes

## notes for the cook

For supercrispy chicken breasts, we pounded them to an even thickness and started them in a cold skillet to give the fat under the skin time to render.

The chicken pairs well with an earthy salad of carrots, chickpeas, feta, and oranges balanced by a tart lemon-harissa dressing.

Harissa is a traditional North African condiment made from a blend of hot chile peppers; spiciness will vary greatly by brand. If you can't find harissa, you can make your own (see page 7).

You will need a 12-inch skillet with a tight-fitting lid for this recipe.

Use a coarse grater to shred the carrots for just the right texture.

4 (10- to 12-ounce) bone-in split chicken breasts
Salt and pepper
2 oranges
1 lemon
2 tablespoons harissa
1 pound carrots
3 ounces feta cheese
Fresh mint
1 (15-ounce) can chickpeas
2 tablespoons extra-virgin olive oil

**1 Prep Chicken** Trim chicken and pat dry with paper towels. Place breasts on cutting board, bone side down, and cover with plastic wrap. Using meat pounder, pound thick ends of breasts to ¾- to 1-inch thickness. Season chicken with salt and pepper.

**2 Cook Chicken** Place chicken, skin side down, in cold 12-inch nonstick skillet. Cover skillet and place over medium heat. Cook chicken, without moving, until skin is light golden brown, about 15 minutes.

**3 Prep Oranges and Make Dressing** While chicken cooks, cut away peel and pith from oranges. Holding fruit over bowl, use paring knife to slice between membranes to release segments. Cut segments in half crosswise and let drain in fine-mesh strainer set over large bowl, reserving juice. Squeeze 1 tablespoon lemon juice. Whisk harissa, lemon juice, and ½ teaspoon salt into reserved orange juice; add orange segments to bowl and set aside.

4 **Finish Chicken** Increase heat to medium-high and continue to cook, covered, until skin is deep golden brown and crispy and breasts register 160 degrees, 10 to 15 minutes, rotating skillet halfway through cooking. Transfer chicken, skin side up, to platter, tent with aluminum foil, and let rest.

5 **Prep Salad** Meanwhile, peel and shred carrots. Cut feta into ½-inch pieces (¾ cup). Mince 2 tablespoons mint. Drain and rinse chickpeas. Add carrots to dressing in bowl and gently toss to coat. Let sit until liquid starts to pool in bottom of bowl, 3 to 5 minutes.

6 **Finish Dish** Drain salad in fine-mesh strainer and return to now-empty bowl. Stir in oil, feta, chickpeas, and mint and season with salt and pepper to taste. Serve with chicken.

# Apricot-Glazed Chicken with Chickpeas, Chorizo, and Spinach

serves 4; total time 1 hour

## notes for the cook

For a sophisticated chicken dinner, we created a complex flavor profile with sweetness from apricot preserves, spice from chorizo sausage, smokiness from smoked paprika, and a hint of fresh bitterness from lemon zest.

Bone-in split chicken breasts are easy to cook and still have deep, rich flavor.

The simple addition of canned chickpeas rounds out this hearty dish.

Other varieties of hard, cured sausage (such as linguiça) can be substituted for the Spanish chorizo; we do not recommend using fresh chorizo.

1 lemon

1 onion

6 ounces Spanish-style chorizo sausage

1 (15-ounce) can chickpeas

¼ cup apricot preserves

Salt and pepper

4 (10- to 12-ounce) bone-in split chicken breasts

1 tablespoon vegetable oil

1½ teaspoons smoked paprika

8 ounces (8 cups) baby spinach

**1 Prep Vegetables and Chorizo** Adjust oven rack to middle position and heat oven to 450 degrees. Grate 2 teaspoons lemon zest, then cut lemon into wedges for serving. Chop onion. Cut chorizo into ½-inch pieces. Drain and rinse chickpeas.

**2 Make Sauce and Prep Chicken** Combine preserves, lemon zest, ⅛ teaspoon salt, and ⅛ teaspoon pepper in bowl; set aside. Trim chicken and cut each breast in half crosswise. Pat chicken dry with paper towels and season with salt and pepper.

**3 Sear Chicken** Heat oil in 12-inch ovensafe skillet over medium-high heat until just smoking. Cook chicken, skin side down, until lightly browned, about 4 minutes. Transfer to plate, skin side up.

**4** **Build Base** Off heat, combine paprika, onion, chorizo, chickpeas, ⅛ teaspoon salt, and ⅛ teaspoon pepper in now-empty skillet.

**5** **Cook Chicken** Return chicken to skillet, skin side up, and brush apricot mixture over chicken skin. Transfer pan to oven and bake until chicken registers 160 degrees, 20 to 25 minutes. Transfer chicken to platter, tent with aluminum foil, and let rest.

**6** **Finish Dish** While chicken rests, return skillet with chickpea mixture to medium-high heat (skillet handle will be hot), add spinach, and cook until wilted, about 2 minutes. Season with salt and pepper to taste. Serve chicken with chickpea mixture and lemon wedges.

# Lemon-Thyme Roasted Chicken with Ratatouille

serves 4; total time 45 minutes

## notes for the cook

This streamlined version of roasted chicken and vegetables requires just one pan and is almost entirely hands-off once the pan is in the oven.

The large surface area of a sheet pan can accommodate both the chicken and the makings of ratatouille, and the dry heat of the oven prevents the vegetables from becoming soggy as they cook.

To get nicely golden skin, we preheat the baking sheet, oil it to prevent sticking, and place the chicken breasts skin side down on the pan to sear.

You can substitute 1½ teaspoons dried thyme for the fresh thyme in this recipe.

12 ounces eggplant

2 zucchini

2 garlic cloves

Fresh thyme

1 (14.5-ounce) can diced tomatoes

4 (10- to 12-ounce) bone-in split chicken breasts

Salt and pepper

3 tablespoons extra-virgin olive oil

1 lemon

Fresh parsley

1 **Prep Vegetables** Adjust oven rack to upper-middle position, place rimmed baking sheet on rack, and heat oven to 450 degrees. Cut eggplant into ½-inch pieces. Cut zucchini into ½-inch pieces. Mince garlic. Mince 1 tablespoon thyme. Drain tomatoes.

2 **Prep Chicken** Trim chicken. Pat chicken dry with paper towels and season with 2 teaspoons thyme, salt, and pepper. Toss 2 tablespoons oil, eggplant, zucchini, garlic, remaining 1 teaspoon thyme, tomatoes, ½ teaspoon salt, and ¼ teaspoon pepper together in bowl.

3 **Begin Roasting Chicken and Vegetables** Remove sheet from oven and brush remaining 1 tablespoon oil evenly over hot sheet. Place chicken, skin side down, on 1 side of sheet and spread vegetables in single layer on other side. Roast until chicken releases from sheet and vegetables begin to soften, about 10 minutes. Meanwhile, cut lemon into quarters.

**4** **Flip Chicken and Finish Roasting** Flip chicken, skin side up, and stir vegetables on sheet. Place lemon quarters, cut side down, on sheet. Continue to roast, stirring vegetables occasionally, until chicken registers 160 degrees and vegetables are tender, 10 to 15 minutes. Remove sheet from oven, tent with aluminum foil, and let rest.

**5** **Prep Parsley** While chicken rests, mince 2 tablespoons parsley.

**6** **Finish Dish** Transfer chicken and lemon wedges to platter. Toss vegetables with pan juices, season with salt and pepper to taste, and transfer to platter with chicken. Sprinkle parsley over vegetables and serve with roasted lemon wedges.

# Pomegranate-Glazed Chicken with Warm Farro Salad

serves 4; total time 1 hour

## notes for the cook

A glaze of spiced pomegranate molasses adds a new dimension to simple pan-roasted chicken.

The Mediterranean-inspired ingredients in our farro salad complement the pomegranate glaze on the chicken.

If you can't find pomegranate molasses, you can make your own (see page 7).

We prefer the flavor and texture of whole farro; pearled farro can be used, but the texture may be softer. Do not use quick-cooking or presteamed farro (read the ingredient list on the package to determine this) in this recipe. The cooking time for farro can vary greatly among different brands, so we recommend beginning to check for doneness after 10 minutes.

1½ cups whole farro

Salt and pepper

4 (10- to 12-ounce) bone-in split chicken breasts

3 tablespoons extra-virgin olive oil

6 tablespoons pomegranate molasses

1 teaspoon ground cinnamon

1 shallot

1 lemon

2 tablespoons plain Greek yogurt

1 English cucumber

6 ounces cherry tomatoes

Fresh mint

1 **Cook Farro** Adjust oven rack to middle position and heat oven to 450 degrees. Set wire rack in aluminum foil–lined rimmed baking sheet. Bring 4 quarts water to boil in Dutch oven. Add farro and 1 tablespoon salt, return to boil, and cook until grains are tender with slight chew, 15 to 30 minutes. Drain farro, spread in second rimmed baking sheet, and let cool completely, about 15 minutes.

2 **Prep and Sear Chicken** While farro cooks, trim chicken and cut each breast in half crosswise. Pat dry with paper towels and season with salt and pepper. Heat 1 teaspoon oil in 12-inch skillet over medium-high heat until just smoking. Place chicken, skin side down, in skillet and cook until well browned, 6 to 8 minutes. Transfer chicken, skin side up, to prepared rack.

3 **Roast Chicken** While chicken sears, combine pomegranate molasses, cinnamon, and ⅛ teaspoon salt in bowl. Brush top of browned chicken skin with half of pomegranate glaze. Transfer to oven and roast for 10 minutes. Brush chicken with remaining pomegranate glaze and continue to roast until chicken registers 160 degrees, 5 to 10 minutes. Cover with aluminum foil and let rest.

**4 Make Vinaigrette** While chicken roasts, mince shallot and squeeze 2 tablespoons lemon juice. Whisk yogurt, shallot, lemon juice, remaining 8 teaspoons oil, ¼ teaspoon salt, and ¼ teaspoon pepper together in large bowl; set aside.

**5 Prep Vegetables** Cut cucumber in half lengthwise, then seed and cut into ¼-inch pieces. Halve tomatoes. Chop ¼ cup mint.

**6 Finish Dish** Add cooled farro, cucumber, tomatoes, and mint to bowl with vinaigrette, toss gently to combine, and season with salt and pepper to taste. Serve with chicken.

# Chicken with Creamy Butternut Squash Orzo

serves 4; total time 45 minutes

## notes for the cook

The ultracrispy skin on these chicken breasts pairs beautifully with the sweet-savory profile of our orzo side dish.

To prep the butternut squash, start by cutting off both ends, then remove the skin with a vegetable peeler and cut the squash in half, separating the bulb from the neck. Cut the bulb in half through the base, remove the seeds with a spoon, and cut the peeled and seeded squash into pieces.

We made a super-creamy orzo side dish by cooking the squash with the pasta and stirring in just the right amount of Parmesan cheese at the end of cooking.

You will need a 12-inch skillet with a tight-fitting lid for this recipe.

1 small (1 pound) butternut squash
3 garlic cloves
4 (10- to 12-ounce) bone-in split chicken breasts
Salt and pepper
2 tablespoons butter
1 cup orzo
3½ cups chicken broth
2 ounces Parmesan cheese
Fresh chives
1 lemon
4 ounces (4 cups) baby spinach
¼ teaspoon ground nutmeg

**1 Prep Vegetables** Peel and seed squash, then cut into ½-inch pieces. Mince garlic.

**2 Prep Chicken** Trim chicken and pat dry with paper towels. Place breasts on cutting board, bone side down, and cover with plastic wrap. Using meat pounder, pound thick ends of breasts to ¾- to 1-inch thickness. Season chicken with salt and pepper.

**3 Cook Chicken** Place chicken, skin side down, in cold 12-inch nonstick skillet. Cover and place over medium heat. Cook, without moving, until skin is light golden brown, about 15 minutes. Increase heat to medium-high. Continue to cook, covered, until skin is deep golden brown and breasts register 160 degrees, 10 to 15 minutes, rotating skillet halfway through cooking. Transfer chicken, skin side up, to platter, and tent with aluminum foil.

4 **Cook Orzo and Squash** While chicken cooks, melt butter in large sauce pan over medium heat. Add garlic and cook until fragrant, about 30 seconds. Stir in orzo and cook for 1 minute. Add squash and broth, bring to boil, and cook, stirring often, until orzo and squash are both tender, about 15 minutes.

5 **Prep Parmesan, Chives, and Lemon** While orzo is cooking, grate Parmesan (1 cup), mince 3 tablespoons chives, and squeeze 1 teaspoon lemon juice.

6 **Finish Dish** Off heat, stir in baby spinach, nutmeg, Parmesan, 2 tablespoon chives, and lemon juice. Let sit uncovered for 5 minutes to thicken (Add hot water to loosen texture, if desired). Season with salt and pepper to taste. Sprinkle chicken with remaining 1 tablespoon chives and serve with orzo.

# Za'atar Chicken with Pistachios, Brussels Sprouts, and Pomegranate

serves 4; total time 45 minutes

## notes for the cook

Za'atar is an addictive Mediterranean seasoning made from thyme, sumac, and sesame. Here we brush it on meaty chicken breasts for a complexly flavored dish.

We also skillet-roast Brussels sprouts using fat rendered from pan-searing the chicken.

Pistachios and pomegranate molasses in the Brussels sprouts pair perfectly with the earthy flavors of the za'atar. If you can't find za'atar or pomegranate molasses, you can make your own (see page 7).

Look for Brussels sprouts that are similar in size with small, tight heads, and no more than 1½ inches in diameter, as they're likely to be sweeter and more tender than larger sprouts.

¼ cup shelled pistachios
4 (10- to 12-ounce) bone-in split chicken breasts
Salt and pepper
⅓ cup extra-virgin olive oil
2 tablespoons za'atar
1 pound small Brussels sprouts
1 lemon
2 tablespoons pomegranate seeds
1 tablespoon pomegranate molasses
½ teaspoon ground cumin

1 **Toast Pistachios** Adjust oven rack to lowest position and heat oven to 450 degrees. Toast pistachios in 12-inch nonstick skillet over medium heat, shaking pan occasionally, until golden and fragrant, 3 to 5 minutes. Transfer to small bowl to cool, then chop cooled nuts.

2 **Prep and Sear Chicken** Trim chicken and cut each breast in half crosswise. Pat chicken dry with paper towels and season with salt and pepper. Heat 1 teaspoon oil in now-empty skillet over medium-high heat until just smoking. Place chicken, skin side down, in skillet and cook until well browned, 6 to 8 minutes. Transfer chicken, skin side up, to rimmed baking sheet (do not wipe out skillet).

3 **Roast Chicken** While chicken browns, combine za'atar and 2 tablespoons oil in small bowl. Brush browned chicken skin with za'atar mixture. Transfer to oven and roast until chicken registers 160 degrees, about 20 minutes. Transfer pieces to platter, tent with aluminum foil, and let rest.

**4** **Prep Brussels Sprouts and Lemon**
While chicken cooks, let skillet cool
for 10 minutes. Trim Brussels sprouts
and cut in half. Cut lemon into wedges.

**5** **Cook Brussels Sprouts** Add
remaining 3 tablespoons oil to cooled
skillet and arrange Brussels sprouts in
single layer, cut side down. Cover skillet,
place over medium-high heat, and cook until
sprouts are bright green and cut sides have
started to brown, about 5 minutes. Continue
to cook, uncovered, until cut side of sprouts
are deeply and evenly browned and paring
knife slides in with little to no resistance, 2 to
3 minutes.

**6** **Finish Dish** Off heat, add pomegranate
seeds, pomegranate molasses, cumin,
pistachios, and ½ teaspoon salt to skillet
and stir to coat evenly. Season with
salt and pepper to taste. Serve with chicken
and lemon wedges.

# Oven-Roasted Chicken Breasts with Chickpeas, Fennel, and Chermoula

serves 4; total time 1 hour

## notes for the cook

Our version of chermoula, a bold Moroccan green sauce, works overtime in this dish, seasoning a side dish of chickpeas and fennel and also serving as a bright, potent topping to drizzle over crispy oven-roasted chicken breasts.

Note that you'll need ¾ cup of cilantro, so shop accordingly.

If you can't find fennel bulbs with their fronds intact, you can substitute minced parsley or omit the fronds altogether.

Fresh cilantro

2 lemons

4 garlic cloves

2 fennel bulbs, fronds intact

2 (15-ounce) cans chickpeas

¼ cup plus 1 teaspoon extra-virgin olive oil

½ teaspoon ground cumin

½ teaspoon paprika

⅛ teaspoon cayenne pepper

Salt and pepper

4 (10- to 12-ounce) bone-in split chicken breasts

1 cup chicken broth

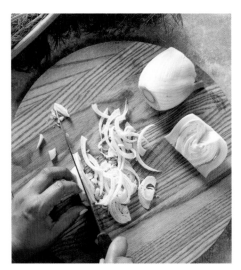

1 **Prep Vegetables** Adjust oven rack to middle position and heat oven to 450 degrees. Pick ¾ cup cilantro leaves. Squeeze 2 tablespoons lemon juice from 1 lemon and cut remaining lemon into wedges. Mince garlic. Discard fennel stalks and reserve fronds. Halve fennel bulb, core, and slice thin. Mince 2 tablespoons fennel fronds. Drain and rinse chickpeas.

2 **Make Chermoula** Process ¼ cup oil, cumin, paprika, cayenne, cilantro, lemon juice, garlic, and ¼ teaspoon salt in food processor until combined, about 1 minute, scraping down sides of bowl as needed; set aside.

3 **Prep and Sear Chicken** Trim chicken and cut breasts in half crosswise. Pat dry with paper towels and season with salt and pepper. Heat remaining 1 teaspoon oil in 12-inch skillet over medium-high heat until just smoking. Place chicken, skin side down, in skillet and cook until well browned, 6 to 8 minutes.

**4** **Roast Chicken** Transfer browned chicken pieces, skin side up, to rimmed baking sheet (do not wipe out skillet). Transfer sheet to oven and roast until chicken registers 160 degrees, about 20 minutes, rotating sheet halfway through cooking. Tent with aluminum foil and let rest.

**5** **Cook Fennel** While chicken roasts, pour off all but 1 tablespoon fat from skillet and heat over medium-high until shimmering. Add fennel and cook until softened, about 5 minutes. Stir in broth and chickpeas and bring to simmer. Reduce heat to medium-low, cover, and cook until chickpeas are warmed through, 3 to 5 minutes. Uncover, increase heat to high and cook until nearly all liquid has evaporated, about 3 minutes.

**6** **Finish Dish** Off heat, stir fennel fronds and 1 tablespoon chermoula into chickpeas; transfer chickpeas to serving dish. Drizzle chicken with remaining chermoula and serve with chickpeas and lemon wedges.

# Chicken Thighs with White Beans, Pancetta, and Baby Kale

serves 4; total time 45 minutes

## notes for the cook

This hearty, satisfying dish has a triple dose of savory flavor from meaty chicken thighs, salty pancetta, and creamy white beans.

Cooking the beans with rendered chicken fat and crisped pancetta gives them deep meaty flavor.

The pan will seem overly crowded with chicken at first—don't worry. The fat from the chicken skin renders quickly, shrinking the thighs.

Don't be shy when drizzling the olive oil over the beans in step 6. Using at least a tablespoon will boost the creaminess of the bean mixture considerably.

8 (5- to 7-ounce) bone-in chicken thighs
Salt and pepper
2 teaspoons extra-virgin olive oil
2 ounces pancetta
5 garlic cloves
2 (15-ounce) cans cannellini beans
Fresh rosemary
1 cup chicken broth
Fresh parsley
1 lemon
6 ounces (6 cups) baby kale

**1 Sear Chicken** Adjust oven rack to upper-middle position and heat oven to 450 degrees. Trim chicken, pat dry with paper towels, and season with salt and pepper. Heat oil in 12-inch skillet over medium-high heat until just smoking. Add chicken, skin side down, and cook until well browned, 6 to 8 minutes.

**2 Roast Chicken** Transfer chicken to rimmed baking sheet, skin side up (do not wipe out skillet). Transfer to oven and roast until chicken registers 175 degrees, 15 to 20 minutes. Remove chicken from oven, tent with aluminum foil, and let rest.

**3 Prep Pancetta, Garlic, and Beans** While chicken roasts, chop pancetta fine. Peel and smash garlic cloves. Drain and rinse beans.

**4** **Cook Beans** Pour off all but 1 tablespoon fat from skillet and heat over medium heat until shimmering. Add 2 rosemary sprigs, pancetta, and garlic and cook until garlic is golden brown, about 3 minutes. Stir in broth, beans, and ¼ teaspoon pepper. Bring to simmer and cook until slightly thickened, 5 to 7 minutes. Discard rosemary sprigs.

**5** **Prep Garnishes** While beans cook, chop 1 tablespoon parsley and cut lemon into wedges.

**6** **Finish Dish** Stir baby kale into beans, reduce heat to medium-low, and cook until mostly wilted, about 2 minutes. Season with salt and pepper to taste. Transfer beans to serving platter and drizzle with extra oil to taste. Top with chicken, sprinkle with parsley, and serve with lemon wedges.

# Roasted Chicken Thighs with Brussels Sprouts and Carrots

serves 4; total time 45 minutes

## notes for the cook

Pairing meaty chicken thighs with a mixture of hearty root vegetables makes for a classic, foolproof, ultraflavorful dinner.

A bright herb-and-lemon yogurt sauce provides just the right tangy complement to the rich thighs and earthy roasted veggies.

Searing the chicken thighs before roasting ensures crispy skin, and finishing them on the same pan as the vegetables in the oven helps the whole dish develop great flavor.

Look for Brussels sprouts that are similar in size with small, tight heads, and no more than 1½ inches in diameter, as they're likely to be sweeter and more tender than larger sprouts.

1 pound carrots

8 ounces Brussels sprouts

4 shallots

¼ cup extra-virgin olive oil

Salt and pepper

8 (5- to 7-ounce) bone-in chicken thighs

1 lemon

2 garlic cloves

Fresh dill

½ cup plain whole-milk yogurt

**1 Prep Vegetables** Adjust oven rack to lower-middle position and heat oven to 425 degrees. Peel carrots and halve lengthwise. Trim Brussels sprouts and cut in half. Halve shallots.

**2 Roast Vegetables** Toss 2 tablespoons oil, carrots, Brussels sprouts, shallots, 1 teaspoon salt, and ¾ teaspoon pepper together on rimmed baking sheet. Spread vegetables in single layer and roast for 8 minutes.

**3 Prep Chicken** While vegetables roast, trim chicken. Pat dry with paper towels and season with salt and pepper.

**4** **Sear Chicken** Heat 1 tablespoon oil in 12-inch skillet over medium-high heat until just smoking. Add chicken, skin side down, and cook until well browned, 6 to 8 minutes.

**5** **Roast Chicken** Remove sheet from oven and push vegetables to edges of baking sheet. Add chicken, skin side up, to middle of sheet. Roast until chicken registers 175 degrees and vegetables are fully tender, 15 to 20 minutes. Tent with aluminum foil and let rest.

**6** **Make Sauce and Finish Dish** Meanwhile, squeeze 1 tablespoon lemon juice. Mince garlic. Mince 1 tablespoon dill. Whisk yogurt, remaining 1 tablespoon oil, lemon juice, garlic, and dill together in small bowl. Season with salt and pepper to taste. Serve yogurt sauce with chicken and vegetables.

# Cumin-Crusted Chicken Thighs with Cauliflower Rice

serves 4; total time 45 minutes

## notes for the cook

For a break from traditional chicken and rice, we pair spiced chicken thighs with cauliflower that gets blitzed to small pieces in a food processor. The processed cauliflower makes a fresh and surprisingly satisfying substitute for grains.

Cumin seeds add toastiness, crunch, and a distinctive woodsy aroma to the chicken.

Crush the cumin seeds with a mortar and pestle or a spice grinder, or simply under the bottom of a skillet.

Note that you'll need ½ cup of mint, so shop accordingly.

Be sure to keep the rendered chicken fat in the skillet after step 1; the schmaltz adds flavor and richness to the cauliflower.

8 (5- to 7-ounce) bone-in chicken thighs
Salt and pepper
1 tablespoon vegetable oil
4 teaspoons cumin seeds
1 head cauliflower (2 pounds)
Fresh mint
1 lime
1 teaspoon paprika

**1 Season Chicken** Adjust oven rack to upper-middle position and heat oven to 450 degrees. Pat chicken dry with paper towels and season with salt and pepper.

**2 Cook Chicken** Heat oil in 12-inch nonstick skillet over medium-high heat until just smoking. Add chicken, skin side down, and cook until well browned, 6 to 8 minutes. Transfer chicken, skin side up, to rimmed baking sheet (do not wipe out skillet). Crush cumin seeds and sprinkle 2 teaspoons evenly over chicken. Roast until chicken registers 175 degrees, 15 to 20 minutes. Tent with aluminum foil and let rest.

**3 Prep Cauliflower** While chicken roasts, core cauliflower and cut into ½-inch pieces. Working in 2 batches, pulse cauliflower in food processor to ¼- to ⅛-inch pieces, about 6 pulses.

**4** **Prep Herbs and Lime** Chop ½ cup mint. Grate 1½ teaspoons lime zest, then cut lime into wedges.

**5** **Cook Cauliflower** Heat reserved fat in skillet over medium-high heat until shimmering. Add paprika, remaining 2 teaspoons crushed cumin seeds, cauliflower, ¾ teaspoon salt, and ¾ teaspoon pepper and cook until just tender, about 7 minutes.

**6** **Finish Dish** Off heat, stir mint and lime zest into cauliflower. Serve chicken with cauliflower rice and lime wedges.

# Thai-Style Chicken and Sweet Potato Curry

serves 4; total time 45 minutes

## notes for the cook

The savory-sweet flavors of this Thai-style curry offer a spiced but not spicy take on a classic dish.

Earthy sweet potatoes complement the complexity of the red curry paste and simmering the chicken and potatoes in coconut milk adds richness.

A final garnish of scallions, cilantro, and lime wedges adds a splash of color and brightness.

1½ cups long-grain white rice

Salt and pepper

1 pound sweet potatoes

1½ pounds boneless, skinless chicken thighs

2 tablespoons red curry paste

1 teaspoon vegetable oil

1 cup canned coconut milk

1 tablespoon fish sauce

4 scallions

¼ cup dry-roasted peanuts

Fresh cilantro

1 lime

**1** **Make Rice** Rinse rice in fine-mesh strainer until water runs clear. Bring rice, 2¼ cups water, and ¼ teaspoon salt to simmer in large saucepan over medium heat. Reduce heat to low, cover, and simmer until rice is tender and liquid is absorbed, 16 to 18 minutes. Remove pot from heat, lay clean folded dish towel underneath lid, and let sit for 10 minutes.

**2** **Prep Sweet Potatoes** While rice cooks, peel sweet potatoes and cut into ½-inch pieces.

**3** **Prep Chicken** Trim chicken. Pat dry with paper towels. Cut into 1-inch pieces, then toss with curry paste, ½ teaspoon salt, and ¼ teaspoon pepper.

**4** **Cook Chicken** Heat oil in 12-inch skillet over medium heat until shimmering. Add chicken and cook until chicken is no longer pink and curry is fragrant, about 3 minutes.

**5** **Simmer Chicken and Potatoes** Stir in coconut milk, fish sauce, and potatoes, scraping up any browned bits, and bring to boil. Reduce heat to medium-low and simmer vigorously, stirring occasionally, until chicken and potatoes are tender, about 10 minutes.

**6** **Finish Dish** While chicken and potatoes cook, slice scallions thin on bias. Chop peanuts coarse. Mince 2 tablespoons cilantro and cut lime into wedges. Season curry with salt and pepper to taste. Sprinkle scallions, peanuts, and cilantro over top and serve with rice and lime wedges.

# Chicken Mole with Cilantro-Lime Rice and Beans

serves 4; total time 1 hour

## notes for the cook

With a few key shortcut ingredients, such as chili powder, cocoa powder, and peanut butter, you can make a deeply flavored mole sauce in no time at all.

The brightness of cilantro and lime zest and juice cuts through the richness of the mole sauce. If you have other fresh herbs on hand, feel free to get creative and throw them in to make the rice even more flavorful.

Note that you'll need ½ cup of cilantro, so shop accordingly.

You will need a 12-inch skillet with a tight-fitting lid for this recipe.

1½ cups long-grain white rice
Salt and pepper
1 onion
1 (14.5-ounce) can diced tomatoes
1 tablespoon vegetable oil
⅓ cup raisins
2 tablespoons chili powder
2 tablespoons unsweetened cocoa powder
1 cup chicken broth
2 tablespoons creamy peanut butter
1 (15-ounce) can black beans
2 pounds boneless, skinless chicken thighs
Fresh cilantro
2 limes

**1 Cook Rice** Rinse rice in fine-mesh strainer until water runs clear. Bring rice, 2¼ cups water, and ¼ teaspoon salt to simmer in large saucepan over medium heat. Reduce heat to low, cover, and simmer until rice is tender and liquid is absorbed, 16 to 18 minutes.

**2 Make Mole** While rice cooks, chop onion and drain tomatoes. Microwave oil, raisins, chili powder, cocoa, and onion in bowl, stirring occasionally, until onion is softened, about 3 minutes. Process broth, peanut butter, tomatoes, and onion mixture in blender until smooth, about 1 minute. Transfer puree to 12-inch skillet; set aside.

**3 Add Beans to Rice** Drain and rinse beans. When rice is finished cooking, remove pot from heat, add beans to pot over rice, and cover. Let sit for 10 minutes. Set aside until ready to serve.

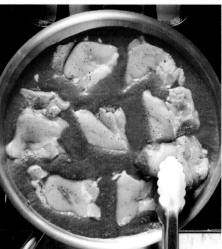

**4** **Cook Chicken** Meanwhile, trim chicken, pat dry with paper towels, and season with salt and pepper. Add chicken to skillet with sauce and bring to simmer over medium heat. Cover skillet, reduce heat to medium-low, and simmer gently, until chicken registers 175 degrees and sauce is slightly thickened, 15 to 20 minutes.

**5** **Prep Garnishes** While chicken cooks, mince ½ cup cilantro. Grate 1 teaspoon lime zest and squeeze 1 tablespoon juice from 1 lime. Cut remaining lime into wedges.

**6** **Finish Dish** Add ¼ cup cilantro and lime zest and juice to rice and beans, fluff with fork to combine, and season with salt and pepper to taste. Season chicken mole with salt and pepper to taste and sprinkle with remaining ¼ cup cilantro. Serve with rice and beans and lime wedges.

# Nepali-Style Chicken Curry with Basmati Rice

serves 4; total time 45 minutes

## notes for the cook

Fresh tomatoes, cardamom, ginger, and garlic are highlighted in this simplified version of the earthy, deeply fragrant curries characteristic of Nepal.

We like chicken thighs in this recipe because they stay moist and tender as they simmer in the sauce.

A half cup of yogurt tempered with sauce (to avoid curdling) and then stirred into the dish at the end of cooking gives our curry just a bit of creaminess and rounds out the flavors.

Long-grain white, jasmine, or Texmati rice can be substituted for the basmati rice.

1½ cups basmati rice

Salt and pepper

1 onion

4 garlic cloves

Fresh ginger

3 tomatoes

1½ pounds boneless, skinless chicken thighs

1 tablespoon yellow curry powder

2 tablespoons vegetable oil

1 teaspoon ground cardamom

¾ cup chicken broth

Fresh cilantro

½ cup plain yogurt

**1 Make Rice** Rinse rice in fine-mesh strainer until water runs clear. Bring rice, 2¼ cups water, and ¼ teaspoon salt to simmer in large saucepan over medium heat. Reduce heat to low, cover, and simmer until rice is tender and liquid is absorbed, 16 to 18 minutes. Remove pot from heat, lay clean folded dish towel underneath lid, and let sit for 10 minutes.

**2 Prep Vegetables and Aromatics** While rice cooks, chop onion fine. Mince garlic. Peel and grate 2 teaspoons ginger. Core tomatoes and chop coarse.

**3 Prep Chicken** Trim chicken, cut into 1-inch cubes, and pat dry with paper towels. Toss chicken with 2 teaspoons curry powder, ½ teaspoon salt, and ¼ teaspoon pepper in bowl and set aside.

**4** **Sauté Onion, Aromatics, and Chicken** Heat oil in 12-inch skillet over medium heat until shimmering. Add onion and ½ teaspoon salt and cook until softened, about 5 minutes. Add cardamom, garlic, ginger, and remaining 1 teaspoon curry powder and cook until fragrant, about 30 seconds. Stir in chicken and cook, stirring often, until lightly browned, about 3 minutes.

**5** **Simmer Chicken** Stir in broth and half of tomatoes, scraping up any browned bits, and bring to boil. Reduce heat to medium-low and simmer until chicken is tender and sauce is slightly thickened and reduced by about half, 8 to 10 minutes.

**6** **Finish Dish** While chicken simmers, chop 2 tablespoons cilantro. Remove skillet from heat. In small bowl, whisk yogurt until smooth. Whisking constantly, slowly ladle about 1 cup hot liquid from skillet into yogurt and whisk until combined, then stir yogurt mixture back into skillet until combined. Stir in cilantro and remaining tomatoes and season with salt and pepper to taste. Fluff rice with fork and serve with curry.

# Chicken Leg Quarters with Cauliflower and Shallots

serves 4; total time 1 hour

## notes for the cook

Chicken leg quarters are an underutilized cut and one that deserves a second look. They work especially well in this one-pan approach when paired with cauliflower, shallots, and grape tomatoes, all of which shine when roasted.

Slashing the chicken lets the seasonings penetrate the meat and helps the fat render.

Some leg quarters are sold with the backbone attached; removing it before cooking makes the chicken easier to serve.

You can substitute 2 teaspoons dried sage for the fresh sage in this recipe.

You can substitute cherry tomatoes for the grape tomatoes, but halve them before adding to the pan.

1 head cauliflower (2 pounds)
6 shallots
Fresh sage
2 garlic cloves
1 lemon
4 (10-ounce) chicken leg quarters
Salt and pepper
¼ cup extra-virgin olive oil
Fresh parsley
8 ounces grape tomatoes

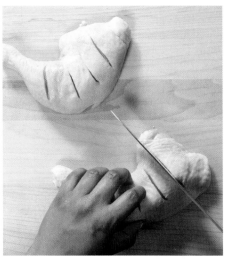

**1 Prep Vegetables** Adjust 1 oven rack to lower-middle position and second rack 6 inches from broiler element and heat oven to 475 degrees. Meanwhile, trim outer leaves of cauliflower and cut stem flush with bottom of head. Cut into 8 equal wedges, keeping core and florets intact. Peel shallots and slice in half through root end. Chop 2 tablespoons sage. Mince garlic. Grate 1 teaspoon lemon zest, then cut lemon into wedges.

**2 Prep Chicken** Trim chicken and pat dry with paper towels. Make 4 diagonal slashes through skin and meat of each leg quarter with sharp knife (each slash should reach bone). Season chicken with salt and pepper.

**3 Arrange Vegetables and Chicken for Roasting** Gently toss 2 tablespoons oil, cauliflower, shallots, 1 tablespoon sage, ½ teaspoon salt, and ½ teaspoon pepper together on rimmed baking sheet. Arrange cauliflower pieces, cut side down, in single layer in center of sheet. Place each piece of chicken, skin side up, in 1 corner of sheet; rest chicken directly on sheet, not on vegetables.

**4** **Roast Chicken and Vegetables**
Whisk garlic, lemon zest, remaining 1 tablespoon sage, and remaining 2 tablespoons oil together in bowl. Brush skin side of chicken with oil mixture. Transfer sheet to lower rack and roast until chicken registers 175 degrees, cauliflower is browned, and shallots are tender, 25 to 30 minutes, rotating sheet halfway through roasting.

**5** **Chop Parsley, Add Tomatoes to Sheet, and Broil** While chicken roasts, chop 1 tablespoon parsley. Remove sheet from oven and heat broiler. Scatter tomatoes over vegetables. Place sheet on upper rack and broil until chicken skin is browned and crisp and tomatoes have begun to wilt, 3 to 5 minutes.

**6** **Finish Dish** Remove sheet from oven and let rest for 5 to 10 minutes. Sprinkle with parsley and serve with lemon wedges.

# Crispy Chicken with Sautéed Radishes, Spinach, and Bacon

serves 4; total time 45 minutes

## notes for the cook

Cooking chicken pieces in rendered bacon fat ensures crisp skin and adds a subtle smoky flavor to the meat.

The pairing of radishes and baby spinach brightened with lemon makes a vibrant side dish, while the crispy bacon pieces add earthy richness.

3 pounds bone-in chicken pieces (split breasts, drumsticks, and/or thighs)

Salt and pepper

2 slices bacon

2 garlic cloves

2 lemons

10 ounces radishes

10 ounces (10 cups) baby spinach

**1 Prep Chicken** Adjust oven rack to middle position and heat oven to 450 degrees. Trim chicken and cut breasts in half crosswise (if using). Pat chicken dry with paper towels and season with salt and pepper.

**2 Cook Bacon** Chop bacon fine. Cook in ovensafe 12-inch skillet over medium-high heat, stirring occasionally, until crispy, 5 to 7 minutes. Using slotted spoon, transfer bacon to paper towel–lined plate (do not wipe out skillet).

**3 Pan-Roast Chicken** Add chicken to skillet, skin side down, and cook until well browned, 6 to 8 minutes. Flip chicken, transfer skillet to oven, and roast until breasts register 160 degrees and drumsticks/thighs register 175 degrees, 15 to 20 minutes.

**4** **Prep Vegetables and Lemons**
While chicken cooks, mince garlic. Squeeze 2 teaspoons lemon juice from 1 lemon and cut remaining lemon into wedges. Trim radishes and cut into quarters.

**5** **Rest Chicken** Transfer chicken to serving platter, tent loosely with aluminum foil, and let rest. Being careful of hot skillet handle, discard all but 1 tablespoon fat from skillet.

**6** **Cook Vegetables and Finish Dish**
While chicken rests, return skillet to medium-high heat, add radishes and ½ teaspoon salt and cook until tender, about 2 minutes. Add garlic, then add spinach, one handful at a time, and cook until wilted, about 2 minutes. Off heat, stir in bacon and lemon juice, and season with salt and pepper to taste. Serve with chicken and lemon wedges.

# Roasted Chicken with Harissa and Warm Bulgur Salad

serves 4; total time 45 minutes

## notes for the cook

We paired quick-cooking bone-in chicken pieces with a robust warm bulgur salad to create an easy and satisfying dinner.

Harissa is a traditional North African condiment made from a blend of hot chile peppers; spiciness will vary greatly by brand. If you can't find harissa, you can make your own (see page 7).

As a creamy, cooling foil to the warmly spiced chicken, we seasoned some Greek yogurt with salt and pepper to make a simple, delicate sauce.

When shopping, don't confuse bulgur with cracked wheat, which has a much longer cooking time and will not work in this recipe.

1 garlic clove

2¼ cups chicken broth

Fresh dill

1½ cups medium-grind bulgur

Salt and pepper

3 pounds bone-in chicken pieces (split breasts, drumsticks, and/or thighs)

2 tablespoons plus 1 teaspoon extra-virgin olive oil

1 lemon

1 English cucumber

8 ounces roasted red peppers

3 tablespoons harissa

1 cup plain Greek yogurt

**1 Cook Bulgur** Peel and crush garlic. Adjust oven rack to middle position and heat oven to 450 degrees. Bring broth, 1 dill sprig, bulgur, garlic, and ¼ teaspoon salt to boil in large saucepan over medium-high heat. Reduce heat to low, cover, and simmer gently until bulgur is tender, 16 to 18 minutes. Off heat, let bulgur sit for 10 minutes. Fluff bulgur gently with fork, discard garlic and dill, and cover to keep warm.

**2 Prep Chicken** While bulgur cooks, trim chicken and cut breasts in half crosswise (if using). Pat chicken dry with paper towels and season with salt and pepper.

**3 Cook Chicken** Heat 1 teaspoon oil in 12-inch ovensafe skillet over medium-high heat until just smoking. Place chicken pieces, skin side down, in skillet and cook until well browned, 6 to 8 minutes. Flip chicken, transfer skillet to oven, and roast until breasts register 160 degrees and drumsticks/thighs register 175 degrees, 15 to 20 minutes.

4 **Make Dressing** While chicken cooks, grate 1 teaspoon lemon zest and squeeze 3 tablespoons juice. Whisk remaining 2 tablespoons oil, lemon zest and juice, ¼ teaspoon salt, and ¼ teaspoon pepper together in large bowl.

5 **Make Salad** Chop cucumber and roasted red peppers. Mince 2 tablespoons dill. Add bulgur, cucumber, red peppers, and minced dill to bowl with dressing, and toss gently to combine. Season with salt and pepper to taste.

6 **Season Yogurt and Finish Dish** Transfer chicken to platter, reserving pan juices in skillet. In small bowl, whisk harissa together with 2 to 4 tablespoons pan juices, 1 tablespoon at a time, until mixture is loose and spreadable. Brush mixture onto chicken, tent with aluminum foil, and let rest for 5 to 10 minutes. Season yogurt with salt and pepper to taste. Serve chicken with bulgur salad and seasoned yogurt.

# Honey-and-Garlic Roasted Chicken with Pearl Couscous Salad

serves 4; total time 1 hour

## notes for the cook

Honey, apple cider vinegar, garlic, and paprika combine to form a sweet and tangy glaze with a gentle kick for this quick and easy roast chicken dish.

A warm pearl couscous salad with carrots and spinach is a hearty complement to the chicken. Deeply flavorful pan juices from the chicken are stirred into the dressing to give it a boost of flavor; be careful when adding pan juices to the dressing as the pan will be very hot.

A fragrant blend of tarragon, olive oil, vinegar, and garlic doubles as a dressing for the couscous and a sauce to drizzle over the chicken.

3 tablespoons plus 1 teaspoon extra-virgin olive oil

1½ cups pearl couscous

Salt and pepper

3 garlic cloves

2 tablespoons honey

2 tablespoons plus ½ teaspoon apple cider vinegar

¼ teaspoon paprika

3 pounds bone-in chicken pieces (split breasts, drumsticks, and/or thighs)

Fresh tarragon

2 carrots

4 ounces (4 cups) baby spinach

**1 Cook Couscous** Adjust rack to middle position and heat oven to 450 degrees. Heat 1 tablespoon oil and couscous in medium saucepan over medium heat, stirring frequently, until half of grains are golden, about 5 minutes. Stir in 2 cups water and ¼ teaspoon salt. Increase heat to high and bring to boil. Reduce heat to low, cover, and simmer until water is absorbed and couscous is tender, 9 to 12 minutes. Off heat, fluff with fork and cover.

**2 Make Glaze and Prep Chicken** While couscous cooks, mince garlic. Whisk honey, ½ teaspoon vinegar, paprika, and two-thirds of garlic together in small bowl. Trim chicken and cut breasts in half crosswise (if using). Pat chicken dry with paper towels and season with salt and pepper.

**3 Cook Chicken** Heat 1 teaspoon oil in 12-inch ovensafe skillet over medium-high heat until just smoking. Place chicken pieces, skin side down, in skillet and cook until well browned, 6 to 8 minutes. Flip chicken and brush with glaze. Transfer skillet to oven and roast until breasts register 160 degrees and drumsticks/thighs register 175 degrees, 15 to 20 minutes.

**4 Make Dressing and Prep Carrots**
While chicken cooks, mince 2 tablespoons tarragon. Whisk remaining garlic, remaining 2 tablespoons oil, remaining 2 tablespoons vinegar, tarragon, ½ teaspoon salt, and ¼ teaspoon pepper together in large bowl. Peel and grate carrots.

**5 Rest Chicken and Finish Dressing**
Transfer chicken to platter, tent with aluminum foil, and let rest, reserving pan juices in skillet. Carefully measure out ¼ cup pan juices from skillet (skillet handle will be hot), then add to dressing in bowl and whisk to combine. Measure out ¼ cup dressing and set aside for serving.

**6 Assemble Salad and Finish Dish** Add spinach, couscous, and carrots to large bowl with remaining dressing and toss to coat. Drizzle chicken with reserved dressing and serve with couscous salad.

# Mustard-Roasted Chicken with Warm Green Bean and Potato Salad

serves 4; total time 1 hour

## notes for the cook

A simple coating of mustard elevates humdrum chicken pieces to flavorful weeknight bistro fare. The best part: The cooking is almost entirely hands-off, leaving you free to create a simple but equally delicious side dish.

Dressing potatoes and green beans while they are still warm ensures that they absorb the vinaigrette, and adding the fond and juices from the roasted chicken to the salad contributes extra meaty, mustardy flavor.

If you can't find baby red potatoes, you can use larger red potatoes cut into 1-inch pieces, but the salad will be slightly drier.

1 garlic clove

Fresh rosemary

3 tablespoons plus 1 teaspoon Dijon mustard

¼ cup extra-virgin olive oil

2 teaspoons soy sauce

Salt and pepper

3 pounds bone-in chicken pieces (split breasts, drumsticks, and/or thighs)

1½ pounds baby red potatoes, 1 to 2 inches in diameter

8 ounces green beans

Fresh parsley

1 tablespoon capers

2 tablespoons white wine vinegar

**1 Make Mustard Sauce** Adjust oven rack to upper-middle position and heat oven to 475 degrees. Meanwhile, mince garlic and mince 1 teaspoon rosemary. Combine 3 tablespoons mustard, 1 tablespoon oil, soy sauce, garlic, rosemary, and ⅛ teaspoon pepper in small bowl.

**2 Prep Chicken** Trim chicken and cut breasts in half crosswise (if using). Pat chicken dry with paper towels and season with salt and pepper. Place chicken, skin side up, on rimmed baking sheet, arranging breast pieces in center and leg and/or thigh pieces around perimeter. Brush chicken with mustard mixture.

**3 Roast Chicken** Roast chicken until breasts register 160 degrees and drumsticks/thighs register 175 degrees, 25 to 30 minutes, rotating pan halfway through cooking. Tent with aluminum foil and let rest.

**4 Cook Vegetables** While chicken cooks, bring 2 quarts water to boil in large saucepan over medium-high heat. Halve potatoes. Trim green beans and cut into 1½-inch lengths. Add potatoes and 1½ tablespoons salt to boiling water; return to boil and cook for 10 minutes. Add green beans and cook until both vegetables are tender, about 5 minutes. Drain well, return to pot, and cover to keep warm.

**5 Make Dressing** While vegetables cook, chop 2 tablespoons parsley. Rinse and mince capers. Whisk vinegar, remaining 1 teaspoon mustard, and capers together in large bowl. Whisking constantly, slowly drizzle in remaining 3 tablespoons oil until incorporated.

**6 Finish Dish** Transfer chicken to serving platter. Scrape up any browned bits and pour any accumulated juices from baking sheet into dressing; whisk to combine. Add warm vegetables to bowl with dressing, toss gently to combine, and season with salt and pepper to taste. Sprinkle chicken and salad with parsley and serve.

# Paprika and Lime–Rubbed Chicken with Grilled Vegetable Succotash

serves 4; total time 1 hour

## notes for the cook

All of the elements of this brightly flavored dish come together quickly on the grill.

Cooking the chicken on the cooler side of the grill avoids flare-ups while still giving it great flavor and char.

To round out our grilled succotash we use convenient canned butter beans, which are superquick to prepare and have a creamy consistency and pleasant mild flavor.

You will need four 12-inch metal skewers for this recipe.

2 limes

3 ears corn

1 red onion

12 ounces cherry tomatoes

¼ cup extra-virgin olive oil

Salt and pepper

Fresh cilantro

2 garlic cloves

1 (15-ounce) can butter beans

1 tablespoon plus ½ teaspoon smoked hot paprika

1½ teaspoons packed dark brown sugar

1 teaspoon ground cumin

3 pounds bone-in chicken pieces (split breasts, drumsticks, and/or thighs)

**1 Heat Grill** Turn all burners to high, cover, and heat grill until hot, about 15 minutes. Leave primary burner on high and turn other burner(s) to low.

**2 Prep Vegetables** While grill heats, grate 4 teaspoons lime zest, then squeeze 2 tablespoons juice from 1 lime. Cut remaining lime into wedges. Remove husks and silk from corn. Cut onion crosswise into ½-inch-thick rounds. Thread tomatoes onto four 12-inch metal skewers. Brush corn, onion, and tomato skewers with 2 tablespoons oil and season with salt and pepper. Mince 3 tablespoons cilantro. Mince garlic. Drain and rinse beans.

**3 Make Spice Rub and Coat Chicken** Combine 1 tablespoon paprika, sugar, cumin, 1 tablespoon lime zest, 1 teaspoon salt, and ½ teaspoon pepper together in large bowl. Trim chicken and cut breasts in half crosswise (if using). Pat chicken dry with paper towels, transfer to bowl with spice mixture, and stir to coat evenly.

4 **Grill Chicken** Clean and oil cooking grate. Place chicken, skin side down, on cooler side of grill. Cover and cook until skin is well browned and slightly charred and breasts register 160 degrees and drumsticks/thighs register 175 degrees, 20 to 30 minutes, flipping as needed and rearranging so all pieces get equal exposure to heat source. Transfer chicken pieces to platter as they finish cooking, tent with aluminum foil, and let rest.

5 **Grill Vegetables** While chicken cooks on cooler side, place corn, onion rounds, and tomato skewers on hotter side of grill. Cook tomatoes, covered, turning as needed, until skins begin to blister, about 2 minutes; transfer to platter. Continue to cook corn and onion, covered, turning occasionally, until lightly charred on all sides, 8 to 10 minutes; transfer corn and onion to platter as they finish cooking and cover with foil.

6 **Finish Dish** Chop grilled onions coarse and cut corn kernels from cobs. Whisk remaining 1 teaspoon lime zest, lime juice, 2 tablespoons cilantro, garlic, remaining ½ teaspoon paprika, and remaining 2 tablespoons oil together in large bowl. Add beans, tomatoes, chopped onion, and corn to bowl and toss to combine. Season with salt and pepper to taste. Sprinkle remaining 1 tablespoon cilantro over chicken. Serve with succotash and lime wedges.

# Indian-Spiced Chicken with Grilled Naan and Radicchio

serves 4; total time 1 hour

## notes for the cook

A simple spice coating, store-bought naan, a quick cooking veg, and a simple yogurt sauce allowed us to create a delicious takeout-worthy weeknight meal at home.

Radicchio makes a surprisingly great pairing for our Indian-spiced chicken; its crispy edges and bitter notes are an excellent complement to the rich chicken and tangy yogurt.

1 lime
Fresh cilantro
¾ cup plain whole-milk yogurt
Salt and pepper
1 tablespoon garam masala
1 head radicchio (10 ounces)
1 tablespoon extra-virgin olive oil
2 naan breads
3 pounds bone-in chicken pieces (split breasts, drumsticks, and/or thighs)

**1 Heat Grill** Turn all burners to high, cover, and heat grill until hot, about 15 minutes. Leave primary burner on high and turn other burner(s) to low.

**2 Make Spice Rub and Sauce** While grill heats, squeeze 2 tablespoons lime juice. Chop 2 tablespoons cilantro. Stir yogurt, lime juice, 1 tablespoon cilantro, and ½ teaspoon salt together in small bowl until smooth; set aside sauce for serving. Mix garam masala and ½ teaspoon salt together in large bowl.

**3 Prep Radicchio and Naan** Cut radicchio into quarters, leaving core intact. Brush with oil and season with salt and pepper. Cut each naan bread in half.

**4** **Prep and Season Chicken**
Trim chicken and cut breasts in half crosswise (if using). Pat dry with paper towels, transfer to bowl with spice mixture, and stir to coat evenly.

**5** **Grill Chicken** Clean and oil cooking grate. Place chicken, skin side down, on cooler side of grill. Cover and cook until skin is well browned and slightly charred and breasts register 160 degrees and drumsticks/thighs register 175 degrees, 20 to 30 minutes, flipping as needed and rearranging so all pieces get equal exposure to heat source. Transfer chicken pieces to platter as they finish cooking. Tent with aluminum foil and let rest.

**6** **Grill Radicchio and Naan and Finish Dish** While chicken cooks on cooler side, place radicchio on hotter side of grill. Cook, flipping as needed, until softened and lightly charred, 3 to 5 minutes. Transfer radicchio to platter and tent with foil. While chicken rests, grill naan on hotter side of grill, uncovered, until warmed through, 1 minute per side. Sprinkle chicken with remaining 1 tablespoon cilantro and serve with reserved sauce and naan.

# Teriyaki Chicken with Grilled Bok Choy and Pineapple

serves 4; total time 1 hour

## notes for the cook

A quick homemade teriyaki sauce beats out the bottled stuff every time.

We brush our teriyaki sauce on the chicken parts toward the end of grilling so that it stays bright and sweet instead of getting burnt.

Grilling baby bok choy gives it a complex bitterness that's perfectly balanced by the caramelized sweetness of grilled pineapple and savory depth of teriyaki chicken.

Many supermarkets carry fresh peeled and cored pineapple; you can use that in this recipe if you prefer. Canned pineapple rings will also work in a pinch.

Fresh ginger

⅓ cup soy sauce

¼ cup sugar

2 tablespoons mirin

1 teaspoon cornstarch

4 heads baby bok choy (4 ounces each)

1 tablespoon vegetable oil

Salt and pepper

2 scallions

1 pineapple (about 4 pounds)

8 (5- to 7-ounce) bone-in chicken thighs

**1 Heat Grill and Make Teriyaki Sauce** Turn all burners to high, cover, and heat grill until hot, about 15 minutes. Leave primary burner on high and turn other burner(s) to low. While grill heats, peel and grate 1 tablespoon ginger. Whisk soy sauce, sugar, mirin, cornstarch, and ginger together in small saucepan. Bring to boil over medium-high heat and cook until thickened, about 2 minutes.

**2 Prep Bok Choy and Scallions** Cut bok choy in half lengthwise. Place bok choy in bowl, cover, and microwave until beginning to soften, 3 to 5 minutes. Drain any liquid from bowl and toss bok choy with oil, ½ teaspoon salt, and ¼ teaspoon pepper. Slice scallions thin on bias.

**3 Prep Pineapple and Chicken** Peel and core pineapple, then cut lengthwise into 1-inch-thick planks. Brush pineapple planks with 2 tablespoons teriyaki sauce. Trim chicken, pat dry with paper towels, and season with salt and pepper.

**4 Grill Chicken** Clean and oil cooking grate. Place chicken, skin side down, on cooler side of grill. Cover and cook until chicken registers 175 degrees, 20 to 25 minutes. Halfway through cooking rearrange so all pieces get equal exposure to heat source.

**5 Grill Bok Choy and Pineapple** While chicken cooks on cooler side, place pineapple and bok choy (in batches, if necessary), on hotter side of grill and cook, covered, until lightly charred and tender, 2 to 5 minutes, flipping halfway through cooking; transfer to platter as they finish cooking and tent with aluminum foil.

**6 Finish Dish** Transfer chicken pieces, skin side up, to hotter side of grill. Brush chicken all over with ¼ cup teriyaki sauce and continue to grill, uncovered and flipping often, until sauce begins to caramelize, about 5 minutes; transfer to platter, and let rest for 5 to 10 minutes. Brush remaining sauce over chicken and pineapple, sprinkle with scallions, and serve with bok choy.

# Turkey Cutlets with Barley and Swiss Chard

serves 4; total time 1 hour

## notes for the cook

For juicy white-meat turkey that's accessible for a weeknight meal, we love thin, quick-cooking cutlets.

Instead of spending time making a complex sauce, we simply sear lemon halves in the skillet and squeeze the deeply flavorful juice over our easy sautéed cutlets. Caramelizing the lemon infuses the cooking oil (and, thus, the cutlets) with flavor.

A fresh, light barley salad enriched with nutty Parmesan and Swiss chard completes this wholesome dinner.

Do not substitute hulled, hull-less, quick-cooking, or presteamed barley for the pearl barley in this recipe.

1½ cups pearl barley

1 small onion

12 ounces Swiss chard

2 garlic cloves

¼ cup extra-virgin olive oil

2½ cups chicken broth

1 lemon

1 ounce Parmesan cheese

Salt and pepper

6 (4-ounce) turkey cutlets

**1 Prep Aromatics and Sauté with Barley** Rinse barley. Chop onion. Stem chard by cutting away leafy green portion from either side of stalks. Set leaves aside. Chop 1 cup chard stalks and mince garlic. Heat 2 tablespoons oil in large saucepan over medium-high heat until shimmering. Add onion and chard stalks and cook until softened, about 5 minutes. Stir in barley and garlic and cook until barley is lightly toasted, about 3 minutes.

**2 Cook Barley** Stir broth into saucepan with barley and bring to simmer. Reduce heat to low, cover, and simmer until barley is tender and broth is absorbed, 20 to 40 minutes.

**3 Prep Salad Ingredients** While barley cooks, cut chard leaves into 1-inch pieces. Grate 1 teaspoon lemon zest, then cut lemon in half and remove seeds. Grate Parmesan (½ cup).

**4 Finish Barley** Fold chard leaves and lemon zest into barley, increase heat to medium-high, and cook, uncovered, stirring gently, until chard is wilted, about 2 minutes. Off heat, stir in ¼ cup Parmesan and season with salt and pepper to taste. Transfer to serving platter and tent with aluminum foil.

**5 Prep Turkey and Sear Lemons** Trim cutlets, pat dry with paper towels, and season with salt and pepper. Heat 2 teaspoons oil in 12-inch nonstick skillet over medium-high heat until shimmering. Add lemon halves, cut side down, and cook until browned, about 2 minutes; transfer to serving platter with barley.

**6 Cook Turkey and Finish Dish** Heat 2 teaspoons oil in now-empty skillet over medium-high heat until shimmering. Add 3 cutlets to skillet and cook until well browned and tender, about 2 minutes per side; transfer to serving platter with barley and lemons. Repeat with remaining 2 teaspoons oil and remaining cutlets. Squeeze lemon halves over cutlets and sprinkle with remaining ¼ cup Parmesan. Serve.

# Crispy Skillet Turkey Burgers with Tomato-Feta Salad

serves 4; total time 45 minutes

## notes for the cook:

A little bit of cheese goes a long way in helping turkey burgers stay moist. Mixing Monterey Jack in with the lean meat creates juicy pockets of fat, and the cheese creates a crunchy, golden crust around the edges of the burger as it cooks.

An easy salad of bright, juicy cherry tomatoes, tangy feta, and aromatic oregano is a perfect complement to the crispy, hearty burgers, and a spoonful of lemon-oregano mayonnaise over the burger ties the whole dish together.

Be sure to use 93 percent lean ground turkey in this recipe, not 99 percent fat-free ground turkey breast, or the burgers will be tough.

1 garlic clove
Fresh oregano
1 lemon
12 ounces cherry tomatoes
1 small red onion
3 tablespoons extra-virgin olive oil
Salt and pepper
6 tablespoons mayonnaise
2 ounces Monterey Jack cheese
1 pound ground turkey
1 cup panko bread crumbs
2 ounces feta cheese
4 hamburger buns
1 cup baby arugula

**1 Prep Salad and Sauce Ingredients** Mince garlic. Mince 1 tablespoon oregano. Grate ¾ teaspoon lemon zest and squeeze 2 tablespoons juice. Halve tomatoes. Halve onion and then slice thin.

**2 Make Dressing and Assemble Salad** Whisk 2 tablespoons oil, garlic, 1½ teaspoons oregano, ½ teaspoon lemon zest, 1 tablespoon lemon juice, ¼ teaspoon salt, and ¼ teaspoon pepper together in medium bowl until combined. Add tomatoes and half of sliced onion to dressing.

**3 Make Lemon-Oregano Mayonnaise** Whisk 3 tablespoons mayonnaise, remaining 1½ teaspoons oregano, remaining ¼ teaspoon lemon zest, remaining 1 tablespoon lemon juice, and ⅛ teaspoon pepper together in small bowl; set aside.

**4 Form Burgers** Grate Monterey Jack (½ cup). Combine turkey, panko, remaining 3 tablespoons mayonnaise, Monterey Jack, ¼ teaspoon salt, and ¼ teaspoon pepper in bowl. Knead until combined. Divide turkey mixtures into 4 equal balls, then flatten into ¾-inch-thick patties, about 4 inches in diameter. Season patties with salt and pepper.

**5 Cook Burgers** Heat remaining 1 tablespoon oil in 12-inch nonstick skillet over medium heat until shimmering. Add patties and cook until well browned and meat registers 160 degrees, 5 to 7 minutes per side.

**6 Finish Dish** Crumble feta (½ cup) over top of salad and toss to combine. Season with salt and pepper to taste; set aside. Place burgers on bottom buns, spread with layer of lemon-oregano mayo, and top with remaining onion and arugula. Serve with tomato-feta salad.

# Roasted Salmon and Broccoli Rabe with Pistachio Gremolata

serves 4; total time 45 minutes

## notes for the cook

This one-pan dinner combines rich oven-roasted salmon with flavorful broccoli rabe.

To accent the flavors of this supper, we top it with a quick gremolata, which is an Italian condiment made with parsley, lemon zest, garlic, and here, hearty pistachios.

Roasting the broccoli rabe tempers its characteristic bitterness into something richer and more well-rounded.

Broccoli rabe is sometimes called rapini.

¼ cup shelled pistachios
1 pound broccoli rabe
2 garlic cloves
2 tablespoons plus 2 teaspoons extra-virgin olive oil
Pinch red pepper flakes
Salt and pepper
4 (6- to 8-ounce) skin-on salmon fillets,
    1 to 1½ inches thick
Fresh parsley
1 lemon

**1 Toast Nuts** Adjust oven rack to middle position and heat oven to 450 degrees. Toast pistachios in 10-inch skillet over medium heat, shaking pan occasionally, until golden and fragrant, 3 to 5 minutes; transfer to small bowl to cool, then chop cooled nuts.

**2 Prep Broccoli Rabe** Trim broccoli rabe, then cut into 1½-inch lengths. Mince garlic. Toss broccoli rabe, 2 tablespoons oil, pepper flakes, half of garlic, ¼ teaspoon salt, and ¼ teaspoon pepper together in bowl.

**3 Prep Salmon** Pat salmon dry with paper towels, then rub all over with remaining 2 teaspoons oil and season with salt and pepper.

**4** **Arrange Ingredients on Baking Sheet** Arrange broccoli rabe on half of rimmed baking sheet. Arrange salmon, skin side down, on other half of sheet.

**5** **Roast Salmon and Broccoli Rabe** Roast until center of salmon is still translucent when checked with tip of paring knife and registers 125 degrees (for medium-rare), and broccoli rabe is tender, about 10 minutes.

**6** **Make Gremolata and Finish Dish** While salmon and broccoli rabe roast, chop 2 tablespoons parsley. Grate 1 teaspoon lemon zest. Combine parsley, lemon zest, chopped pistachios, and remaining garlic in small bowl. Sprinkle over salmon and serve with broccoli rabe.

# Sesame Salmon with Grapefruit Slaw

serves 4; total time 45 minutes

## notes for the cook

Adding a sesame seed crust to pan-seared salmon gives it a great crunch and nutty accent. A bright cabbage and citrus slaw provides the perfect contrast to the rich fish.

Starting the salmon in a cold pan allows the fat to render and the skin to crisp.

You can use either white or black sesame seeds (or a combination of the two) in the coating.

Shred the carrots on the large holes of a box grater.

½ head napa cabbage (1 pound)

3 carrots

3 scallions

1 red grapefruit

1 jalapeño

4 (6- to 8-ounce) skin-on salmon fillets, 1 to 1½ inches thick

Salt and pepper

2 tablespoons sesame seeds

¼ cup vegetable oil

3 tablespoons rice vinegar

**1 Prep Fruit and Vegetables** Remove core from cabbage, then slice thin. Peel then shred carrots. Slice scallions thin. Cut away peel and pith from grapefruit and cut into quarters. Slice quarters crosswise into ¼-inch–thick pieces. Cut jalapeño in half lengthwise, seed, and slice thin.

**2 Prep Salmon** Pat salmon dry with paper towels, then season with salt and pepper. Sprinkle flesh sides of fillets evenly with 1 tablespoon sesame seeds.

**3 Render Salmon Skin** Arrange salmon, skin side down, in 12-inch nonstick skillet. Place skillet over medium-high heat and cook until fat from skin renders, about 7 minutes.

**4 Continue Cooking Salmon** Flip salmon and continue to cook until center is still translucent when checked with tip of paring knife and registers 125 degrees (for medium-rare), about 7 minutes.

**5 Make Dressing** While salmon cooks, whisk oil, vinegar, remaining 1 tablespoon sesame seeds, ½ teaspoon salt, and ¼ teaspoon pepper together in large bowl.

**6 Make Slaw and Finish Dish** Add cabbage, carrots, scallions, grapefruit, and jalapeño to dressing in bowl and toss to combine. Season with salt and pepper to taste. Serve salmon with slaw.

# Black Rice Bowls with Roasted Salmon and Miso Dressing

serves 4; total time 45 minutes

## notes for the cook

Black rice, also known as purple rice or forbidden rice, has a delicious roasted, nutty taste that pairs wonderfully with meaty salmon, rich avocado, and crisp vegetables.

If you can't find black rice, you can use brown rice, although it may need a few extra minutes of cooking.

Our oven-roasted salmon starts on a baking sheet preheated in a 500-degree oven. We turn the oven down to 275 before adding the fish; the initial blast of heat firms up the exterior and the fish cooks through gently as the oven temperature slowly drops.

As an optional garnish, we use crumbled nori, which is dried seaweed; you can find it in the international foods aisle.

1½ cups black rice

Salt and pepper

4 (6- to 8-ounce) skin-on salmon fillets, 1 to 1½ inches thick

Fresh ginger

1 lime

1 (8 by 7½-inch) sheet nori (optional)

4 radishes

1 avocado

1 English cucumber

2 scallions

¼ cup rice vinegar

¼ cup mirin

1 tablespoon white miso

**1 Cook Rice** Bring 4 quarts water to boil in Dutch oven over medium-high heat. Add rice and 1 teaspoon salt and cook until rice is tender, 20 to 25 minutes. Drain rice and transfer to large bowl; cover to keep warm.

**2 Prep Salmon** While rice cooks, adjust oven rack to lowest position, line rimmed baking sheet with aluminum foil and place on rack, and heat oven to 500 degrees. Pat salmon dry with paper towels and season with salt and pepper.

**3 Prep Vegetables** While oven is heating, peel and grate 1 teaspoon ginger. Grate ½ teaspoon lime zest and squeeze 2 tablespoons juice. Tear nori (if using) into small pieces and place in small bowl. Trim and halve radishes, then slice thin. Halve avocado, remove pit, and slice thin. Halve cucumber lengthwise, then slice thin. Slice scallions thin on bias.

**4** **Cook Salmon** Once oven reaches 500 degrees, reduce oven temperature to 275 degrees. Remove sheet from oven and carefully place salmon, skin side down, on hot sheet and roast until center is still translucent when checked with tip of paring knife and registers 125 degrees (for medium-rare), 9 to 13 minutes. Slide fish spatula along underside of fillets and transfer to plate, leaving skin behind; discard skin.

**5** **Make Dressing** While salmon roasts, whisk vinegar, mirin, miso, ginger, and lime zest and juice in small bowl until miso is fully incorporated. Season with salt and pepper to taste. Measure out ¼ cup dressing, drizzle over rice, and toss to combine.

**6** **Finish Dish** Divide rice among individual serving bowls and sprinkle with nori, if using. Top with salmon, radishes, avocado, and cucumber. Sprinkle with scallions and drizzle with remaining dressing. Serve.

# Glazed Salmon with Black-Eyed Peas, Walnuts, and Pomegranate

serves 4; total time 45 minutes

## notes for the cook

Rich, meaty salmon and a sweet glaze are a fantastic pairing, and sweet-tangy pomegranate molasses is a flavor-packed shortcut to the perfect thick, shiny glaze.

Pomegranate molasses is also the key to the punchy dressing on our black-eyed pea salad. The creamy, mild peas make a great base for crunchy additions like toasted nuts, fresh scallions, and tart pomegranate seeds.

If you can't find pomegranate molasses, you can make your own (see page 7).

Note that you'll need ½ cup of parsley, so shop accordingly.

½ cup walnuts

1 lemon

4 scallions

Fresh parsley

4 (6- to 8-ounce) skin-on salmon fillets, 1 to 1½ inches thick

3 tablespoons plus 1 teaspoon extra-virgin olive oil

¼ cup pomegranate molasses

Salt and pepper

2 (15-ounce) cans black-eyed peas

½ cup pomegranate seeds

**1 Heat Oven and Toast Nuts** Adjust oven rack to lowest position, line rimmed baking sheet with aluminum foil and place on rack, and heat oven to 500 degrees. While oven heats, toast walnuts in 10-inch skillet over medium heat, shaking pan occasionally, until golden and fragrant, 3 to 5 minutes; transfer to small bowl to cool, then chop cooled nuts.

**2 Prep Vegetables** Squeeze 2 tablespoons lemon juice. Slice scallions thin. Mince ½ cup parsley.

**3 Season Salmon** Pat salmon dry with paper towels. Brush with 1 teaspoon oil, then brush with 1 tablespoon pomegranate molasses and season with salt and pepper.

**4 Cook Salmon** Once oven reaches 500 degrees, reduce oven temperature to 275 degrees. Remove sheet from oven and carefully place salmon, skin side down, on hot sheet. Roast salmon until center is still translucent when checked with tip of paring knife and registers 125 degrees (for medium-rare), 9 to 13 minutes.

**5 Make Salad** While salmon cooks, drain and rinse black eyed peas. Whisk 2 tablespoons pomegranate molasses, lemon juice, remaining 3 tablespoons oil, ¼ teaspoon salt, and ⅛ teaspoon pepper together in large bowl until combined. Add pomegranate seeds, walnuts, scallions, parsley, and black-eyed peas and toss to combine. Season with salt and pepper to taste.

**6 Finish Dish** Remove salmon from oven and brush with remaining 1 tablespoon pomegranate molasses. Slide fish spatula along underside of fillets and transfer to plate, leaving skin behind; discard skin. Serve with black-eyed pea salad.

# Salmon Tacos with Collard and Radish Slaw

serves 4; total time 45 minutes

## notes for the cook

For a fresh take on fish tacos that didn't require messy frying, we went with salmon treated with a simple spice rub. Paired with a quick slaw and mashed avocado, these are the most flavorful fish tacos you can make in under an hour.

If you have a few extra minutes, try our preferred tortilla-warming method: Using a dry skillet over medium-high heat, warm the tortillas one at a time until softened and speckled brown, 20 to 30 seconds per side.

Jícama is a root vegetable with cool, crisp flesh that tastes like a mix of apple and water chestnut. Its crunchy texture makes it the perfect addition to our slaw.

You can substitute 2 cups of thinly sliced purple cabbage for the collards if desired.

2 limes

4 ounces collard greens

4 ounces jícama

4 radishes

1 shallot

Fresh cilantro

Salt and pepper

1½ teaspoons chili powder

3 (6- to 8-ounce) skin-on salmon fillets, 1 to 1½ inches thick

1 tablespoon vegetable oil

1 ripe avocado

12 (6-inch) corn tortillas

Hot sauce

**1 Prep Ingredients** Grate ¼ teaspoon lime zest and squeeze 3 tablespoons juice. Stem collard greens by cutting away leafy green portion from either side of stalk, then slice leaves thin. Peel jícama and cut into 2-inch-long matchsticks. Trim radishes and cut into 1-inch-long matchsticks. Slice shallot thin. Pick ¼ cup cilantro leaves.

**2 Make Slaw** Whisk lime zest and 2 tablespoons juice and ¼ teaspoon salt together in large bowl. Add collard greens, jícama, radishes, shallot, and cilantro and toss well to combine.

**3 Season Salmon** Combine chili powder, ¾ teaspoon salt, and ¼ teaspoon pepper in small bowl. Pat salmon dry with paper towels and sprinkle evenly with spice mixture.

**4** **Cook Salmon** Heat oil in 12-inch nonstick skillet over medium heat until shimmering. Place salmon in skillet, skin side up, and cook until well browned, 4 to 6 minutes. Flip and continue to cook until center is still translucent when checked with tip of paring knife and registers 125 degrees (for medium-rare), 4 to 6 minutes. Transfer salmon to plate.

**5** **Mash Avocado** While salmon cooks, halve avocado and remove pit. Mash avocado and remaining 1 tablespoon lime juice in bowl with fork until mostly smooth. Season with salt and pepper to taste.

**6** **Warm Tortillas and Finish Dish** Place tortillas on plate, cover with damp dish towel, and microwave for 60 to 90 seconds until warm. Spread mashed avocado over tortillas. Using 2 forks, flake salmon into 2-inch pieces; discard skin. Divide fish evenly among tortillas, top with collard slaw, and drizzle with hot sauce to taste. Serve.

# Salmon Burgers with Asparagus and Lemon-Herb Sauce

serves 4; total time 45 minutes

## notes for the cook

A food processor makes quick work of chopping not just the fish but also our fresh bread crumbs for these salmon burgers. We use just enough bread and mayonnaise (plus some choice flavorings) to bind the burgers together while letting the salmon still shine through.

Broiling the salmon burgers on a sheet pan in the oven allows us to prepare a roasted vegetable side dish in the same pan. We opted for broiler-friendly asparagus, simply seasoned with salt and pepper.

Age affects the flavor of asparagus enormously. For the sweetest taste, look for spears that are bright green and firm, with tightly closed tips.

1 pound asparagus

2 teaspoons capers

1 lemon

2 scallions

Fresh parsley

6 tablespoons mayonnaise

Salt and pepper

1 slice hearty white sandwich bread

1 pound skinless salmon fillets

1 tablespoon Dijon mustard

1 teaspoon extra-virgin olive oil

4 hamburger buns

1 small head Bibb lettuce

**1 Prep Ingredients and Make Sauce** Trim asparagus. Rinse and mince capers. Squeeze 1 tablespoon lemon juice into small bowl. Mince scallions. Chop 3 tablespoons parsley. Add ¼ cup mayonnaise, half of scallions, and 1 tablespoon parsley to bowl with lemon juice. Season with salt and pepper to taste. Cover and refrigerate until serving.

**2 Prep Bread Crumbs** Adjust oven rack 4 inches from broiler element and heat broiler. Tear bread into 1-inch pieces. Pulse bread in food processor to coarse crumbs, about 4 pulses; transfer to large bowl.

**3 Prep Salmon** Cut salmon into 1-inch pieces. Working in 2 batches, pulse salmon in food processor until coarsely ground, about 4 pulses; transfer to bowl with bread crumbs and toss to combine. Add mustard, remaining scallions, remaining 2 tablespoons parsley, capers, remaining 2 tablespoons mayonnaise, ¼ teaspoon salt, and ⅛ teaspoon pepper to bowl; gently fold into salmon mixture until well combined.

**Make Patties** Line rimmed baking sheet with aluminum foil. Divide salmon mixture into 4 equal portions and gently pack into 1-inch-thick patties, about 3½ inches wide. Place patties on 1 side of prepared sheet. Toss asparagus with oil, ¼ teaspoon salt, and ¼ teaspoon pepper and spread in single layer on empty side of sheet.

**Broil Burgers and Asparagus** Broil until burgers are lightly browned on top, 4 to 6 minutes. Flip burgers and asparagus and continue to broil until burgers register 125 degrees (for medium-rare) and asparagus is lightly browned and tender, 3 to 6 minutes.

**Toast Buns and Finish Dish** Transfer salmon burgers and asparagus to platter. Discard foil and arrange buns, cut side up, in single layer on now-empty sheet and broil until lightly browned, 30 seconds to 1 minute. Top bun bottoms with lettuce, burgers, lemon-herb sauce, and bun tops. Serve with asparagus.

# Braised Halibut with Coriander Carrots and Pearl Couscous

serves 4; total time 1 hour

## notes for the cook

Braising is a gentle, forgiving cooking method that guarantees moist, succulent fish. It also works particularly well for the sweet carrots and shallots in this dish.

Our wine- and butter-enriched cooking liquid becomes a velvety sauce for the fish and couscous.

We prefer this recipe with halibut, but another firm-fleshed white fish such as cod, striped bass, or sea bass can be substituted. Look for similarly-shaped fillets that are uniformly 1 inch thick.

Pearl couscous is also known as Israeli couscous.

You will need a 12-inch skillet with a tight-fitting lid for this recipe.

7 tablespoons unsalted butter

1½ cups pearl couscous

Salt and pepper

5 carrots

3 shallots

4 (6- to 8-ounce) skinless halibut fillets, 1 to 1½ inches thick

½ teaspoon ground coriander

¾ cup dry white wine

2 lemons

Fresh cilantro

**1** **Cook Couscous** Melt 1 tablespoon butter in medium saucepan over medium heat. Add couscous and cook, stirring frequently, until half of grains are golden, about 5 minutes. Stir in 2 cups water and ¼ teaspoon salt. Increase heat to high and bring to boil. Reduce heat to low, cover, and simmer until water is absorbed and couscous is tender, 9 to 12 minutes. Off heat, fluff with fork and cover to keep warm.

**2** **Prep Vegetables** While couscous cooks, peel carrots, then shave lengthwise into ribbons with vegetable peeler. Cut shallots in half through root end, then slice thin.

**3** **Parcook Halibut** Pat halibut dry with paper towels and season with ½ teaspoon salt. Melt remaining 6 tablespoons butter in 12-inch skillet over low heat. Place halibut in skillet, skinned side up, increase heat to medium, and cook, shaking pan occasionally, until butter begins to brown (fish should not brown), 3 to 4 minutes. Using spatula, carefully transfer halibut to large plate, skinned side down.

### Braise Vegetables and Halibut

Add coriander, carrots, shallots, and ¼ teaspoon salt to skillet with butter and cook, stirring frequently, until beginning to soften, 2 to 4 minutes. Add wine and bring to gentle simmer. Place halibut, skinned side down, on top of vegetables. Reduce heat to low, cover, and cook until halibut flakes apart when gently prodded with paring knife and registers 140 degrees, 10 to 14 minutes.

### Prep Lemons and Herbs

While halibut cooks, squeeze 1½ teaspoons lemon juice from 1 lemon and cut remaining lemon into wedges. Chop ¼ cup cilantro. Transfer couscous to serving bowl and sprinkle with 3 tablespoons cilantro. When halibut is done, remove from heat and transfer halibut and vegetables to serving platter, leaving sauce in skillet. Tent with aluminum foil.

### Reduce Sauce and Finish Dish

Return skillet with sauce to high heat and cook until sauce is thickened, 2 to 3 minutes. Off heat, stir in lemon juice and season with salt and pepper to taste. Toss couscous with 2 tablespoons sauce and season with salt and pepper to taste. Spoon remaining sauce over fillets and sprinkle with remaining 1 tablespoon cilantro. Serve fillets with couscous and lemon wedges.

# Lemon-Poached Halibut with Roasted Fingerling Potatoes

serves 4; total time 45 minutes

## notes for the cook

Cooking white fish in a foil packet keeps it moist and allows it to pick up the flavors of whatever you add to the packet; we used tomatoes, lemon, and oregano for a bright, fresh dish.

A simple side dish of roasted fingerling potatoes cooks to crispy perfection underneath the foil packets of fish in the oven.

Use potatoes of a similar size to ensure consistent cooking.

You can substitute cod, striped bass, or sea bass for the halibut in this recipe.

1½ pounds fingerling potatoes

8 ounces grape tomatoes

1 lemon

3 tablespoons extra-virgin olive oil

Salt and pepper

4 (6- to 8-ounce) skinless halibut fillets, 1 to 1½ inches thick

½ teaspoon dried oregano

Fresh parsley

**1 Prep Vegetables** Adjust oven rack to lower-middle position and heat oven to 450 degrees. Halve potatoes lengthwise. Halve tomatoes. Cut lemon crosswise into 8 thin slices.

**2 Roast Potatoes** Toss potatoes with 5 teaspoons oil, ½ teaspoon salt, and ½ teaspoon pepper on rimmed baking sheet. Arrange potatoes, cut side down, in even layer. Roast until cut sides are starting to brown, about 10 minutes.

**3 Make Foil Packets** While potatoes cook, lay four 12-inch-long pieces of aluminum foil on counter. Place one-quarter of tomatoes in center of each piece of foil, then place 1 fillet on each tomato pile. Sprinkle each fillet with ⅛ teaspoon oregano and season with salt and pepper, then top each with 2 lemon slices and 1 teaspoon oil. Pull edges of foil up around halibut and tomatoes and crimp to form packet.

**4 Roast Halibut and Finish Potatoes**
Remove sheet from oven, place packets on top of potatoes, and bake until halibut registers 140 degrees and cut sides of potatoes are crisp and skins spotty brown, about 15 minutes. (To check temperature, poke thermometer through foil of 1 packet and into halibut.)

**5 Mince Parsley** While halibut and potatoes roast, mince 2 tablespoons parsley.

**6 Finish Dish** Divide potatoes among 4 shallow serving bowls. Open 1 packet over each bowl and slide halibut and tomatoes onto potatoes along with any accumulated juices. Sprinkle with parsley and serve.

# Cod in Saffron Broth with Chorizo and Potatoes

serves 4; total time 1 hour

## notes for the cook

This Spanish-inspired seafood dish is a simple one-pot meal.

You can substitute halibut, sea bass, or haddock for the cod in this recipe.

Other varieties of hard, cured sausage (such as linguiça) can be substituted for the Spanish chorizo; we do not recommend using fresh chorizo.

When shopping for saffron, look for dark red threads without any interspersion of yellow or orange threads, and be prepared for some sticker shock—they don't call it the most expensive spice in the world for nothing, but its distinctive flavor is worth it.

You will need a 12-inch skillet with a tight-fitting lid for this recipe.

4 ounces small red potatoes
1 onion
4 garlic cloves
3 ounces Spanish-style chorizo sausage
1 tablespoon extra-virgin olive oil
¼ teaspoon saffron threads
1 (8-ounce) bottle clam juice
½ cup dry white wine
1 bay leaf
4 (6- to 8-ounce) skinless cod fillets, 1 to 1½ inches thick
Salt and pepper
1 lemon
Fresh parsley
1 loaf rustic bread

**1  Prep Vegetables and Chorizo**
Slice potatoes ¼ inch thick. Chop onion fine and mince garlic. Slice chorizo into ¼-inch-thick rounds.

**2  Sauté Aromatics and Chorizo**
Heat oil in 12-inch skillet over medium heat until shimmering. Add onion and chorizo and cook until onion is softened and lightly browned, 5 to 7 minutes. Stir in garlic and crumble saffron into skillet and cook until fragrant, about 30 seconds.

**3  Build Saffron Broth and Add Potatoes** Stir in clam juice, ¾ cup water, wine, potatoes, and bay leaf and bring to simmer. Reduce heat to medium-low, cover, and cook until potatoes are almost tender, about 10 minutes.

**4 Season Cod and Add to Broth**
Pat cod dry with paper towels and season with salt and pepper. Nestle cod, skinned side down, into skillet and spoon some broth over top. Bring to simmer, cover, and cook until potatoes are fully tender and cod flakes apart when gently prodded with paring knife and registers 140 degrees, 10 to 15 minutes.

**5 Prep Lemon and Parsley**
While cod cooks, squeeze 1 teaspoon lemon juice. Mince 2 tablespoons parsley.

**6 Finish Dish** Carefully transfer cod to individual shallow bowls. Using slotted spoon, divide potatoes and chorizo evenly among bowls. Discard bay leaf. Stir lemon juice into broth and season with salt and pepper to taste. Spoon broth over cod, sprinkle with parsley, and drizzle with extra oil. Slice bread and serve with cod.

# Pan-Seared Cod with Herb-Butter Sauce and Roasted Green Beans

serves 4; total time 1 hour

## notes for the cook

Using one skillet for both the fish and the sauce makes for easy cleanup and also builds layers of deep flavor in this recipe.

For perfect roasted green beans, we start them covered with foil to let them gently steam for 10 minutes. A little bit of sugar promotes browning when the foil is removed to let the beans blister in the oven's high heat.

You can substitute halibut, sea bass, or haddock for the cod in this recipe.

2 garlic cloves

1 lemon

7 tablespoons extra-virgin olive oil

1 teaspoon Dijon mustard

Salt and pepper

1½ pounds green beans

¾ teaspoon sugar

1 shallot

Fresh basil

4 tablespoons unsalted butter

½ cup all-purpose flour

4 (6- to 8-ounce) skinless cod fillets, 1 to 1½ inches thick

⅓ cup dry white wine

**1 Make Dressing** Adjust oven rack to lowest position and heat oven to 475 degrees. Mince garlic. Grate 2 teaspoons lemon zest and squeeze 2 tablespoons juice. Combine 3 tablespoons oil, garlic, and 1 teaspoon lemon zest in large bowl and microwave until bubbling, about 1 minute. Whisk mustard, 1 tablespoon lemon juice, ¼ teaspoon salt, and ¼ teaspoon pepper into garlic mixture; set aside.

**2 Prep and Steam Green Beans** Trim green beans. Toss sugar, 1 tablespoon oil, green beans, ¼ teaspoon salt, and ¼ teaspoon pepper together on rimmed baking sheet. Spread green beans into even layer. Cover sheet tightly with aluminum foil and roast for 10 minutes.

**3 Prep Cod and Sauce Ingredients** While green beans steam, mince shallot. Chop ¼ cup basil. Cut butter into 4 pieces. Place flour in shallow dish. Pat cod dry with paper towels and season with salt and pepper. Dredge fillets lightly with flour.

**4** **Finish Roasting Green Beans and Add Dressing** Remove foil from green beans, stir, and continue to roast until green beans are spotty brown, 10 to 12 minutes. Transfer green beans to bowl with dressing, add 2 tablespoons chopped basil, and toss to combine. Transfer to serving platter and tent with foil to keep warm.

**5** **Cook Cod** While green beans roast, heat 2 tablespoons oil in 12-inch nonstick skillet over medium heat until just smoking. Place cod in skillet and cook until fish is golden and flakes apart when gently prodded with paring knife and registers 140 degrees, 4 to 6 minutes per side. Transfer to serving plate and tent with foil.

**6** **Make Sauce and Finish Dish** Add remaining 1 tablespoon oil, shallot, and ¼ teaspoon salt to now-empty skillet. Cook over medium heat until softened, about 1 minute. Add wine, remaining 1 teaspoon lemon zest, and remaining 1 tablespoon lemon juice and simmer until reduced by half, about 2 minutes. Off heat, whisk in butter and remaining 2 tablespoons basil. Season with salt and pepper to taste, and pour over cod. Serve with green beans.

# Thai Curry Rice with Cod

serves 4; total time 45 minutes

## notes for the cook

This one-skillet dish infuses mild cod with all the zesty, aromatic flavors of Thai curry alongside a hearty rice-and-vegetable side.

The cod's natural juices are exuded during cooking and add flavor to the rice, tying the dish together.

You will need a 12-inch nonstick skillet with a tight-fitting lid for this recipe.

You can substitute halibut, sea bass, or haddock for the cod in this recipe.

8 ounces white mushrooms
Fresh ginger
3 scallions
1 (8-ounce) can bamboo shoots
1 ½ cups long-grain white rice
1 tablespoon vegetable oil
Salt and pepper
¾ cup canned coconut milk
3 tablespoons red curry paste
4 (6- to 8-ounce) skinless cod fillets, 1 to 1 ½ inches thick
1 lime

1 **Prep Vegetables** Trim mushrooms then slice thin. Peel and grate 2 teaspoons ginger. Slice scallions thin; keep whites and greens separate. Rinse bamboo shoots. Rinse rice in fine mesh strainer until water runs clear.

2 **Cook Vegetables and Rice** Heat oil in 12-inch nonstick skillet over medium heat until shimmering. Add mushrooms, ginger, scallion whites, bamboo shoots, and rice. Cook, stirring often, until edges of rice begin to turn translucent, about 2 minutes. Add 2¼ cups water and ½ teaspoon salt and bring to boil. Cover, reduce heat to medium-low, and simmer for 10 minutes.

3 **Prep Cod** While rice and vegetables cook, whisk coconut milk and curry paste together in bowl. Pat cod dry with paper towels and season with salt and pepper.

4 **Cook Cod** Nestle fillets, skinned side down, into rice mixture and drizzle with one-third of coconut-curry sauce. Cover and cook until liquid is absorbed and cod flakes apart when gently prodded with paring knife and registers 140 degrees, 10 to 12 minutes.

5 **Heat Remaining Sauce and Slice Lime** While cod cooks, microwave remaining coconut-curry sauce mixture until warm, about 1 minute; cover to keep warm. Cut lime into wedges.

6 **Finish Dish** Off heat, sprinkle scallion greens over cod and rice mixture. Serve with remaining warm coconut-curry sauce and lime wedges.

# Cod Cakes with Garlic-Basil Aïoli and Arugula-Celery Salad

serves 4; total time 45 minutes

## notes for the cook

For fish cakes that taste more like fish and less like filler, we process fresh cod in the food processor and then add an egg and just enough crunchy panko bread crumbs to hold the cakes together.

A quick garlicky aïoli with basil dresses up the fish cakes, and we also use a few tablespoons of the aïoli to add a touch more binding power (as well as a pop of flavor) to the cakes.

A simple salad of peppery arugula and crisp celery complements the rich cod cakes.

Note that you'll need ½ cup of basil, so shop accordingly.

Fresh basil
1 lemon
1 garlic clove
½ cup mayonnaise
Salt and pepper
5 tablespoons extra-virgin olive oil
1 tablespoon apricot jam
2 celery ribs
2 scallions
1 pound skinless cod fillets
1 egg
1½ cups panko bread crumbs
5 ounces (5 cups) baby arugula

**1 Make Garlic-Basil Aïoli** Pick ½ cup basil leaves. Squeeze 3 tablespoons lemon juice. Mince garlic. Process mayonnaise, basil, 2 tablespoons lemon juice, and garlic in food processor until smooth and pale green, about 20 seconds; transfer to bowl and season with salt and pepper to taste.

**2 Make Dressing and Prep Celery** Whisk 1 tablespoon oil, apricot jam, remaining 1 tablespoon lemon juice, ½ teaspoon salt, and ¼ teaspoon pepper together in serving bowl. Slice celery thin on bias and add to bowl with dressing. Chop scallions fine.

**3 Prep Cod** Cut cod into 1-inch pieces. Working in 2 batches, pulse cod in now-empty food processor until some is finely minced and some is coarsely chopped, about 3 pulses; transfer to large bowl.

**4 Make Cod Cakes** Lightly beat egg. Gently fold ¾ cup panko, 3 tablespoons garlic-basil aïoli, scallions, egg, ½ teaspoon salt, and ¼ teaspoon pepper into cod in bowl until combined. Divide cod mixture into 4 equal portions and gently pack into 1-inch-thick cakes, about 3½ inches wide. Spread remaining ¾ cup panko in shallow dish. Dredge patties in panko, pressing gently to adhere.

**5 Cook Cakes** Heat remaining ¼ cup oil in 12-inch nonstick skillet over medium heat until shimmering. Lay patties in skillet and cook until golden on first side, 3 to 5 minutes. Flip and continue to cook until golden on second side and cakes register 140 degrees, 3 to 5 minutes.

**6 Toss Salad and Finish Dish** Add arugula to bowl with celery and toss gently to coat. Serve cod cakes with salad and remaining aïoli.

# Blackened Snapper with Sautéed Spinach and Black Rice

serves 4; total time 1 hour

## notes for the cook

To get all the deep flavor of blackened fish without a smoky mess in the kitchen, we cook our snapper under the broiler.

Garlicky sautéed spinach and nutty black rice complement the spiced fish, while a yogurt sauce provides a cooling contrast.

If you can't find black rice, you can use brown rice, although it may need a few extra minutes of cooking.

If you don't have a microwave-safe bowl large enough to accommodate the entire amount of spinach, cook it in two batches. Reduce the water to 2 tablespoons per batch and cook each for about 1½ minutes.

1½ cups black rice

Salt and pepper

1 lemon

½ cup plain yogurt

3 tablespoons extra-virgin olive oil

1½ teaspoons smoked paprika

½ teaspoon ground coriander

½ teaspoon ground fennel

¼ teaspoon cayenne pepper

⅛ teaspoon ground cloves

18 ounces (18 cups) baby spinach

2 garlic cloves

4 (6- to 8-ounce) skin-on red snapper fillets,
  ¾ to 1 inch thick

**1 Cook Rice** Bring 4 quarts water to boil in Dutch oven over medium-high heat. Add rice and 1 teaspoon salt and cook until rice is tender, 20 to 25 minutes. Drain rice, transfer to bowl and season with salt and pepper to taste; cover to keep warm.

**2 Make Sauce and Spice Rub** While rice cooks, grate 2 teaspoons lemon zest and squeeze 1 teaspoon juice. Stir yogurt and lemon zest and juice together in bowl and season with salt and pepper to taste; set aside for serving. Microwave 1 tablespoon oil, paprika, coriander, fennel, cayenne, cloves, ½ teaspoon salt, and ¼ teaspoon pepper in small bowl until fragrant, about 30 seconds; let cool slightly.

**3 Parcook Spinach** Microwave spinach and ¼ cup water in large bowl, covered, until spinach is wilted and decreased in volume by half, 3 to 4 minutes. Remove bowl from microwave and keep covered for 1 minute. Carefully remove cover and transfer spinach to colander. Using back of rubber spatula, gently press spinach against colander to release excess liquid. Slice garlic thin.

**4 Prep Red Snapper** Adjust oven rack 4 inches from broiler element and heat broiler. Pat red snapper dry with paper towels and brush flesh side evenly with spice mixture.

**5 Cook Red Snapper** Line rimmed baking sheet with aluminum foil. Arrange snapper, skin side down, on prepared sheet. Broil until snapper flakes apart when gently prodded with paring knife, 6 to 8 minutes.

**6 Sauté Spinach and Finish Dish** While snapper cooks, heat remaining 2 tablespoons oil in 12-inch skillet over medium heat until shimmering. Stir in garlic and cook until fragrant, about 30 seconds. Add spinach and toss to coat. Season with ¼ teaspoon salt and continue stirring with tongs until spinach is glossy green, about 2 minutes. Season with salt and pepper to taste. Serve with snapper, rice, and yogurt sauce.

# Roasted Trout with White Bean and Tomato Salad

serves 4; total time 45 minutes

## notes for the cook

By starting with trout that have already been boned and butterflied, you can focus on roasting this rich, flavorful fish and creating a complementary side dish.

Adding the trout to a preheated baking sheet in the oven ensures that it will develop a nice crisp skin.

Given the trout's brief roasting time, we partnered it with an equally quick accompaniment: creamy cannellini beans tossed with the bright, fresh flavors of shallots, parsley, lemon juice, capers, rosemary, and garlic.

We like cannellini beans for this salad, but any canned small white beans will work.

2 shallots

2 garlic cloves

Fresh rosemary

2 tablespoons capers

3 lemons

12 ounces cherry tomatoes

Fresh parsley

½ cup extra-virgin olive oil

4 (7- to 10-ounce) boneless, butterflied whole trout

Salt and pepper

2 (15-ounce) cans cannellini beans

**1 Prep Vegetables and Aromatics** Adjust oven rack to middle position, place rimmed baking sheet on rack, and heat oven to 450 degrees. Mince shallots and garlic. Mince 4 teaspoons rosemary. Rinse capers, then chop. Squeeze ¼ cup lemon juice from 2 lemons. Cut remaining lemon into wedges. Cut tomatoes in half. Chop ¼ cup parsley.

**2 Make Dressing** Whisk ¼ cup oil, shallots, garlic, rosemary, capers, and lemon juice together in large bowl.

**3 Season Trout** Pat trout dry with paper towels and season with salt and pepper.

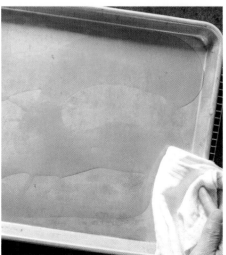

**4** **Heat Oil** Add remaining ¼ cup oil to preheated sheet, tilting to coat evenly, and return to oven for 4 minutes.

**5** **Roast Trout** Carefully place trout, skin side down, on hot sheet; return to oven and cook until trout flakes apart when gently prodded with paring knife, 7 to 9 minutes.

**6** **Make Salad and Finish Dish** While trout roasts, drain and rinse beans. Add beans, tomatoes, and parsley to dressing in bowl and toss to coat. Season with salt and pepper to taste. Serve with trout and lemon wedges and drizzle with extra oil to taste.

# Seared Tuna Steaks with Wilted Frisée and Mushroom Salad

serves 4; total time 1 hour

## notes for the cook

Harissa is a bright, spicy traditional North African condiment that adds a jolt of potent flavor to any recipe it's used in. It works well with the meaty tuna steaks and earthy mushrooms in this dish.

Use harissa paste for this recipe rather than harissa sauce. Note that spiciness will vary greatly by brand. If you can't find harissa, you can make your own (see page 7).

White mushrooms can be substituted for the creminis, if you prefer.

We prefer our tuna cooked rare. If you like yours medium-rare, cook the fish in step 5 until it is opaque at the perimeter and reddish pink at the center when checked with the tip of a paring knife and it registers 125 degrees, 2 to 3 minutes per side.

1 shallot

1¼ pounds cremini mushrooms

12 ounces shiitake mushrooms

1 head frisée (6 ounces)

6 tablespoons extra-virgin olive oil

Salt and pepper

2 lemons

3 tablespoons harissa

Fresh mint

4 (6- to 8-ounce) tuna steaks, 1 inch thick

½ teaspoon sugar

**1 Prep Vegetables** Halve shallot through root end and slice thin. Trim cremini mushrooms and halve if small or quarter if large. Stem shiitake mushrooms and slice ½ inch thick. Cut frisée into 1-inch pieces and transfer to large serving bowl.

**2 Cook Mushrooms** Heat 2 tablespoons oil in 12-inch nonstick skillet over medium heat until shimmering. Add shallot and cook until softened, about 2 minutes. Add cremini mushrooms, shiitake mushrooms, and ½ teaspoon salt, cover, and cook, stirring occasionally, until mushrooms have released their liquid, 8 to 10 minutes.

**3 Make Sauce and Chop Mint** While mushrooms cook, squeeze 1 tablespoon juice from 1 lemon into small bowl and cut remaining lemon into wedges. Add 1 tablespoon oil and 2 tablespoons harissa to lemon juice in bowl. Whisk in hot water, 1 tablespoon at a time (up to 3 tablespoons), until sauce is pourable; set aside. Chop 2 tablespoons mint.

**4** **Finish Cooking Mushrooms and Assemble Salad** Uncover skillet, add 2 tablespoons oil, and cook, stirring occasionally, until mushrooms are deep golden brown and tender, 10 to 12 minutes. Add remaining 1 tablespoon harissa and cook until fragrant, about 30 seconds. Transfer mushrooms to bowl with frisée and toss to combine; set aside. Wipe skillet clean with paper towels.

**5** **Cook Tuna** Pat tuna dry with paper towels and season with salt and pepper. Sprinkle ⅛ teaspoon sugar evenly over 1 side of each steak. Heat remaining 1 tablespoon oil in now-empty skillet over medium-high heat until just smoking. Place steaks in skillet, sugared sides down, and cook until translucent red at center when checked with tip of paring knife and register 110 degrees (for rare), 1 to 2 minutes per side.

**6** **Finish Dish** Transfer tuna to cutting board and slice ½ inch thick. Sprinkle mint over mushroom mixture and season with salt and pepper to taste. Drizzle tuna with reserved harissa sauce and serve with salad and lemon wedges.

# Swordfish Kebabs with Zucchini Ribbon Salad

serves 4; total time 45 minutes

## notes for the cook

Swordfish has a robust taste all its own and needs co-starring ingredients with just as much oomph. For these skewers, we paired swordfish with a fresh, vibrant salad containing thinly shaved zucchini, earthy baby kale, and nutty ricotta salata.

To prevent the salad from becoming watery, wait until just before serving to toss the ingredients together.

You will need four 12-inch metal skewers for this recipe.

We like the flavor of swordfish here but you can substitute other firm-fleshed fish such as mahi-mahi or halibut.

2 lemons

7 tablespoons extra-virgin olive oil

1 ½ teaspoons dried oregano

2 pounds skinless swordfish steaks, 1 inch thick

Salt and pepper

3 zucchini (8 ounces each)

3 ounces ricotta salata

Fresh mint

3 ounces (3 cups) baby kale

**1 Heat Grill** Turn all burners to high, cover, and heat grill until hot, about 15 minutes. Leave all burners on high.

**2 Make Marinade** While grill heats, squeeze ¼ cup lemon juice. Whisk ¼ cup oil, oregano, and 2 tablespoons lemon juice together in large bowl.

**3 Prep Swordfish** Cut swordfish into 1-inch chunks and pat dry with paper towels. Add to bowl with marinade and toss to coat. Let sit for 10 minutes.

**4 Make Dressing and Prep Vegetables** While swordfish marinates, whisk remaining 3 tablespoons oil, remaining 2 tablespoons lemon juice, 1 teaspoon salt, and 1 teaspoon pepper together in serving bowl; set dressing aside. Trim zucchini, then shave into thin ribbons with vegetable peeler. Shave ricotta salata with vegetable peeler. Chop 2 tablespoons mint. Thread marinated swordfish evenly onto 4 metal skewers.

**5 Grill Skewers** Clean and oil cooking grate. Grill swordfish skewers, covered, turning often, until swordfish registers 140 degrees, 9 to 12 minutes. Transfer to platter.

**6 Finish Dish** Add kale, zucchini, ricotta salata, and mint to bowl with dressing and toss to coat. Season with salt and pepper to taste. Slide swordfish off skewers and serve immediately with salad.

# Grilled Swordfish with Eggplant, Tomato, and Chickpea Salad

serves 4; total time 1 hour

## notes for the cook

Meaty swordfish stands up particularly well to grilling. Here, we give it a flavor boost by coating it with a paste of cilantro, onion, garlic, and warm spices that bloom over the hot fire.

A smoky salad of charred eggplant, juicy cherry tomatoes, and chickpeas dressed with the same herb and spice mixture complements the fish perfectly.

Note that you'll need 1 cup of cilantro, so shop accordingly.

We like the flavor of swordfish here but you can substitute other firm-fleshed fish such as mahi-mahi or halibut.

Fresh cilantro

½ red onion

4 garlic cloves

1 lemon

6 tablespoons extra-virgin olive oil

1 teaspoon ground cumin

1 teaspoon paprika

¼ teaspoon cayenne pepper

⅛ teaspoon ground cinnamon

Salt and pepper

1½ pounds eggplant

6 ounces cherry tomatoes

1 (15-ounce) can chickpeas

4 (6- to 8-ounce) skin-on swordfish steaks, 1 to 1½ inches thick

**1 Heat Grill** Turn all burners to high, cover, and heat grill until hot, about 15 minutes. Leave primary burner on high and turn other burner(s) to medium-high.

**2 Make Dressing** Pick 1 cup cilantro leaves. Chop onion coarse. Chop garlic. Squeeze 3 tablespoons lemon juice. Process 3 tablespoons oil, cumin, paprika, cayenne, cinnamon, cilantro, onion, garlic, lemon juice, and ½ teaspoon salt in food processor until smooth, about 2 minutes, scraping down sides of bowl as needed. Measure out and reserve ½ cup cilantro mixture. Transfer remaining cilantro mixture to large bowl.

**3 Prep Vegetables and Swordfish** Slice eggplant into ½-inch-thick rounds. Brush eggplant with remaining 3 tablespoons oil and season with salt and pepper. Halve tomatoes. Drain and rinse chickpeas. Pat swordfish dry with paper towels and brush evenly with reserved ½ cup cilantro mixture.

**Grill Swordfish and Eggplant**
Clean and oil cooking grate. Place swordfish on hotter side of grill and eggplant on cooler side of grill. Cook swordfish, uncovered, until streaked with dark grill marks, 6 to 9 minutes, gently flipping steaks halfway through cooking. Cook eggplant, flipping as needed, until softened and lightly charred, about 8 to 10 minutes; transfer eggplant to serving platter and tent with aluminum foil.

**Finish Swordfish** Gently move swordfish to cooler side of grill and continue to cook, uncovered, until fish flakes apart when gently prodded with paring knife and registers 140 degrees, 1 to 3 minutes per side; transfer to platter and tent with foil while finishing salad.

**Make Salad and Finish Dish** Chop eggplant coarse and add to bowl with cilantro mixture. Add tomatoes and chickpeas and gently toss to combine. Season with salt and pepper to taste. Serve with swordfish.

# Pan-Seared Scallops with Sugar Snap Pea Slaw

serves 4; total time 45 minutes

## notes for the cook

To accompany sweet, juicy caramelized scallops, we made a fresh take on vegetable slaw with thinly sliced snap peas, cucumber, and radishes.

Using a hot skillet and just-smoking oil are the keys to perfectly seared scallops.

We recommend buying "dry" scallops, which don't have chemical additives and taste better than "wet." Dry scallops will also sear much faster and develop a better crust. Dry scallops will look ivory or pinkish; wet scallops are bright white.

8 ounces sugar snap peas

1 English cucumber

6 radishes

Fresh chives

1 lemon

¼ cup mayonnaise

Salt and pepper

1½ pounds large sea scallops

2 tablespoons vegetable oil

**1 Prep Vegetables** Remove strings from snap peas, then slice thin on bias. Cut cucumber in half lengthwise, remove seeds, then slice thin crosswise. Trim radishes, cut in half, and slice thin.

**2 Make Dressing** Chop 2 tablespoons chives. Grate ¼ teaspoon lemon zest, then squeeze 2 tablespoons juice into large serving bowl. Whisk mayonnaise, chives, and ¼ teaspoon salt together into lemon juice and zest in bowl.

**3 Assemble Slaw** Add snap peas, cucumber, and radishes to bowl with dressing and toss until thoroughly combined.

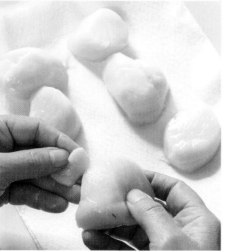

4 **Prep Scallops** Remove tendons from scallops. Pat scallops dry with paper towels and season with salt and pepper.

5 **Sear First Batch of Scallops** Heat 1 tablespoon oil in 12-inch nonstick skillet over high heat until just smoking. Add half of scallops in single layer and cook, without moving, until well browned, 1½ to 2 minutes. Flip and continue to cook until sides of scallops are firm and centers are opaque, 1 to 1½ minutes (remove smaller scallops as they finish cooking). Transfer to plate and tent with aluminum foil.

6 **Sear Second Batch of Scallops and Finish Dish** Wipe out skillet with paper towels and repeat searing with remaining 1 tablespoon oil and remaining scallops. Serve scallops with slaw.

# Lemony Shrimp with Orzo, Feta, and Olives

serves 4; total time 45 minutes

## notes for the cook

Tossing shrimp with a simple combination of salt, pepper, and lemon zest before cooking infuses them with clean citrus flavor.

Cooking orzo with sautéed onion and garlic gives it extra flavor and creates a creamy consistency that pairs well with the rich shrimp, which finish cooking right in the skillet with the orzo.

Kalamata olives are a perfect briny counterpoint to the toasty orzo and lemony shrimp, and a judicious amount of feta cheese gives the dish some tang and just enough richness.

You will need a 12-inch nonstick skillet with a tight-fitting lid for this recipe.

1 lemon

1 onion

2 garlic cloves

1 cup pitted kalamata olives

4 ounces feta cheese

Fresh parsley

1½ pounds extra-large shrimp (21 to 25 per pound)

Salt and pepper

2 tablespoons extra-virgin olive oil

2 cups orzo

4 cups chicken broth

**1 Prep Aromatics and Vegetables** Grate 1 tablespoon lemon zest and squeeze 1 tablespoon juice. Chop onion fine. Mince garlic. Chop olives coarse. Crumble feta (1 cup). Chop 2 tablespoons parsley.

**2 Prep Shrimp** Peel and devein shrimp. Pat shrimp dry with paper towels then toss with lemon zest, ½ teaspoon salt, and ½ teaspoon pepper in bowl; set aside.

**3 Cook Aromatics** Heat 1 tablespoon oil in 12-inch nonstick skillet over medium-high heat until shimmering. Add onion and cook until softened, about 5 minutes. Stir in garlic and cook until fragrant, about 30 seconds.

4 **Cook Orzo** Stir in orzo and cook, stirring frequently, until orzo is coated with oil and lightly browned, about 4 minutes. Add broth, bring to boil, and cook, uncovered, until orzo is al dente, about 6 minutes.

5 **Finish Orzo** Stir in lemon juice, olives, and ½ cup feta. Season with salt and pepper to taste.

6 **Add Shrimp and Finish Dish** Reduce heat to medium-low, nestle shrimp into orzo, cover, and cook until shrimp are pink and cooked through, about 5 minutes. Sprinkle with remaining ½ cup feta and parsley and drizzle with extra oil to taste. Serve.

# Seared Shrimp with Tomato, Avocado, and Lime Quinoa

serves 4; total time 1 hour

## notes for the cook

For a main-course quinoa and seafood dish, we paired this quick-cooking supergrain with seared shrimp and flavorful Southwestern-inspired ingredients.

Cooking the shrimp in two batches ensures that they will brown, not steam.

A quick, fresh tomato sauce pulls together the smoky shrimp and nutty quinoa.

Note that you'll need ½ cup of cilantro, so shop accordingly.

We like the convenience of prewashed quinoa; rinsing removes the quinoa's bitter protective coating (called saponin). If you buy unwashed quinoa, rinse it and then spread it out on a clean dish towel to dry for 15 minutes.

1½ cups prewashed white quinoa

Salt and pepper

2 limes

Fresh cilantro

1 pound tomatoes

3 scallions

3 garlic cloves

1 avocado

1½ pounds extra-large shrimp (21 to 25 per pound)

½ teaspoon chipotle chile powder

2 tablespoons extra-virgin olive oil

**1 Cook Quinoa** Toast quinoa in medium saucepan over medium-high heat, stirring frequently, until quinoa is very fragrant and makes continuous popping sound, 5 to 7 minutes. Stir in 1¾ cups water and ¼ teaspoon salt and bring to simmer. Cover, reduce heat to low, and simmer until quinoa is tender and liquid is absorbed, 18 to 22 minutes, stirring once halfway through cooking.

**2 Prep Vegetables** While quinoa cooks, grate ¼ teaspoon lime zest and squeeze 2 tablespoons juice from 1 lime. Cut remaining lime into wedges. Chop ½ cup cilantro. Core tomatoes and cut into ½-inch pieces. Slice scallions thin; keep whites and greens separate. Mince garlic. Halve avocado, remove pit, and cut into ½-inch pieces.

**3 Finish Quinoa** Remove quinoa from heat and let sit, covered, for 10 minutes. Fluff quinoa with fork, stir in lime zest, 1 tablespoon lime juice, and ¼ cup cilantro; cover to keep warm.

4 **Prep Shrimp** Peel and devein shrimp. Pat shrimp dry with paper towels, then toss with chile powder, ¼ teaspoon salt, and ¼ teaspoon pepper in bowl.

5 **Cook Shrimp** Heat 1 tablespoon oil in 12-inch nonstick skillet over medium-high heat until just smoking. Add half of shrimp in single layer and cook, without stirring, until spotty brown and edges turn pink on bottom side, about 1 minute. Flip shrimp and continue to cook until all but very center is opaque, about 30 seconds. Transfer shrimp to large plate. Repeat with remaining 1 tablespoon oil and remaining shrimp.

6 **Finish Dish** Return now-empty skillet to medium-high heat. Add tomatoes, scallion whites, garlic, remaining ¼ cup cilantro, remaining 1 tablespoon lime juice, and ¼ teaspoon salt. Cook until tomatoes soften slightly, about 1 minute. Stir in shrimp and cook until shrimp are opaque throughout, about 1 minute. Transfer to platter, sprinkle with scallion greens and top with avocado. Serve with quinoa and lime wedges, drizzling with extra oil to taste.

# Garlicky Roasted Shrimp with Napa Cabbage and Orange Salad

serves 4; total time 1 hour

## notes for the cook

To get quick-cooking shrimp to develop great color and flavor in just minutes, we briefly brine the shrimp, then coat them in a potent mixture of aromatics before roasting them under the broiler. The superhot broiler ensures that the shrimp brown quickly and avoid steaming in their own juices.

Keeping the shrimp in their shells during cooking protects them from drying out and contributes extra flavor; make sure you buy shell-on shrimp for this recipe.

A bright shredded cabbage salad, studded with citrus and fresh basil, contrasts nicely with the rich, sweet shrimp.

Note that you'll need ½ cup of basil, so shop accordingly.

Salt and pepper
2 pounds shell-on jumbo shrimp (16 to 20 per pound)
3 scallions
2 garlic cloves
3 oranges
½ small head napa cabbage (12 ounces)
Fresh basil
10 tablespoons extra-virgin olive oil
1 tablespoon cider vinegar
1 teaspoon fennel seeds
½ teaspoon red pepper flakes

**1 Brine Shrimp** Dissolve ¼ cup salt in 1 quart cold water in large container. Using kitchen shears or sharp paring knife, cut through shell of shrimp and devein but do not remove shell. Using paring knife, cut ½-inch-deep slit in each shrimp, taking care not to cut shrimp in half completely. Submerge shrimp in brine, cover, and refrigerate for 15 minutes.

**2 Prep Vegetables** While shrimp brines, slice scallions thin; keep white and green parts separate. Mince garlic. Cut away peel and pith from oranges. Quarter oranges, then slice crosswise ½ inch thick. Remove core from cabbage and slice thin crosswise. Shred ½ cup basil.

**3 Make Dressing** Whisk 2 tablespoons oil, vinegar, scallion whites, ¼ teaspoon salt, and ⅛ teaspoon pepper together in large bowl; set aside.

**4 Flavor Shrimp** Adjust oven rack 4 inches from broiler element and heat broiler. Combine fennel seeds, pepper flakes, scallion greens, garlic, and remaining ½ cup oil in large bowl. Remove shrimp from brine and pat dry with paper towels. Add shrimp to oil mixture; toss well, making sure oil mixture gets into interior of shrimp. Arrange shrimp in single layer on wire rack set in rimmed baking sheet.

**5 Cook Shrimp** Broil shrimp until first side is opaque and shells are beginning to brown, 2 to 4 minutes, rotating sheet halfway through broiling. Flip shrimp and continue to broil until second side is opaque and shells are beginning to brown, 2 to 4 minutes, rotating sheet halfway through broiling. Transfer shrimp to serving platter.

**6 Finish Dish** Add orange pieces, cabbage, and basil to dressing in bowl and toss to combine. Serve with shrimp.

# Quick Paella

serves 4; total time 1 hour

## notes for the cook

Paella, Spain's famous rice and seafood dish, is not something you'd usually want to attempt for a weeknight dinner, but we streamlined this classic for a quick version that packs all of the flavor with minimal prep and fuss.

To build deep flavor in our quick paella, we use fat from the chorizo to cook the aromatics and herbs before toasting the rice, which then soaks up the flavors of the clam juice, tomatoes, and saffron.

Other varieties of hard, cured sausage (such as linguiça) can be substituted for the Spanish chorizo; we do not recommend using fresh chorizo.

You will need a 12-inch nonstick skillet with a tight-fitting lid for this recipe.

1 onion
3 garlic cloves
1 cup long-grain white rice
1 (14.5-ounce) can diced tomatoes
8 ounces Spanish-style chorizo sausage
1 pound extra-large shrimp (21 to 25 per pound)
½ teaspoon chili powder
¼ teaspoon pepper
12 mussels
2 tablespoons vegetable oil
2 (8-ounce) bottles clam juice
¼ teaspoon saffron threads
Fresh parsley
½ cup frozen peas

**1 Prep Aromatics, Rice, Tomatoes, and Chorizo** Chop onion fine. Mince garlic. Rinse rice in fine-mesh strainer until water runs clear. Drain tomatoes. Slice chorizo ½ inch thick.

**2 Prep Shrimp and Mussels** Peel and devein shrimp. Pat dry with paper towels and toss with chili powder and pepper in bowl. Scrub mussels and remove weedy beards protruding from between shells using paring knife.

**3 Cook Shrimp** Heat 1 tablespoon oil in 12-inch nonstick skillet over medium-high heat until just smoking. Add shrimp in single layer and cook, without stirring, until spotty brown and edges turn pink on bottom side, about 1 minute. Flip shrimp and continue to cook until all but very center is opaque, about 30 seconds. Transfer to bowl and cover with aluminum foil.

 **Cook Chorizo** Add remaining 1 tablespoon oil to now-empty skillet and heat until just smoking. Add chorizo and cook until browned, about 3 minutes. Using slotted spoon, transfer chorizo to bowl with shrimp and cover to keep warm (do not wipe out skillet).

 **Cook Rice** Add onion to fat left in skillet and cook over medium heat until softened, about 5 minutes. Stir in garlic and cook until fragrant, about 30 seconds. Stir in rice and cook until grains are lightly toasted, about 1 minute. Stir in clam juice and tomatoes, scraping up any browned bits. Crumble saffron over top, bring to boil, then cover, reduce heat to low, and cook until rice is tender and liquid is absorbed, 12 to 15 minutes.

 **Finish Dish** While rice cooks, chop 2 tablespoons parsley. Off heat, stir cooked shrimp and chorizo into rice. Arrange mussels over top and sprinkle with peas. Cover and cook over medium heat until mussels have opened, about 7 minutes, discarding any that don't open. Sprinkle with parsley and serve.

# Clams with Pearl Couscous, Chorizo, and Leeks

serves 4 to 6; total time 1 hour

## notes for the cook

This simple seafood dish gets big flavor from chorizo, thyme, and dry vermouth (dry white wine can be used as a substitute).

Pearl couscous is also known as Israeli couscous.

To wash sliced leeks, put them in a bowl of cold water and rub the pieces together until the layers separate. Let the grit settle for 1 minute, then lift the leeks from the water and transfer them to a colander to drain.

Other hard, cured sausages (like linguiça) can be substituted for the Spanish chorizo.

Note that you'll need ½ cup of parsley, so shop accordingly.

You can substitute 1 teaspoon dried thyme for the fresh thyme.

2 cups pearl couscous

Salt and pepper

1½ pounds leeks

3 garlic cloves

Fresh thyme

3 tomatoes

6 ounces Spanish-style chorizo sausage

4 pounds littleneck clams

2 tablespoons extra-virgin olive oil

1 cup dry vermouth

Fresh parsley

**1 Cook Couscous** Bring 2 quarts water to boil in large saucepan. Stir in couscous and 2 teaspoons salt and cook until al dente, about 8 minutes; drain well and set aside.

**2 Prep Ingredients** While couscous cooks, cut off dark green stalks from leeks and discard. Slice leeks in half lengthwise, then slice thin and wash thoroughly. Mince garlic. Mince 1 tablespoon thyme. Core and seed tomatoes, then chop. Cut chorizo in half lengthwise then slice thin. Scrub clams.

**3 Cook Leeks and Chorizo** Heat oil in Dutch oven over medium heat until shimmering. Add leeks and chorizo and cook until leeks are tender, about 4 minutes. Stir in garlic and thyme and cook until fragrant, about 30 seconds. Stir in vermouth and cook until slightly reduced, about 1 minute.

**4** **Add Tomatoes and Clams** Stir in tomatoes and clams, cover, and cook until clams open, 8 to 12 minutes.

**5** **Chop Parsley and Remove Clams** While clams cook, mince ½ cup parsley. Once clams open, use slotted spoon to transfer to large serving bowl, discarding any clams that refuse to open.

**6** **Finish Dish** Stir couscous and parsley into pot to warm through. Season with salt and pepper to taste. Portion couscous mixture into individual bowls. Top with clams, drizzle with extra oil to taste, and serve.

Pasta & Noodles

# Grown-Up Macaroni and Cheese with Swiss Chard

serves 4; total time 45 minutes

## notes for the cook

Everyone loves a bowl of mac and cheese, but sometimes the boxed stuff just doesn't cut it, so we dressed up this classic with three kinds of cheese and hearty greens.

A bit of American cheese mixed in with the more flavorful Gruyère and Parmesan helps keep the sauce smooth and creamy.

You can get unsliced block American cheese at the deli counter.

We cook the macaroni in a smaller-than-usual amount of water (with some milk), so the pasta doesn't need to be drained; just enough liquid remains to make the sauce.

We don't recommend using different shapes or sizes of pasta in this recipe; stick to elbow macaroni.

¼ ounce Parmesan cheese

1 (5-ounce) block American cheese

5 ounces Gruyère cheese

1 pound Swiss chard

1¾ cups whole milk

⅓ cup panko bread crumbs

2 tablespoons extra-virgin olive oil

Salt and pepper

8 ounces elbow macaroni

½ teaspoon Dijon mustard

Pinch cayenne pepper

**1 Prep Cheese and Swiss Chard** Grate Parmesan (2 tablespoons). Shred American cheese (1¼ cups) and shred Gruyère (1¼ cups). Stem chard by cutting away leafy green portion from either side of stalk, then chop leaves into 1-inch pieces. Bring milk and 1¾ cups water to boil in medium saucepan over high heat.

**2 Make Panko Topping** While water and milk come to boil, stir panko, 1 tablespoon oil, ⅛ teaspoon salt, and ⅛ teaspoon pepper together in 12-inch nonstick skillet until panko is evenly moistened. Cook over medium-high heat, stirring frequently, until evenly browned, 3 to 5 minutes. Off heat, sprinkle Parmesan over panko mixture and stir to combine. Transfer to small bowl and wipe skillet clean with paper towels.

**3 Cook Macaroni** Stir macaroni into boiling milk mixture and reduce heat to medium-low. Cook, stirring frequently, until macaroni is soft (slightly past al dente), 6 to 8 minutes.

**4 Add Cheeses** Add mustard, cayenne, and American cheese to macaroni and cook, stirring constantly, until cheese is completely melted, about 1 minute. Off heat, stir in Gruyère until evenly distributed but not melted. Cover saucepan and let sit for 5 minutes.

**5 Cook Swiss Chard** While macaroni sits, heat remaining 1 tablespoon oil in now-empty skillet over medium heat until shimmering. Add chard and cook until wilted, about 4 minutes; remove skillet from heat.

**6 Finish Dish** Stir macaroni until sauce is smooth (sauce may look loose but will thicken as it cools). Stir chard into macaroni and season with salt and pepper to taste. Sprinkle panko mixture over top of individual servings. Serve immediately.

# Bucatini with Peas, Kale, and Pancetta

serves 4 to 6; total time 45 minutes

## notes for the cook

Cooking pasta in a broth infused with richness from crisped pancetta and garlic creates an ultraflavorful one-pot dish with a minimal amount of effort.

We use bucatini for this recipe; you may be less familiar with this long pasta than its cousin spaghetti, but we like how its thick, hollow strands absorb plenty of flavorful sauce. You can substitute 1 pound of spaghetti or linguine for the bucatini if you prefer.

Baby kale and frozen peas, added at the end of cooking, contribute freshness without any fussy prep required.

2 garlic cloves

1 lemon

1½ ounces Parmesan cheese

2 ounces pancetta

½ cup dry white wine

2 cups chicken broth

1 pound bucatini

½ cup panko bread crumbs

1 tablespoon extra-virgin olive oil

Salt and pepper

5 ounces (5 cups) baby kale

1 cup frozen peas

**1** **Prep Ingredients** Mince garlic. Grate 1 tablespoon lemon zest. Grate Parmesan (¾ cup). Cut pancetta into ½-inch pieces.

**2** **Cook Pancetta** Cook pancetta in Dutch oven over medium heat until crisp, 6 to 8 minutes; transfer to paper towel–lined plate.

**3** **Add Aromatics and Liquids** Add garlic and 2 teaspoons lemon zest to fat left in pot and cook until fragrant, about 30 seconds. Stir in wine, scraping up any browned bits, and cook until nearly evaporated, about 3 minutes. Stir in broth and 2½ cups water.

**Cook Pasta** Increase heat to high and bring to boil. Stir in pasta, reduce heat to medium, and simmer vigorously, stirring often, until pasta is nearly tender, 8 to 10 minutes.

**Toast Panko and Add Parmesan** While pasta cooks, toss panko with oil in bowl and season with salt and pepper. Microwave panko stirring often, until crumbs are golden brown, 3 to 5 minutes. Stir in ¼ cup Parmesan and remaining 1 teaspoon lemon zest; set aside.

**Finish Dish** Stir kale and peas into pot and continue to simmer until pasta and kale are tender, about 4 minutes. Add remaining ½ cup Parmesan and stir vigorously until pasta is creamy and well coated, about 30 seconds. Season with salt and pepper to taste. Serve, sprinkling individual portions with crisp pancetta and panko mixture.

# Linguine with Broccoli Rabe, Capers, and Lemon

serves 4 to 6; total time 45 minutes

## notes for the cook

This is not your average bland weeknight pasta: Plenty of capers, garlic, and cheese together with slightly bitter broccoli rabe make for a sophisticated, flavor-packed dish that comes together quickly and easily.

We sauté the broccoli rabe with garlic, salt, and pepper until just tender to ensure that it doesn't overcook when added to the pasta.

You can substitute 1 pound of spaghetti or bucatini for the linguine, if desired.

4 garlic cloves

1 pound broccoli rabe

3 ounces Pecorino Romano cheese

½ cup capers

1 lemon

3 tablespoons extra-virgin olive oil

Salt and pepper

1 pound linguine

1 cup chicken broth

¼ cup dry white wine

**1 Prep Broccoli Rabe and Sauce Ingredients** Bring 4 quarts water to boil in large pot. Meanwhile, slice garlic thin. Trim broccoli rabe and cut into 2-inch pieces. Grate Pecorino (1½ cups). Rinse and mince capers. Squeeze 1½ teaspoons lemon juice.

**2 Cook Broccoli Rabe** Heat 2 tablespoons oil in 12-inch skillet over medium-high heat until shimmering. Add garlic and cook until fragrant and lightly golden, about 1 minute. Add broccoli rabe, ½ teaspoon salt, and ½ teaspoon pepper and cook until broccoli rabe is just tender, about 4 minutes. Transfer broccoli rabe mixture to bowl.

**3 Cook Pasta** While broccoli rabe cooks, add pasta and 1 tablespoon salt to boiling water and cook, stirring often, until al dente. Reserve ½ cup cooking water, then drain pasta and return it to pot.

4 **Make Sauce** Add broth and wine to now-empty skillet and bring to simmer. Cook until sauce is reduced to about 1 cup, 4 to 6 minutes.

5 **Add Sauce and Toppings to Pasta** Add sauce to pasta and toss to combine. Stir in broccoli rabe mixture, 1 cup Pecorino, capers, lemon juice, and remaining 1 tablespoon oil and toss to combine.

6 **Finish Dish** Adjust consistency of pasta with reserved cooking water as needed. Season with salt and pepper to taste. Drizzle with extra oil to taste and serve, passing remaining ½ cup grated Pecorino separately.

# Skillet Penne with Chickpeas and Cauliflower

serves 4; total time 45 minutes

## notes for the cook

Skillet pastas where the pasta is cooked right in the sauce are a great way to make flavorful one-dish meals.

Browning cauliflower and onion deepens the flavor of the sauce in this dish, and chickpeas add substance.

You will need a 12-inch nonstick skillet with a tight-fitting lid for this recipe.

You can substitute 2 teaspoons dried oregano for the fresh oregano.

You can substitute 12 ounces of other pasta (such as orecchiette, ziti, campanelle, medium shells, or farfalle) for the penne; however, the cup amounts will vary for different shapes. Make sure you measure by weight.

½ head cauliflower (1 pound)
1 small onion
5 garlic cloves
Fresh oregano
1 (15-ounce) can chickpeas
3 tablespoons extra-virgin olive oil
Salt and pepper
1 (28-ounce) can crushed tomatoes
2¼ cups chicken broth
12 ounces (3¾ cups) penne
1 ounce Parmesan cheese
Fresh basil

**1** **Prep Sauce Ingredients** Core cauliflower, then cut florets into 1-inch pieces. Halve onion, then slice thin. Mince garlic. Mince 1½ tablespoons oregano. Drain and rinse chickpeas.

**2** **Cook Cauliflower and Onion** Heat oil in 12-inch nonstick skillet over medium-high heat until shimmering. Add cauliflower, onion, and ½ teaspoon salt and cook until vegetables are spotty brown, about 8 minutes.

**3** **Add Aromatics** Stir in garlic and oregano and cook until fragrant, about 30 seconds.

**4** **Cook Pasta** Add tomatoes, broth, pasta, chickpeas, ½ teaspoon salt, and ¼ teaspoon pepper to skillet and stir to combine. Bring to simmer, reduce heat to medium, cover, and simmer vigorously, stirring often, until pasta is al dente, 15 to 17 minutes.

**5** **Prep Parmesan and Basil** While pasta cooks, grate Parmesan (½ cup). Chop 2 tablespoons basil.

**6** **Finish Dish** Off heat, stir ¼ cup Parmesan into pasta. Season with salt and pepper to taste. Serve, sprinkling individual portions with basil and remaining ¼ cup Parmesan and drizzling with extra oil to taste.

# Garlicky Spaghetti with Basil and Broiled Tomatoes

serves 4 to 6; total time 1 hour

## notes for the cook

This take on *aglio e olio*, an Italian pasta dish packed with garlic flavor, is a classic pantry dinner.

Broiled tomato slices sprinkled with a mixture of Parmesan and pine nuts are a perfect foil to the simple garlicky pasta.

A serrated knife makes quick work of cutting tomatoes.

Since broilers vary so much in their output, we included a wide time range to broil the tomatoes. Watch them carefully to get them to a crispy, golden brown without burning.

You can substitute 1 pound of linguine or bucatini for the spaghetti, if desired.

Note that you'll need 1 cup of basil, so shop accordingly.

6 garlic cloves
¼ cup extra-virgin olive oil
¼ teaspoon red pepper flakes
2 ounces Parmesan
2 tablespoons pine nuts
Fresh basil
1 lemon
1 pound spaghetti
Salt and pepper
6 Roma tomatoes
½ teaspoon sugar

**1** **Make Garlic Oil** Bring 4 quarts water to boil in large pot. Meanwhile, mince garlic. Heat garlic, oil, and pepper flakes in 8-inch nonstick skillet over low heat, stirring often, until garlic is pale golden brown, 9 to 12 minutes; remove from heat and set aside.

**2** **Prep Sauce, Topping, and Garnish Ingredients** While the garlic cooks, grate Parmesan (1 cup). Chop pine nuts. Combine ½ cup Parmesan and pine nuts in bowl and set aside. Chop 1 cup basil. Grate 2 teaspoons lemon zest and squeeze 2 tablespoons juice.

**3** **Cook Pasta** Add pasta and 1 tablespoon salt to boiling water and cook, stirring occasionally, until al dente. Reserve 1 cup cooking water, then drain pasta and return it to pot.

**Prep Tomatoes** While pasta cooks, adjust oven rack 6 inches from broiler element and heat broiler. Core and cut tomatoes crosswise into ¼-inch thick slices (slicing off and discarding ends) and place in large bowl. Add sugar, ½ teaspoon salt, and ½ teaspoon pepper and toss to coat. Arrange tomatoes in even layer on wire rack set in rimmed baking sheet. Top tomatoes evenly with Parmesan–pine nut mixture.

**Broil Tomatoes** Broil tomatoes until topping is golden brown, rotating sheet halfway through cooking, 3 to 6 minutes.

**Sauce Pasta and Finish Dish** Add lemon zest and juice, reserved garlic-oil mixture, and reserved cooking water to pasta. Stir until well coated with oil and no water remains in pot. Add ¾ cup basil and remaining ½ cup Parmesan and toss to combine. Season with salt and pepper to taste. Divide pasta among individual bowls, top with tomatoes, drizzle with extra oil to taste, and sprinkle with remaining ¼ cup basil. Serve.

# Spaghetti with Spring Vegetables
serves 4 to 6; total time 45 minutes

## notes for the cook

We build up a deeply flavorful sauce for our version of pasta primavera by cooking the vegetables in stages.

Do not be alarmed when the zucchini slices turn soft and creamy and lose their shape as they cook. Overcooking the zucchini lets it break down, creating a silky texture that nicely coats the rest of the dish.

Cherry tomatoes, briefly marinated in a bit of garlic and oil, make the perfect finishing touch for this lively pasta.

You can substitute 1 pound of linguine or bucatini for the spaghetti, if desired.

1 cup frozen peas

6 ounces cherry tomatoes

5 garlic cloves

6 tablespoons extra-virgin olive oil

Salt and pepper

1 zucchini

1 pound asparagus

⅛ teaspoon red pepper flakes

1 pound spaghetti

Fresh chives

1 lemon

1 ounce Pecorino Romano cheese

Fresh mint

**1** **Prep Vegetables** Bring 4 quarts water to boil in large pot. Meanwhile, bring peas to room temperature. Halve tomatoes. Mince 1 garlic clove and slice remaining 4 cloves thin. Toss 1 tablespoon oil, tomatoes, minced garlic, ¼ teaspoon salt, and ¼ teaspoon pepper together in bowl; set aside. Cut zucchini in half lengthwise, then slice ¼ inch thick. Trim asparagus, then cut on bias into 1-inch lengths.

**2** **Cook Zucchini** Heat 3 tablespoons oil in 12-inch nonstick skillet over medium-low heat until shimmering. Add pepper flakes, sliced garlic, zucchini, and ½ teaspoon salt, cover, and cook, stirring occasionally, until zucchini softens and breaks down, 10 to 15 minutes.

**3** **Cook Pasta** While zucchini cooks, add pasta and 1 tablespoon salt to boiling water and cook, stirring often, until al dente. Reserve ½ cup cooking water, then drain pasta and return it to pot.

**4 Prep Herbs, Lemon, and Pecorino**
While pasta cooks, mince ¼ cup chives. Squeeze 1 tablespoon lemon juice. Grate Pecorino (½ cup). Chop 2 tablespoons mint.

**5 Cook Asparagus and Peas** Stir peas, asparagus, and ¾ cup water into skillet with zucchini and bring to simmer over medium-high heat. Cover and cook until asparagus is crisp-tender, about 2 minutes.

**6 Finish Dish** Add remaining 2 tablespoons oil, vegetable mixture, chives, and lemon juice to pasta and toss to combine. Adjust consistency with reserved cooking water as needed. Transfer to serving bowl, sprinkle with ¼ cup Pecorino, and drizzle with extra oil to taste. Spoon tomatoes and their juices over top and sprinkle with mint. Serve, passing remaining ¼ cup Pecorino separately.

# Spaghetti with Fried Eggs, Asparagus, and Bread Crumbs

serves 4; total time 1 hour

## notes for the cook

This combination of spaghetti, olive oil, garlic, crispy bread crumbs, Parmesan, and a soft-fried egg is a classic Italian dish sometimes referred to as Salerno-style pasta and it makes a perfect weeknight dinner. We added asparagus to round out the dish with something green.

Breaking the egg yolk over the pasta instantly creates a rich sauce.

For a spicier dish, double the amount of red pepper flakes.

You can substitute 1 pound of linguine or bucatini for the spaghetti, if desired.

You will need a 12-inch nonstick skillet with a tight-fitting lid for this recipe.

4 garlic cloves
1 pound asparagus
1½ ounces Parmesan cheese
Fresh parsley
½ cup panko bread crumbs
5 tablespoons plus 2 teaspoons extra-virgin olive oil
Salt and pepper
¼ teaspoon red pepper flakes
1 pound spaghetti
4 large eggs

**1 Prep Asparagus and Toppings**
Bring 4 quarts water to boil in large pot. Meanwhile, mince garlic. Trim asparagus and cut on bias into 1-inch lengths. Grate Parmesan (¾ cup). Mince ¼ cup parsley. Stir panko, 1 tablespoon oil, ⅛ teaspoon salt, and ⅛ teaspoon pepper together in 12-inch nonstick skillet. Cook over medium-high heat, stirring often, until evenly browned, 3 to 5 minutes. Transfer to small bowl, and wipe skillet clean.

**2 Make Garlic Oil** Heat pepper flakes, garlic, 3 tablespoons oil, and ¼ teaspoon salt in now-empty skillet over low heat, stirring often, until garlic is pale golden brown, 8 to 10 minutes; transfer to small bowl and set aside.

**3 Cook Asparagus** Heat 1 tablespoon oil in now-empty skillet over medium-high heat until shimmering. Add asparagus and pinch salt and cook until crisp-tender, 3 to 5 minutes. Transfer to separate bowl. Wipe out skillet with paper towels.

**4** **Cook Pasta** Add pasta and 1 tablespoon salt to boiling water and cook, stirring often, until al dente. Reserve 1 cup cooking water, then drain pasta and return it to pot. Off heat, add asparagus, ½ cup Parmesan, parsley, garlic mixture, ½ cup reserved cooking water, and ½ teaspoon salt to pasta and toss to combine. Cover to keep warm.

**5** **Cook Eggs** Crack 2 eggs into small bowl and season with salt and pepper. Repeat with remaining 2 eggs and second small bowl. Heat remaining 2 teaspoons oil in now-empty skillet over medium-high heat until shimmering. Working quickly, pour 1 bowl of eggs in 1 side of pan and second bowl of eggs in other side. Cover and cook for 1 minute. Remove skillet from heat and let stand, covered, about 30 seconds for runny yolks.

**6** **Finish Dish** Adjust consistency of pasta with remaining reserved cooking water as needed, then divide among serving bowls. Sprinkle each serving with 2 tablespoons panko mixture. Top each bowl with 1 fried egg and serve immediately, passing remaining ¼ cup Parmesan separately.

# Penne with Butternut Squash and Radicchio

serves 4 to 6; total time 45 minutes

## notes for the cook

The slight bitterness of radicchio makes a perfect foil for the creamy sauce, caramelized squash, and toasted almonds in this hearty dish.

Don't be tempted to use dried sage in this recipe; its flavor just doesn't hold up.

You can substitute 1 pound of other pasta (such as orecchiette, ziti, campanelle, medium shells, or farfalle) for the penne; however, the cup amounts will vary for different shapes. Make sure you measure by weight.

1 medium (2-pound) butternut squash
Fresh sage leaves
½ head radicchio (5 ounces)
½ ounce Parmesan cheese
1 lemon
⅓ cup sliced almonds
3 tablespoons extra-virgin olive oil
Salt and pepper
1 pound penne
1 teaspoon sugar
¼ teaspoon ground nutmeg
1½ cups chicken broth
1 cup heavy cream

**1 Prep Squash and Sauce Ingredients** Bring 4 quarts water to boil in large pot. Meanwhile, peel and seed butternut squash, then dice into ½-inch pieces. Mince 1 tablespoon sage. Core radicchio and slice thin. Grate Parmesan (¼ cup). Squeeze 4 teaspoons lemon juice.

**2 Toast Nuts** Toast almonds in 12-inch nonstick skillet over medium heat, shaking pan occasionally, until golden and fragrant, 3 to 5 minutes. Transfer to bowl. Wipe skillet clean with paper towels.

**3 Cook Squash** Return now-empty skillet to high heat, add 2 tablespoons oil, and heat until shimmering. Add squash, ½ teaspoon salt, and ¾ teaspoon pepper; spread in even layer, and cook, without stirring, until beginning to caramelize, 4 to 5 minutes. Continue cooking, stirring occasionally, until spotty brown, 3 to 4 minutes.

**4** **Cook Pasta** While squash cooks, add pasta and 1 tablespoon salt to boiling water and cook, stirring often, until al dente. Reserve ½ cup cooking water, then drain pasta and return it to pot.

**5** **Finish Sauce** Stir in sugar, nutmeg, sage, and remaining 1 tablespoon oil and cook until fragrant, about 30 seconds. Stir in broth and cream, bring to simmer, and cook until squash is tender, 1 to 3 minutes.

**6** **Finish Dish** Add squash mixture, radicchio, Parmesan, and lemon juice to pasta and toss until radicchio is just wilted. Adjust consistency with reserved cooking water as needed. Sprinkle with almonds. Serve.

# Penne with Chicken, Artichokes, Cherry Tomatoes, and Olives

serves 4; total time 1 hour

## notes for the cook

We embraced a Mediterranean-inspired flavor profile for this lightly sauced one-pot pasta. Penne pairs well with brothy sauces because the liquid binds to the tubes, inside and out.

If necessary, add hot water, 1 tablespoon at a time, to adjust the consistency of the sauce before serving.

You can substitute ¼ teaspoon dried oregano for the fresh oregano.

You can substitute 8 ounces of other pasta (such as orecchiette, ziti, campanelle, medium shells, or farfalle) for the penne; however, the cup amounts will vary for different shapes. Make sure you measure by weight.

1 onion
6 garlic cloves
Fresh oregano
1 pound boneless, skinless chicken breasts
Salt and pepper
3 tablespoons extra-virgin olive oil
⅛ teaspoon red pepper flakes
½ cup dry white wine
2 cups chicken broth
8 ounces (2½ cups) penne
12 ounces cherry tomatoes
2 ounces Parmesan cheese
Fresh parsley
1½ cups jarred whole artichoke hearts packed in water
½ cup pitted kalamata olives

**1 Prep Aromatics and Chicken** Chop onion fine. Mince garlic. Mince 1 teaspoon oregano. Trim chicken and pat dry with paper towels. Slice thin crosswise and season with salt and pepper.

**2 Cook Chicken** Heat 2 tablespoons oil in Dutch oven over medium-high heat until just smoking. Add chicken, breaking up any clumps, and cook without stirring until lightly browned and just cooked through, 2 to 3 minutes; transfer to bowl and cover to keep warm.

**3 Cook Aromatics** Add remaining 1 tablespoon oil and onion to now-empty pot and cook over medium heat until onion is softened, about 5 minutes. Stir in pepper flakes, garlic, and oregano and cook until fragrant, about 30 seconds. Stir in wine, scraping up any browned bits, and cook until nearly evaporated, about 1 minute.

4 **Cook Pasta** Stir in broth, 1¾ cups water, pasta, and ½ teaspoon salt, increase heat to high, and bring to boil. Reduce heat to medium and simmer vigorously, stirring often, for 10 minutes.

5 **Prep Sauce Ingredients** While pasta cooks, quarter tomatoes. Grate Parmesan (1 cup). Mince 2 tablespoons parsley. Drain artichokes, cut in half, and pat dry. After pasta has cooked for 10 minutes, stir in artichokes and continue to cook until pasta is tender and sauce is thickened, 5 to 8 minutes.

6 **Finish Dish** Reduce heat to low and stir in olives, cooked chicken and any accumulated juices, tomatoes, and Parmesan. Cook, tossing pasta gently, until well coated, 1 to 2 minutes. Season with salt and pepper to taste. Sprinkle with parsley and serve.

# Farfalle with Crispy Prosciutto and Peas

serves 4; total time 45 minutes

## notes for the cook

The fat from crisped prosciutto adds depth to the simple, flavorful tomato sauce for this pasta dinner.

Crisping the prosciutto not only develops its flavor but also creates a pleasing textural contrast in this dish.

The addition of sweet, quick-cooking frozen peas and fresh basil gives this rich pasta a bright finish.

You can substitute 12 ounces of other pasta (such as orecchiette, ziti, campanelle, medium shells, or penne) for the farfalle; however, the cup amounts will vary for different shapes. Make sure you measure by weight.

1 onion

3 garlic cloves

1 (28-ounce) can whole peeled tomatoes

6 ounces thinly sliced prosciutto

2 tablespoons extra-virgin olive oil

¼ teaspoon red pepper flakes

Salt and pepper

12 ounces (4¾ cups) farfalle

2 ounces Parmesan cheese

Fresh basil

1½ cups frozen peas

**1 Prep Sauce Ingredients** Bring 4 quarts water to boil in large pot. Meanwhile, chop onion. Mince garlic. Drain tomatoes, then chop coarse. Cut prosciutto into ½-inch pieces.

**2 Cook Prosciutto** Heat oil in 12-inch skillet over medium heat until shimmering. Add prosciutto and cook, stirring to break up pieces, until crispy, about 10 minutes. Using slotted spoon, transfer prosciutto to paper towel–lined plate, leaving fat in skillet.

**3 Cook Sauce** Add pepper flakes, onion, ⅛ teaspoon salt, and ¼ teaspoon pepper to fat left in skillet and cook over medium heat until onion is softened, about 5 minutes. Stir in garlic and cook until fragrant, about 30 seconds. Add tomatoes and cook, stirring occasionally, until sauce is thickened, about 10 minutes.

4 **Cook Pasta** While sauce cooks, add pasta and 1 tablespoon salt to boiling water and cook, stirring often, until al dente. Reserve ½ cup cooking water, then drain pasta and return it to pot.

5 **Grate Parmesan and Chop Basil** While pasta cooks, grate Parmesan (1 cup). Chop 2 tablespoons basil.

6 **Finish Dish** Add peas, ¼ cup reserved cooking water, sauce, and ¾ cup Parmesan to pasta and toss to combine. Adjust consistency with remaining reserved cooking water as needed. Season with salt, pepper, and extra oil to taste. Serve, sprinkling individual portions with basil, prosciutto, and remaining ¼ cup Parmesan.

# Pasta with Sausage, Kale, and White Beans

serves 4; total time 1 hour

## notes for the cook

We streamlined the elements of this hearty pasta dish to make it a one-pot meal and built layers of deep flavor in the process.

Incorporating the kale in stages lets half of it blend into the sauce, while the other half contributes nice texture to the finished dish.

Orecchiette's ear-like shape traps the sauce without getting too entwined with the kale.

You can substitute 8 ounces of other pasta (such as penne, ziti, campanelle, medium shells, or farfalle) for the orecchiette; however, the cup amounts will vary for different shapes. Make sure you measure by weight.

You can substitute ½ teaspoon dried oregano for the fresh oregano.

1 onion
6 garlic cloves
Fresh oregano
12 ounces kale
1 pound hot or sweet Italian sausage
1 (15-ounce) can cannellini beans
2 tablespoons extra-virgin olive oil
½ teaspoon fennel seeds
⅛ teaspoon red pepper flakes
3 cups chicken broth
8 ounces (2¼ cups) orecchiette
1 ounce Pecorino Romano cheese
Salt and pepper

**1** **Prep Ingredients** Chop onion fine. Mince garlic. Mince 1½ teaspoons oregano. Stem kale by cutting away leafy green portion from either side of stalk, then chop leaves into even-size pieces. Remove casings from sausage. Drain and rinse beans.

**2** **Cook Sausage** Heat 1 tablespoon oil in Dutch oven over medium-high heat until just smoking. Add sausage and cook, breaking meat into ½-inch pieces, until lightly browned, 5 to 7 minutes.

**3** **Add Beans and Aromatics** Stir in beans and onion and cook until onion is softened, 5 to 7 minutes. Stir in fennel seeds, pepper flakes, garlic, and oregano and cook until fragrant, about 30 seconds.

**4 Cook Pasta** Stir in broth and 1 cup water, increase heat to high, and bring to boil. Stir in pasta and half of kale. Cover, reduce heat to medium, and simmer vigorously for 4 minutes. Place remaining kale in pot without stirring, cover, and continue to cook until kale is just tender, about 4 minutes.

**5 Grate Pecorino** While pasta cooks, grate Pecorino (½ cup).

**6 Finish Dish** Uncover, stir to incorporate kale, and simmer, uncovered and stirring occasionally, until most of liquid is absorbed and orecchiette is tender, 3 to 6 minutes. Off heat, stir in Pecorino and remaining 1 tablespoon oil. Season with salt and pepper to taste, and serve.

# "Baked" Ziti with Spinach and Sausage

serves 4; total time 1 hour

## notes for the cook

This streamlined recipe makes cheesy, saucy ziti without the hassle of a traditional casserole. Simmering the pasta until it is only partially cooked keeps it from getting mushy under the broiler.

You can substitute 12 ounces of ziti or medium shells for the penne; however, the cup amounts will vary for different shapes. Make sure you measure by weight.

Part-skim ricotta and part-skim mozzarella cheese can be substituted here if desired. Do not use preshredded cheese.

If sodium is an issue for you, opt for no salt added tomato products in this recipe.

You can substitute ½ teaspoon dried oregano for the fresh.

3 garlic cloves
Fresh oregano
7 ounces (7 cups) baby spinach
8 ounces hot or sweet Italian sausage
1 (28-ounce) can tomato sauce
1 (14.5-ounce) can diced tomatoes
¾ teaspoon salt
½ teaspoon sugar
⅛ teaspoon red pepper flakes
6 ounces whole-milk mozzarella cheese
2 ounces Parmesan cheese
Fresh basil
12 ounces (3¾ cups) ziti
8 ounces (1 cup) whole-milk ricotta cheese

**1 Prep Ingredients** Mince garlic. Mince 1½ teaspoons oregano. Chop spinach coarse. Remove casings from sausage.

**2 Make Sauce** Cook sausage in Dutch oven over medium-high heat, breaking meat into ½-inch pieces, until lightly browned, about 5 minutes. Stir in garlic and cook until fragrant, about 30 seconds. Stir in tomato sauce, tomatoes and their juice, salt, sugar, pepper flakes, and oregano and bring mixture to boil. Reduce heat to medium-low and simmer until thickened, about 10 minutes.

**3 Prep Toppings** While sauce cooks, cut mozzarella into ¼-inch pieces (1½ cups). Grate Parmesan (1 cup). Chop 6 tablespoons basil. Adjust oven rack 8 inches from broiler element and heat broiler.

4  **Cook Pasta in Sauce** Stir pasta, 2 cups water, and ¼ cup basil into pot, increase heat to high, and bring to boil. Reduce heat to medium and simmer vigorously, stirring often, until pasta is still very firm but just starting to soften, 6 to 8 minutes.

5  **Add Spinach and Cheeses** Off heat, stir in spinach, ¾ cup mozzarella, and ½ cup Parmesan. Dollop surface of pasta evenly with ricotta. Top with remaining ¾ cup mozzarella and remaining ½ cup Parmesan.

6  **Broil and Finish Dish** Broil ziti until cheese is bubbling and beginning to brown, 5 to 7 minutes. Transfer pot to wire rack and let cool for 10 minutes. Sprinkle with remaining 2 tablespoons basil and serve.

# Ricotta Gnocchi with Garlicky Cherry Tomato Sauce and Arugula

serves 4; total time 1 hour

## notes for the cook

You probably don't think of homemade ricotta gnocchi as an approachable weeknight dinner, but think again; they're way easier than potato gnocchi and come together surprisingly quickly for a sophisticated weeknight meal.

We pair these gnocchi with a simple sauce made from garlic, fresh cherry tomatoes, olive oil, and a splash of red wine vinegar (plus a bit of sugar to balance the acidity of the tomatoes and vinegar).

When rolling the gnocchi, use just enough flour to keep the dough from sticking to your hands and work surface; using too much flour will result in tough gnocchi.

Make sure to use whole-milk ricotta in this recipe.

1 ounce Parmesan cheese

5 garlic cloves

1 pound cherry tomatoes

Fresh basil

1 pound (2 cups) whole-milk ricotta cheese

1 large egg

⅛ teaspoon ground nutmeg

Salt and pepper

1 cup plus 2 tablespoons (5⅔ ounces) all-purpose flour

2 tablespoons extra-virgin olive oil

1½ teaspoons red wine vinegar

1½ teaspoons packed light brown sugar

3 ounces (3 cups) baby arugula

**1 Prep Sauce Ingredients** Bring 4 quarts water to boil in large pot. Meanwhile, grate Parmesan (½ cup). Mince garlic. Halve tomatoes. Chop ½ cup basil.

**2 Make Gnocchi Dough** Whisk ricotta, egg, nutmeg, ¼ cup Parmesan, 1 teaspoon salt, and ½ teaspoon pepper together in large bowl until thoroughly combined. Add flour and fold with rubber spatula until just combined into shaggy dough. Press dough into rough ball and transfer to well-floured counter. Gently knead dough into smooth ball, dusting counter with flour as needed to prevent sticking.

**3 Shape Gnocchi** Line rimmed baking sheet with parchment paper and dust liberally with flour. Cut dough into 8 pieces. Lightly dust counter with flour. Working with 1 piece of dough at a time, gently roll dough into ½-inch-thick rope. Cut rope into ¾-inch lengths. Transfer formed gnocchi to prepared sheet; set aside.

**Make Sauce** Heat oil in 12-inch skillet over medium heat until shimmering. Add garlic and cook until fragrant and lightly browned, about 1 minute. Stir in tomatoes and ½ teaspoon salt and cook, stirring frequently, until tomatoes have softened and released their juices, about 3 minutes. Off heat, stir in vinegar and sugar, transfer to large serving bowl, and cover to keep warm.

**Cook Gnocchi** Add 1 tablespoon salt to boiling water. Using parchment paper as funnel, pour gnocchi into pot. Once all gnocchi float to surface, cook for 2 minutes longer, then using slotted spoon, transfer cooked gnocchi to bowl with sauce.

**Finish Dish** Gently toss gnocchi with sauce. Fold in basil and arugula and season with salt and pepper to taste. Sprinkle with remaining ¼ cup Parmesan. Serve immediately.

# Fideos with Chickpeas, Fennel, and Kale

serves 4; total time 45 minutes

## notes for the cook

*Fideos* is a lesser-known cousin of Spanish paella (see page 256) that features toasted broken noodles simmered in a smoky tomato sauce. Our weeknight-friendly version takes a vegetarian approach with a hearty dose of chickpeas, fennel, and kale.

If you can't find a fennel bulb with its fronds intact, you can substitute minced parsley or omit the garnish altogether.

You will need a 12-inch broiler-safe skillet for this recipe.

The pan will be quite full once you add the pasta; we recommend using a straight-sided skillet or sauté pan for easier stirring.

8 ounces spaghettini or thin spaghetti
12 ounces kale
1 fennel bulb, fronds intact
1 onion
3 garlic cloves
2 teaspoons plus 2 tablespoons extra-virgin olive oil
Salt and pepper
1 (14.5-ounce) can diced tomatoes
1 (15-ounce) can chickpeas
1½ teaspoons smoked paprika
½ cup dry white wine
1 lemon

**1 Prep Pasta and Vegetables** Break pasta into 1- to 2-inch lengths. Stem kale by cutting away leafy green portion from either side of stalk, then chop leaves into 1-inch pieces. Mince 2 tablespoons fennel fronds, then discard fennel stalks. Halve bulb, core, and slice thin. Chop onion fine. Mince garlic.

**2 Toast Pasta** Toss pasta and 2 teaspoons oil in 12-inch broiler-safe skillet until pasta is evenly coated. Toast pasta over medium-high heat, stirring often, until browned and releases nutty aroma (pasta should be color of peanut butter), 6 to 10 minutes; transfer to bowl.

**3 Cook Kale, Fennel, and Onion** Add remaining 2 tablespoons oil to now-empty skillet and heat over medium heat until shimmering. Add kale, a handful at a time, sliced fennel, onion, and ¼ teaspoon salt and cook until vegetables are softened, about 5 minutes.

**Add Tomatoes and Chickpeas** While vegetables cook, drain tomatoes, reserving juice, then chop tomatoes fine. Drain and rinse chickpeas. Stir chopped tomatoes into softened vegetables and cook until mixture is thick, dry, and slightly darkened in color, 4 to 6 minutes. Stir in paprika and garlic and cook until fragrant, about 30 seconds.

**Cook Pasta** Stir in toasted pasta until thoroughly combined. Stir in wine, 2¾ cups water, reserved tomato juice, chickpeas, ¼ teaspoon salt, and ½ teaspoon pepper. Increase heat to medium-high and simmer, stirring occasionally, until liquid is slightly thickened and pasta is just tender, 8 to 10 minutes.

**Broil and Finish Dish** While pasta cooks, adjust oven rack 6 inches from broiler element and heat broiler. Transfer skillet to oven and broil until surface of pasta is dry with crisped, browned spots, 5 to 7 minutes. Remove skillet from oven (skillet handle will be hot). Let cool for 5 minutes. While pasta cools, cut lemon into wedges. Sprinkle pasta with fennel fronds and serve with lemon wedges.

# Garlicky Shrimp Pasta with Cherry Tomatoes and Tarragon

serves 4 to 6; total time 45 minutes

## notes for the cook

Tarragon and lemon juice brighten this creamy pasta dish while quick-cooking shrimp make it weeknight-friendly.

Pan searing is one of our favorite ways to cook shrimp; they end up plump, moist, and well caramelized.

Cooking the shrimp in batches before adding them to the pasta ensures plenty of browning on each side of every piece of shrimp.

The acidity of the cherry tomatoes and wine in the sauce balances the richness of the cream and shrimp.

You can substitute 1 pound of linguine or bucatini for the spaghetti, if desired.

1 shallot

3 garlic cloves

12 ounces cherry tomatoes

Fresh tarragon

1 lemon

1½ pounds extra-large shrimp (21 to 25 per pound)

Salt and pepper

3 tablespoons extra-virgin olive oil

1 pound spaghetti

¼ cup dry white wine

½ cup heavy cream

**1 Prep Sauce Ingredients** Bring 4 quarts water to boil in large pot. Meanwhile, mince shallot and garlic. Halve tomatoes. Chop 2 tablespoons tarragon. Squeeze 2 teaspoons lemon juice.

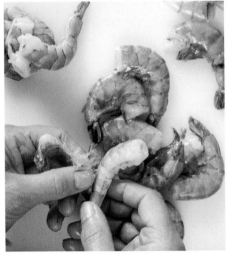

**2 Prep Shrimp** Peel and devein shrimp. Pat dry with paper towels and season with salt and pepper.

**3 Cook Shrimp** Heat 1 tablespoon oil in 12-inch nonstick skillet over medium-high heat until just smoking. Add half of shrimp to skillet in single layer and cook, without stirring, until spotty brown and cooked through, about 2 minutes per side. Transfer shrimp to plate and tent loosely with aluminum foil. Repeat with 1 tablespoon oil and remaining shrimp.

**4** **Cook Pasta** While shrimp cooks, add pasta and 1 tablespoon salt to boiling water and cook, stirring often, until al dente. Reserve ½ cup cooking water, then drain pasta and return it to pot.

**5** **Make Sauce** Add remaining 1 tablespoon oil to now-empty skillet. Add shallot and cook over medium-high heat until softened, about 2 minutes. Add garlic and cook until fragrant, about 30 seconds. Add wine, bring to boil, and cook until reduced by half, about 2 minutes. Stir in cream, tomatoes, and ¼ cup reserved cooking water and return to boil.

**6** **Finish Dish** Off heat, stir in tarragon, lemon juice, shrimp, ¼ teaspoon salt, and ¼ teaspoon pepper. Add sauce to pasta in pot and toss to combine. Adjust consistency with remaining reserved cooking water as needed. Serve.

# Linguine with Mussels and Fennel

serves 4 to 6; total time 1 hour

## notes for the cook

Don't be intimidated by mussels; they're easier to prepare than you think and they make a great weeknight option. The mussels here are cooked in a flavorful broth that becomes a light sauce for the pasta.

The addition of fresh tarragon underscores the anise flavor of the sautéed fennel in the sauce.

When cleaning the mussels, throw out any that won't close or have broken shells.

You can substitute 1 pound of spaghetti or bucatini for the linguine, if desired.

1 fennel bulb

½ onion

Fresh tarragon

2 pounds mussels

3 tablespoons extra-virgin olive oil

¼ teaspoon red pepper flakes

1 (28-ounce) can diced tomatoes

½ cup white wine

1 pound linguine

Salt

**1 Prep Vegetables** Bring 4 quarts water to boil in large pot. Meanwhile, discard fennel stalks. Halve bulb, core, and chop fine. Chop onion fine. Chop 2 tablespoons tarragon.

**2 Prep Mussels** Scrub mussels and remove weedy beards protruding from between shells using paring knife.

**3 Build Sauce** Heat 2 tablespoons oil in Dutch oven over medium heat until shimmering. Add pepper flakes, fennel, and onion and cook until softened, about 5 minutes. Add tomatoes with their juice and wine, bring to simmer, and cook until sauce reduces slightly, about 10 minutes.

**4** **Cook Pasta** While sauce cooks, add pasta and 1 tablespoon salt to boiling water and cook, stirring often, until al dente. Reserve ½ cup cooking water, then drain pasta and return it to pot.

**5** **Cook Mussels** When sauce is reduced slightly, stir mussels into sauce, cover, and steam until fully open, 6 to 7 minutes. Using slotted spoon, transfer mussels to bowl, discarding any that do not open; cover to keep warm.

**6** **Finish Dish** Off heat, add pasta to sauce, along with tarragon and remaining 1 tablespoon oil and toss to combine. Adjust consistency with reserved cooking water as needed. Season with salt to taste. Divide pasta among individual serving bowls and top with mussels. Serve immediately.

# Scallops Fra Diavolo with Fennel and Linguine

serves 4 to 6; total time 1 hour

## notes for the cook

The name of this Italian dish calls to mind the devil, as does its hot, spicy, wine-infused tomato sauce. This version is studded with sweet, firm scallops and served over simple linguine.

We recommend buying "dry" scallops, which don't have chemical additives and taste better than "wet." Dry scallops will also sear much faster and develop a better crust. Dry scallops will look ivory or pinkish; wet scallops are bright white.

One teaspoon of red pepper flakes will give the sauce a little kick, but you can use more if you'd like an even spicier dish.

You can substitute 1 pound of spaghetti or bucatini for the linguine, if desired.

2 fennel bulbs
12 garlic cloves
Fresh parsley
1 (28-ounce) can diced tomatoes
1½ pounds large sea scallops
Salt and pepper
6 tablespoons extra-virgin olive oil
1 teaspoon red pepper flakes
½ teaspoon sugar
1 cup dry white wine
1 pound linguine

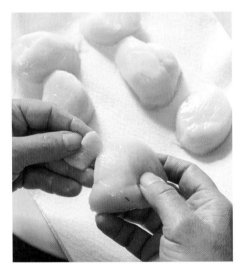

**1 Prep Scallops and Vegetables**
Bring 4 quarts water to boil in large pot. Meanwhile, discard fennel stalks. Halve bulbs, core, and slice thin. Mince garlic. Mince ¼ cup parsley. Drain tomatoes. Remove tendons from scallops, pat dry with paper towels, and season with salt and pepper.

**2 Cook Scallops** Heat 1 tablespoon oil in 12-inch nonstick skillet over high heat until just smoking. Add scallops in single layer and cook, without moving, until well browned, 2 to 4 minutes. Flip and continue to cook until sides of scallops are firm and centers are opaque, about 2 minutes (remove smaller scallops as they finish cooking). Transfer scallops to large bowl.

**3 Cook Fennel** Heat 1 tablespoon oil in now-empty skillet over medium-high heat until shimmering. Add fennel and cook until tender and lightly browned, 7 to 10 minutes; transfer to bowl with scallops. Let skillet cool for 2 minutes.

**4** **Make Sauce** Combine pepper flakes, sugar, three-quarters of garlic, 3 tablespoons oil, and ¾ teaspoon salt in now-empty skillet and cook over low heat until fragrant and beginning to brown, 1 to 2 minutes. Add wine and tomatoes, increase heat to medium-high, and simmer until thickened, about 8 minutes.

**5** **Cook and Sauce Pasta** While sauce simmers, add pasta and 1 tablespoon salt to boiling water and cook, stirring often, until al dente. Reserve ½ cup cooking water, then drain pasta and return it to pot. Add ½ cup sauce to pasta and toss to coat. Adjust consistency with reserved cooking water as needed. Stir in remaining 1 tablespoon oil; transfer sauced pasta to serving dish.

**6** **Finish Dish** Gently stir scallop-fennel mixture and any accumulated juices, remaining garlic, and parsley into remaining sauce and simmer until scallops are warmed through, about 1 minute. Pour sauce over pasta and scallops and serve immediately.

# Soba Noodles with Roasted Eggplant and Sesame

serves 4; total time 45 minutes

## notes for the cook

Rich, nutty soba noodles and creamy roasted eggplant make a perfect pairing in this recipe.

A quick and easy combination of oyster sauce, soy sauce, sugar, Asian chili-garlic sauce, toasted sesame oil, and sake provides just the right spicy-sweet balance in our sauce.

To make this dish vegetarian, make sure you use vegetarian oyster sauce.

Vermouth can be substituted for the sake if necessary.

Note that you'll need ¾ cup of cilantro, so shop accordingly.

Do not substitute other types of noodles for the soba noodles here.

3 pounds eggplant
¼ cup vegetable oil
⅓ cup soy sauce
2 teaspoons sesame seeds
⅓ cup sugar
3 tablespoons oyster sauce
3 tablespoons toasted sesame oil
5 teaspoons sake
1½ tablespoons Asian chili-garlic sauce
12 ounces dried soba noodles
Fresh cilantro

**1 Prep Eggplant** Adjust oven racks to upper-middle and lower-middle positions and heat oven to 450 degrees. Line 2 rimmed baking sheets with aluminum foil and spray with vegetable oil spray. Cut eggplant into 1-inch pieces.

**2 Roast Eggplant** Toss eggplant with vegetable oil and 1 tablespoon soy sauce, then spread evenly on prepared baking sheets. Roast until eggplant is well browned and tender, 25 to 30 minutes, stirring eggplant and switching sheets halfway through roasting.

**3 Toast Sesame Seeds** While eggplant cooks, bring 4 quarts water to boil in large pot. Toast sesame seeds in 8-inch skillet over medium heat, shaking pan occasionally, until golden and fragrant, 3 to 5 minutes; transfer to small bowl to cool.

**4 Make Sauce** Combine sugar, oyster sauce, sesame oil, sake, chili-garlic sauce, and remaining soy sauce in now-empty skillet. Cook over medium heat, whisking often, until sugar has dissolved, about 1 minute; cover and set aside.

**5 Cook Noodles** Add noodles to boiling water and cook, stirring often, until tender. Reserve ½ cup cooking water, then drain noodles and return them to pot.

**6 Finish Dish** While noodles cook, pick ¾ cup cilantro leaves. Add roasted eggplant and sauce to noodles and toss to combine. Adjust consistency with reserved cooking water as needed. Sprinkle individual portions with cilantro and sesame seeds. Serve.

# Sesame Noodles with Snow Peas, Radishes, and Bell Peppers

serves 4 to 6; total time 45 minutes

## notes for the cook

Our recipe for better-than-takeout sesame noodles relies on a set of pantry staples to deliver the requisite sweet, nutty flavor.

You can use chunky or creamy peanut butter in this recipe.

If you can't find tahini, you can make your own (see page 7).

Rinsing the cooked noodles helps rid them of excess starch, which can otherwise make them gummy.

We liked thin chow mein noodles in this recipe, but thicker lo mein noodles can also be used.

Snow peas, red bell pepper, and thinly sliced radishes add crunch, bulk, and freshness to this vegetarian dinner.

4 limes
Fresh ginger
4 garlic cloves
½ cup peanut butter
6 tablespoons tahini
2 tablespoons soy sauce
2 tablespoons honey
1 teaspoon toasted sesame oil
Salt and pepper
6 ounces snow peas
1 red bell pepper
5 radishes
Fresh cilantro
1 pound fresh Chinese noodles

**1 Prep Dressing Ingredients** Bring 4 quarts water to boil in large pot. Meanwhile, squeeze 6 tablespoons lime juice from 3 limes and cut remaining lime into wedges for serving. Peel and grate 2 tablespoons ginger. Mince garlic.

**2 Make Dressing** Whisk peanut butter, tahini, soy sauce, honey, sesame oil, lime juice, ginger, garlic, and ½ teaspoon salt together in large bowl until well combined. Whisking constantly, add hot water, 1 tablespoon at a time (up to ¾ cup), until dressing has consistency of heavy cream.

**3 Prep Vegetables** Remove strings from snow peas and cut in half lengthwise. Stem and seed bell pepper, then cut into ¼-inch-wide strips. Trim radishes, then halve and slice thin. Chop ¼ cup cilantro.

4 **Cook Noodles** Add noodles to boiling water and cook, stirring often, until almost tender, 2 to 3 minutes.

5 **Drain and Rinse Noodles** Drain noodles and rinse under cold running water until water runs clear. Drain well.

6 **Finish Dish** Add noodles, snow peas, bell pepper, and radishes to bowl with sauce and toss well to combine. Season with salt and pepper to taste and sprinkle with cilantro. Serve with lime wedges.

# Japanese-Style Yakisoba Noodles with Beef

serves 4 to 6; total time 45 minutes

## notes for the cook

*Yakisoba* is a popular Japanese dish made by stir-frying vegetables and meat with springy egg noodles in a tangy sauce.

Treating thinly sliced flank steak with baking soda helps keep the meat tender and juicy.

Authentic yakisoba sauce is a made from a combination of tomatoes, prunes, apples, vinegar, onions, carrots, garlic, ginger, and other aromatics. For our pantry-friendly version, we combine chicken broth, Worcestershire sauce, oyster sauce, ketchup, soy sauce, and a bit of hot sauce for a similar sweet-savory flavor profile.

If you can't find fresh noodles, you can use 8 ounces of dried lo mein noodles; increase the cooking time in step 3 to 8 to 10 minutes.

1 pound flank steak
⅛ teaspoon baking soda
½ cup chicken broth
¼ cup Worcestershire sauce
3 tablespoons oyster sauce
2 tablespoons ketchup
2 tablespoons soy sauce
1 tablespoon hot sauce
6 ounces shiitake mushrooms
1 carrot
½ head napa cabbage (1 pound)
7 scallions
1 pound fresh lo mein noodles
1 tablespoon vegetable oil

**1 Prep Beef and Sauce** Bring 4 quarts water to boil in large pot. Meanwhile, trim steak and cut into thirds lengthwise, then slice crosswise ¼ inch thick. Combine 1 tablespoon water and baking soda in medium bowl. Add beef and toss to coat. Whisk broth, Worcestershire, oyster sauce, ketchup, soy sauce, and hot sauce together in small bowl. Stir 2 tablespoons sauce into beef mixture and set aside remaining sauce.

**2 Prep Vegetables** Stem mushrooms and slice ¼ inch thick. Peel carrot and slice ⅛ inch thick on bias. Remove core from cabbage, then slice (you should have about 5 cups). Cut scallions into 1-inch lengths.

**3 Cook Noodles** Add noodles to boiling water and cook, stirring often, until almost tender, 2 to 3 minutes. Drain noodles and rinse under cold running water until water runs clear. Drain well and set aside.

**4** **Cook Vegetables** Heat ½ teaspoon oil in 12-inch nonstick skillet over high heat until just smoking. Add mushrooms and carrot and cook, stirring occasionally, until spotty brown, about 2 minutes; transfer to large bowl. Heat ½ teaspoon oil in now-empty skillet until just smoking. Add cabbage and scallions and cook, stirring occasionally, until spotty brown, about 2 minutes; transfer to bowl with mushroom mixture.

**5** **Cook Beef** Heat 1 teaspoon oil in now-empty skillet over high heat until just smoking. Add half of beef in single layer. Cook, without stirring, for 30 seconds, then cook, stirring occasionally, until beef is spotty brown, 1 to 2 minutes. Transfer to bowl with vegetables. Repeat with remaining 1 teaspoon oil and remaining beef.

**6** **Finish Dish** Add reserved sauce and noodles to now-empty skillet and cook over high heat, stirring often, until sauce has thickened and noodles are well coated and tender, about 1 minute. Transfer noodle mixture to bowl with beef and vegetables and toss to combine. Serve.

# Rice Noodles with Crisp Tofu and Cabbage

serves 4; total time 45 minutes

## notes for the cook

This dish takes tofu to a whole new level by pan-frying it to crispy perfection and pairing it with chewy rice noodles, wilted cabbage, and a zesty sauce.

For optimal flavor, we season the tofu by briefly marinating it in fish sauce. Dredging the marinated tofu in cornstarch before frying creates the perfect crispy crust, providing a nice contrast to its creamy interior.

To make this dish vegetarian, substitute Bragg Liquid Aminos for the fish sauce.

14 ounces firm tofu

6 tablespoons fish sauce

6 tablespoons cornstarch

8 ounces (¼-inch-wide) rice noodles

2 limes

¼ cup packed brown sugar

¼ head green cabbage (8 ounces)

1 carrot

¼ cup vegetable oil

Fresh mint

Sriracha sauce

**1 Prep Tofu** Cut tofu into 1-inch cubes. Spread tofu over paper towel–lined baking sheet and let drain for 20 minutes. Gently press dry with paper towels, then toss with 2 tablespoons fish sauce. Place cornstarch in shallow dish.

**2 Soak Noodles** While tofu drains, bring 3 quarts water to boil in large saucepan. Place noodles in large bowl. Pour boiling water over noodles. Stir, then let soak until noodles are soft and pliable but not fully tender, stirring once halfway through soaking, 8 to 10 minutes. Drain noodles and rinse under cold running water until water runs clear. Drain well and set aside.

**3 Make Sauce and Prep Vegetables** Squeeze ¼ cup lime juice into bowl. Whisk sugar, ¼ cup water, and remaining ¼ cup fish sauce into bowl with lime juice. Remove core from cabbage and slice thin (3 cups). Peel and grate carrot.

**Dredge and Fry Tofu** Dredge tofu in cornstarch, shaking off any excess. Heat 2 tablespoons oil in 12-inch nonstick skillet over medium-high heat until shimmering. Cook tofu until crisp and golden on all sides, about 5 minutes; transfer to paper towel–lined plate. Discard oil in skillet.

**Sauce Noodles** Heat remaining 2 tablespoons oil in now-empty skillet over medium-high heat until shimmering. Add lime juice mixture, noodles, cabbage, and carrot to skillet. Cook until cabbage is just wilted and noodles are well coated and tender, about 5 minutes.

**Chop Mint and Finish Dish** Chop ¼ cup mint. Divide noodles evenly among individual serving bowls and top with tofu and mint. Drizzle with Sriracha and extra fish sauce to taste before serving.

# One-Pan Shrimp Pad Thai
serves 4; total time 1 hour

## notes for the cook
Our version of this take-out classic is surprisingly easy to make and requires just one skillet.

While truly authentic pad thai, with its sweet, sour, and salty flavors, requires hard-to-find ingredients like preserved daikon, palm sugar, and dried shrimp, our simplified weeknight recipe uses accessible ingredients to create a similar flavor profile.

8 ounces (⅜-inch-wide) rice noodles

3 limes

⅓ cup packed brown sugar

¼ cup fish sauce

4 garlic cloves

Fresh cilantro

¼ cup dry-roasted peanuts

1 pound extra-large shrimp (21 to 25 per pound)

2 tablespoons vegetable oil

8 ounces (4 cups) bean sprouts

**1 Soak Noodles** Bring 3 quarts water to boil in large saucepan. Place noodles in large bowl. Pour boiling water over noodles. Stir, then let soak until noodles are soft and pliable but not fully tender, stirring once halfway through soaking, 12 to 15 minutes. Drain noodles and rinse under cold running water until water runs clear. Drain well and set aside.

**2 Make Sauce and Prep Toppings** While noodles soak, squeeze ⅓ cup lime juice. Whisk sugar, fish sauce, and lime juice together in bowl. Mince garlic. Chop ¼ cup cilantro. Chop peanuts.

**3 Prep Shrimp** Peel and devein shrimp. Pat shrimp dry with paper towels.

4 **Cook Shrimp** Heat oil in 12-inch nonstick skillet over medium-high heat until just smoking. Add shrimp in single layer and cook until spotty brown and cooked through, about 2 minutes per side. Stir in garlic during last minute of cooking. Transfer shrimp to plate and tent loosely with aluminum foil.

5 **Sauce Noodles** Add noodles and lime juice mixture to now-empty skillet and cook over medium heat until sauce is thickened slightly, about 4 minutes.

6 **Finish Dish** Add sprouts and shrimp to skillet and cook until shrimp and sprouts are warmed through and noodles are well coated and tender, about 3 minutes. Sprinkle with cilantro and peanuts and serve.

# Pad Kee Mao with Pork (Drunken Noodles)

serves 4; total time 45 minutes

## notes for the cook

*Pad kee mao*, also known as drunken noodles for its reputation as an ideal hangover remedy, is a deeply flavorful, satisfying Thai dish made from rice noodles, meat, and vegetables in a savory, sweet, and spicy sauce.

This recipe uses pantry-friendly ingredients to replicate the savory, sweet, and slightly bitter flavor of the traditional Thai sweet soy sauce, which can be difficult to find.

Note that you'll need ½ cup of Thai basil, so shop accordingly. While we prefer the unique flavor of Thai basil, Italian basil can be used in its place.

If fresh Thai chiles are unavailable, substitute two medium jalapeños.

12 ounces (⅜-inch-wide) rice noodles

4 limes

¼ cup chicken broth

¼ cup soy sauce

¼ cup molasses

2 tablespoons fish sauce

2 large yellow bell peppers

1 large onion

4 garlic cloves

4 Thai chiles

1 tablespoon vegetable oil

1 pound ground pork

Fresh Thai basil

**1 Soak Noodles** Bring 3 quarts water to boil in large saucepan. Place noodles in large bowl. Pour boiling water over noodles. Stir, then let soak until noodles are soft and pliable but not fully tender, stirring once halfway through soaking, 12 to 15 minutes. Drain noodles and rinse under cold running water until water runs clear. Drain well and set aside.

**2 Make Sauce and Prep Vegetables and Aromatics** While noodles soak, squeeze ⅓ cup lime juice from 3 limes into small bowl; cut remaining lime into wedges. Whisk broth, soy sauce, molasses, and fish sauce into bowl with lime juice; set aside. Stem and seed bell peppers, then cut into 1-inch pieces. Slice onion in half, then cut into ¼-inch-thick slices. Mince garlic. Stem chiles and slice into thin rings.

**3 Cook Bell Peppers** Heat 1 teaspoon oil in 12-inch nonstick skillet over high heat until just smoking. Add peppers and cook, stirring occasionally, until spotty brown and tender, 4 to 5 minutes; transfer to large serving bowl.

**4 Cook Onion and Aromatics** Heat remaining 2 teaspoons oil in now-empty skillet over high heat until just smoking. Add onion and cook, stirring occasionally, until softened and lightly browned, about 3 minutes. Stir in garlic and chiles and cook, stirring constantly, until fragrant, about 30 seconds.

**5 Cook Pork** Stir pork into onion mixture in skillet and cook, breaking up meat with wooden spoon and stirring occasionally, until lightly browned, 3 to 5 minutes. Stir in ¼ cup sauce and cook, stirring often, until sauce is thick and syrupy, 1 to 2 minutes. Transfer pork mixture to bowl with peppers.

**6 Finish Dish** Add remaining sauce and noodles to now-empty skillet and cook over high heat, stirring often, until sauce has thickened and noodles are well coated and tender, about 3 minutes. Transfer noodle mixture to bowl with vegetables and pork and toss to combine. Tear ½ cup basil leaves over noodles. Serve with lime wedges.

# Vietnamese Lemon Grass Beef and Rice Noodles

serves 4; total time 45 minutes

## notes for the cook

This recipe is based on Vietnamese *bun bo xao*—a savory, aromatic salad composed of rice noodles topped with pickled and fresh vegetables, herbs, beef, and peanuts. The dish is served at room temperature, which makes it forgiving for weeknight cooks.

If you can't find skirt steak, use a 1-pound piece of flank steak in its place. Slice the flank steak in half lengthwise and cut each piece in half crosswise to create four steaks.

We prefer the unique flavor of Thai basil, but Italian basil can be used in its place.

Be sure to drain noodles thoroughly in step 2 to avoid diluting the flavors of the sauce.

1 lemon grass stalk
¼ cup fish sauce
1 tablespoon plus 1 teaspoon vegetable oil
1 tablespoon sugar
1½ teaspoons Asian chili-garlic sauce
1 pound skirt steak
8 ounces rice vermicelli
3 limes
1 carrot
1 cucumber
2 ounces (1 cup) bean sprouts
Fresh Thai basil
Fresh mint
2 tablespoons dry-roasted peanuts

**1 Prep Steak** Trim lemon grass to bottom 6 inches and mince 5 teaspoons. Whisk ½ tablespoon fish sauce, 1 tablespoon oil, 1 teaspoon sugar, ½ teaspoon chili-garlic sauce, and 1 tablespoon lemon grass together in medium bowl. Trim steak. Cut crosswise into thirds with grain, then add to bowl with lemon grass mixture and toss to coat. Transfer steak to cutting board, cover with plastic wrap, and pound ¼ inch thick; return to bowl.

**2 Soak Noodles** Bring 2 quarts water to boil in large saucepan. Off heat, add noodles to hot water and let stand until tender, about 5 minutes. Drain noodles in colander and rinse under cold running water until water runs clear. Drain well and divide among 4 individual serving bowls.

**3 Make Sauce** While water comes to boil, squeeze ¼ cup lime juice from 2 limes into small bowl and cut remaining lime into wedges. Whisk remaining 2 teaspoons lemon grass, remaining 3½ tablespoons fish sauce, remaining 2 teaspoons sugar, and remaining 1 teaspoon chili-garlic sauce into bowl with lime juice until sugar is dissolved; set aside.

**4** **Prep Vegetables** Peel and shred carrot. Cut cucumber into 2-inch-long matchsticks. Divide carrots, cucumber, and bean sprouts evenly over noodles in serving bowls.

**5** **Cook Steak** Heat remaining 1 teaspoon oil in 12-inch skillet over medium-high heat until just smoking. Cook steak until well browned and meat registers 130 degrees, 2 to 3 minutes per side. Transfer steak to carving board, tent with aluminum foil, and let rest.

**6** **Prep Garnishes and Finish Dish** While steak is resting, pick ¼ cup basil leaves and ¼ cup mint leaves. Chop peanuts. Slice steak thin against grain and divide evenly over noodles and vegetables in bowls. Whisk any accumulated juices from steak into sauce, and drizzle 2 tablespoons sauce evenly over each bowl. Sprinkle with basil, mint, and peanuts. Serve with lime wedges.

# Red Curry Noodles with Shrimp, Summer Squash, and Bell Peppers

serves 4; total time 1 hour

## notes for the cook

This vibrant shrimp-and-noodles dish is packed with bold, contrasting flavors typical of Thai-style curries: Aromatic red curry paste, lime juice, and fresh cilantro are balanced by umami-rich fish sauce and chicken broth, while coconut milk provides a rich, smooth finish.

Store-bought red curry paste—a blend of red chili, garlic, lemon grass, galangal, kaffir lime, and coriander—helps keep the shopping list in check.

If you prefer, you can substitute small, firm zucchini for the yellow summer squash and red, orange, or yellow bell peppers for the green bell pepper.

12 ounces (¼-inch-wide) rice noodles

1 tablespoon vegetable oil

2 green bell peppers

2 yellow summer squash

2 limes

Fresh cilantro

¼ cup dry-roasted peanuts

2 tablespoons red curry paste

2 tablespoons fish sauce

1 tablespoon packed brown sugar

1 cup canned coconut milk

1 cup chicken broth

1 pound large shrimp (26 to 30 per pound)

**1 Soak Noodles** Bring 3 quarts water to boil in large saucepan. Place noodles in large bowl. Pour boiling water over noodles. Stir, then let soak until noodles are soft and pliable but not fully tender, 8 to 10 minutes, stirring once halfway through soaking. Drain noodles and rinse under cold running water until water runs clear. Drain well and set aside.

**2 Prep Vegetables and Aromatics** While noodles soak, stem and seed bell peppers, then chop into 1-inch pieces. Quarter summer squash lengthwise and slice into ¼-inch-thick pieces. Squeeze 2 tablespoons lime juice from 1 lime and cut remaining lime into wedges. Chop ¼ cup cilantro. Chop peanuts.

**3 Cook Vegetables** Heat ½ teaspoon oil in 12-inch nonstick skillet over high heat until just smoking. Add bell peppers and cook, stirring occasionally, until spotty brown, 2 to 3 minutes; transfer to large serving bowl. Add ½ teaspoon oil to now-empty skillet, and heat until just smoking. Add squash and cook, stirring occasionally, until spotty brown, 3 to 4 minutes; transfer to bowl with peppers.

**4 Make Sauce** Add remaining 2 teaspoons oil to now-empty skillet and reduce heat to medium. Add curry paste and cook, stirring constantly, until fragrant, about 30 seconds. Stir in fish sauce and sugar and cook for 30 seconds. Stir in coconut milk and broth and bring to simmer. Reduce heat to medium-low and gently simmer until sauce is thickened and reduced by about a quarter, 8 to 10 minutes.

**5 Prep and Cook Shrimp** While sauce simmers, peel and devein shrimp. When sauce has reduced by about a quarter, stir shrimp into sauce and cook, stirring occasionally, until shrimp are opaque, 2 to 3 minutes. Using slotted spoon, transfer shrimp to bowl with peppers and squash.

**6 Finish Dish** Return sauce to simmer over high heat. Add noodles and cook, stirring often, until sauce has thickened and noodles are well coated and tender, 2 to 3 minutes. Off heat, stir in lime juice. Transfer noodle mixture to bowl with shrimp and vegetables and toss to combine. Sprinkle with cilantro and peanuts. Serve with lime wedges.

# Rice Noodle Bowl with Pork and Scallions

serves 4; total time 45 minutes

## notes for the cook

We keep all the elements of this savory noodle bowl in harmony by using the same soy sauce mixture both as a sauce to cook the ground pork in and as a dressing for the noodles.

For best results, make sure to shake off all excess water from the noodles after rinsing them.

Long matchsticks of cool, quick-pickled cucumber and whole cilantro leaves provide a fresh finish for this dish.

Fresh ginger

3 garlic cloves

1 English cucumber

4 scallions

Fresh cilantro

8 ounces rice vermicelli

5 tablespoons soy sauce

3 tablespoons toasted sesame oil

2 tablespoons rice vinegar

1 pound ground pork

**1 Prep Aromatics and Toppings** Bring 2 quarts water to boil in large saucepan. Meanwhile, peel and grate 1½ tablespoons ginger. Mince garlic. Cut cucumber into 2-inch-long matchsticks. Cut scallions into 1-inch pieces. Pick ¼ cup cilantro leaves.

**2 Soak Noodles** Off heat, add noodles to hot water, and let stand until tender, about 5 minutes. Drain noodles in colander and rinse under cold running water until water runs clear. Drain well and set aside.

**3 Make Sauce and Pickle Cucumber** Whisk soy sauce, 2 tablespoons oil, ginger, and garlic together in large bowl. Combine vinegar and cucumber in second bowl.

**4** **Cook Pork** Heat remaining 1 tablespoon oil in 12-inch nonstick skillet over medium-high heat until shimmering. Add pork and cook, breaking up meat with wooden spoon, until browned, about 7 minutes.

**5** **Cook Scallions** Stir scallions and 2 tablespoons soy sauce mixture into skillet and cook until scallions have softened, about 2 minutes.

**6** **Finish Dish** Add noodles to remaining soy sauce mixture and toss to combine. Divide noodles evenly among individual serving bowls and top with pork, cucumber, and cilantro. Serve.

# Farro Bowl with Tofu, Mushrooms, and Spinach

serves 4; total time 1 hour

## notes for the cook

Hearty, nutty farro is traditionally associated with Italy and flavor profiles of the Mediterranean, but it also adapts well to bold Asian ingredients, as in this bowl featuring crispy seared tofu and a simple miso-ginger sauce.

We prefer the flavor and texture of whole-grain farro; pearled farro can be used, but the texture may be softer.

We found a wide variety of cooking times among different brands of farro, so start checking for doneness after 10 minutes. Do not use quick-cooking farro in this recipe.

1 ½ cups whole farro

Salt and pepper

5 teaspoons toasted sesame oil

2½ teaspoons sherry vinegar

14 ounces firm tofu

10 ounces cremini mushrooms

2 scallions

Fresh ginger

¼ cup mayonnaise

3 tablespoons red miso

1 tablespoon maple syrup

⅓ cup cornstarch

6 tablespoons vegetable oil

2 tablespoons dry sherry

10 ounces (10 cups) baby spinach

**1 Cook Farro** Bring 4 quarts water to boil in large pot. Stir in farro and 1 tablespoon salt, return to boil, and cook until grains are tender with slight chew, 15 to 30 minutes. Drain farro and return to now-empty pot. Drizzle with 2 teaspoons sesame oil and 1 teaspoon vinegar, toss to coat, and cover to keep warm.

**2 Prep Tofu** While farro cooks, cut tofu crosswise into 8 equal slabs. Spread tofu over paper towel–lined baking sheet and let drain for 20 minutes. Gently press dry with paper towels and season with salt and pepper.

**3 Prep Vegetables and Make Sauce** While tofu drains, trim mushrooms, then chop coarse. Slice scallions thin. Peel and grate 1½ teaspoons ginger. Whisk mayonnaise, miso, maple syrup, 2 tablespoons water, remaining 1 tablespoon sesame oil, remaining 1½ teaspoons vinegar, and ginger together in small bowl until combined; set aside.

**4 Cook Tofu** Spread cornstarch in shallow dish. Coat tofu thoroughly in cornstarch, pressing gently to adhere; transfer to plate. Heat 3 tablespoons vegetable oil in 12-inch nonstick skillet over medium-high heat until just smoking. Add tofu and cook until both sides are crisp and browned, about 4 minutes per side. Transfer to paper towel–lined plate and tent with aluminum foil.

**5 Cook Vegetables** Heat 2 tablespoons vegetable oil in now-empty skillet over medium-high heat until shimmering. Stir in mushrooms and ⅛ teaspoon salt and cook until mushrooms begin to brown, 5 to 8 minutes. Stir in sherry and cook, scraping up any browned bits, until skillet is nearly dry, about 1 minute; transfer to bowl.

**6 Cook Spinach and Finish Dish** Heat remaining 1 tablespoon vegetable oil in now-empty skillet over medium-high heat until shimmering. Add spinach, 1 handful at a time, and cook until just wilted, about 1 minute. Divide farro among individual serving bowls, then top with tofu, mushrooms, and spinach. Drizzle with miso-ginger sauce, sprinkle with scallions, and serve.

# Hearty Pearl Couscous Bowl with Eggplant, Spinach, and Beans

serves 4; total time 1 hour

## notes for the cook

A superflavorful spice blend made with zesty sumac, nutty-sweet fenugreek, and floral cardamom gives this grain bowl a Middle Eastern profile and pairs beautifully with sautéed eggplant and white beans.

We toss the eggplant with some of the spice blend and then microwave it, which blooms the spices' flavors and quickly cooks off the eggplant's excess moisture.

Pearl couscous is also called Israeli couscous. Do not substitute regular couscous in this dish, as it requires a different cooking method and will not work in this recipe.

You will need a 12-inch nonstick skillet with tight-fitting lid for this recipe.

1 pound eggplant
1 onion
3 garlic cloves
1 (15-ounce) can great Northern beans
1 teaspoon ground sumac
1 teaspoon ground fenugreek
¼ teaspoon ground cardamom
Salt and pepper
1½ cups pearl couscous
5 tablespoons extra-virgin olive oil
1 tablespoon tomato paste
2 cups vegetable broth
3 ounces (3 cups) baby spinach

**1 Microwave Eggplant** Cut eggplant into ½-inch pieces. Chop onion. Mince garlic. Drain and rinse beans. Line plate with double layer of coffee filters and spray with vegetable oil spray. Combine sumac, fenugreek, cardamom, ½ teaspoon salt, and ½ teaspoon pepper in bowl. Toss eggplant with ½ teaspoon spice mixture and spread over coffee filters. Microwave, uncovered, until dry to touch, 7 to 10 minutes, stirring halfway through.

**2 Toast Couscous** While eggplant microwaves, heat couscous and 2 tablespoons oil in 12-inch nonstick skillet over medium heat, stirring frequently, until about half of grains are golden brown, about 5 minutes. Transfer to bowl and wipe skillet clean with paper towels.

**3 Sauté Eggplant** Heat 1 tablespoon oil in now-empty skillet over medium-high heat until shimmering. Add eggplant and additional 1 teaspoon spice mixture and cook, stirring occasionally, until well browned, 5 to 7 minutes; transfer to second bowl.

**4** **Sauté Aromatics** Heat remaining 2 tablespoons oil in now-empty skillet over medium heat until shimmering. Add onion and cook until softened and lightly browned, 5 to 7 minutes. Stir in tomato paste, garlic, and remaining spice mixture and cook until fragrant, about 1 minute.

**5** **Cook Couscous and Beans** Stir in broth, beans, and couscous and bring to simmer. Reduce heat to medium-low, cover, and simmer, stirring occasionally, until broth is absorbed and couscous is tender, 9 to 12 minutes.

**6** **Finish Dish** Off heat, stir in spinach and eggplant, cover, and let sit for 3 minutes. Season with salt and pepper and drizzle with extra oil to taste. Serve.

# Quinoa Bowl with Mushrooms, Swiss Chard, and Tahini-Lemon Dressing

serves 4; total time 45 minutes

## notes for the cook

For a dinner bowl that would take full advantage of earthy quinoa, we paired it with meaty mushrooms, hearty Swiss chard, and a bright tahini-lemon dressing.

Toasting the quinoa in before adding any water helps develop its natural nutty flavor.

If you can't find tahini, you can make your own (see page 7).

White mushrooms can be substituted for the cremini mushrooms if you prefer.

We like the convenience of prewashed quinoa; rinsing removes the quinoa's bitter protective coating (called saponin). If you buy unwashed quinoa, rinse it and then spread it out on a clean dish towel to dry for 15 minutes.

1½ cups prewashed white quinoa

1½ teaspoons ground cumin

Salt and pepper

2 lemons

1 garlic clove

2 tablespoons tahini

½ cup extra-virgin olive oil

1 pound cremini mushrooms

1 pound Swiss chard

1 shallot

**1 Cook Quinoa** Toast quinoa and cumin in medium saucepan over medium-high heat, stirring frequently, until very fragrant and makes continuous popping sound, 5 to 7 minutes. Stir in 1¾ cups water and ½ teaspoon salt and bring to simmer. Cover, reduce heat to low, and simmer until grains are just tender and liquid is absorbed, 18 to 20 minutes. Remove pan from heat and let sit, covered, for 10 minutes.

**2 Make Dressing** While quinoa cooks, squeeze 2½ tablespoons juice from 1 lemon and cut remaining lemon into wedges. Mince garlic. Whisk tahini, 2 tablespoons water, lemon juice, and garlic, together in bowl until smooth. Whisking constantly, slowly drizzle in ¼ cup oil until combined. Season with salt and pepper to taste and set aside.

**3 Prep Vegetables** Trim mushrooms and halve if small or quarter if large. Stem chard by cutting away leafy green portion from either side of stalk, then cut leaves into ½-inch-wide strips. Slice shallot thin.

4 **Cook Mushrooms** Heat 2 tablespoons oil in 12-inch nonstick skillet over medium heat until shimmering. Add mushrooms, shallot, and ¼ teaspoon salt, cover, and cook, stirring occasionally, until mushrooms release their liquid, 5 to 7 minutes. Uncover, add 1 tablespoon oil, and cook until mushrooms are deep golden brown, 5 to 7 minutes. Transfer to bowl, season with salt and pepper to taste, and cover with aluminum foil.

5 **Sauté Chard** Heat remaining 1 tablespoon oil in now-empty skillet over medium heat until shimmering. Add chard and ¼ teaspoon salt and cook, stirring frequently, until leaves are wilted and tender, about 3 minutes. Remove pan from heat.

6 **Finish Dish** Fluff quinoa with fork, drizzle with extra oil to taste and divide among individual serving bowls. Top with chard and mushrooms and drizzle with tahini dressing. Serve with lemon wedges.

# Crispy Falafel Pitas with Chopped Salad

serves 4; total time 45 minutes

## notes for the cook

To bring crispy, well-spiced falafel from Mediterranean street carts to the home kitchen, we turn to convenient canned chickpeas and the food processor.

Pita bread plays a double role in this recipe; not only does it serve as the sandwich base for the finished falafel, but we also grind up some extra pita and use it as a starchy binder to hold the falafel patties together and help prevent the canned chickpeas from making the falafel too mushy.

Note that you will only use 2½ pita breads in this recipe, so you'll have one half bread left over.

A chopped salad with Mediterranean ingredients makes a bright pairing with the falafel sandwiches.

1 romaine lettuce heart (6 ounces)
1 English cucumber
8 ounces cherry tomatoes
Fresh parsley
1 lemon
1 (15-ounce) can chickpeas
¾ cup plain whole-milk yogurt
1¼ teaspoons ground cumin
Salt and pepper
3 (8-inch) pita breads
1 large egg
2 tablespoons plus ½ cup extra-virgin olive oil
2 ounces feta cheese

**1 Prep Vegetables and Make Sauce** Chop lettuce into 1-inch pieces. Chop cucumber into ½-inch pieces. Halve tomatoes. Chop 6 tablespoons parsley. Squeeze 2 tablespoons lemon juice. Drain and rinse chickpeas. Whisk yogurt, ¼ teaspoon cumin, 2 tablespoons parsley, and 1 tablespoon lemon juice together in small bowl. Season with salt and pepper to taste and set aside.

**2 Make Falafel Mixture** Cut 1 pita in half; reserve one half for another use. Tear other half into small pieces. Process torn pita pieces in food processor until finely ground, about 15 seconds. Add egg, 2 tablespoons parsley, chickpeas, remaining 1 teaspoon cumin, ½ teaspoon salt, and ½ teaspoon pepper and pulse until chickpeas are coarsely chopped and mixture is cohesive, about 10 pulses.

**3 Form Patties** Working with 1 tablespoon at a time, use your hands to form chickpea mixture into patties about 2 inches in diameter (you should have 16 patties). Set aside. Adjust oven rack to upper-middle position and heat broiler.

**4** **Make Salad** Whisk 2 tablespoons oil, remaining 1 tablespoon lemon juice, ¼ teaspoon salt, and ¼ teaspoon pepper together in large bowl. Add lettuce, cucumbers, and remaining 2 tablespoons parsley. Crumble feta (½ cup) over top and toss to coat; set aside.

**5** **Fry Falafel** Heat remaining ½ cup oil in 12-inch nonstick skillet over medium-high heat until just smoking. Fry patties until deep golden brown on both sides, about 3 minutes per side. Transfer falafel to paper towel–lined plate to drain briefly.

**6** **Finish Dish** Cut remaining 2 pitas in half and place on rimmed baking sheet. Broil until lightly browned on first side, 1 to 2 minutes. Flip and continue to broil until lightly browned on second side, 1 to 2 minutes. Stuff each pita pocket with ¼ cup tomatoes and 4 falafel. Drizzle with yogurt sauce. Serve falafel pitas with salad and remaining yogurt sauce.

# Polenta with Broccoli Rabe and Fried Eggs

serves 4; total time 1 hour

## notes for the cook

Creamy polenta provides a savory bed for broiled broccoli rabe and an Italian flavor profile suits both elements. Add a fried egg on top and it's a hearty dinner in a bowl.

A pinch of baking soda helps the cornmeal break down so it cooks much faster.

Make sure to scrape down the bottom and sides of the pan while cooking the polenta.

Keep an eye on the broccoli rabe as it cooks. If the leaves get too dark or are not browning in the time specified, adjust the distance of the oven rack from the broiler.

If you like your fried eggs less runny, use the following resting times in step 6: Let sit 45 to 60 seconds for soft but set yolks, or about 2 minutes for medium-set yolks.

Pinch baking soda

Salt and pepper

1 cup coarse-ground cornmeal

¼ cup plus 2 teaspoons extra-virgin olive oil

1 pound broccoli rabe

1½ ounces Parmesan cheese

½ cup oil-packed sun-dried tomatoes

1 garlic clove

¼ teaspoon red pepper flakes

4 large eggs

**1 Cook Polenta** Bring 5 cups water to boil in large saucepan over medium-high heat. Stir in baking soda and 1 teaspoon salt. Slowly pour cornmeal into water in steady stream while whisking constantly and bring to boil. Reduce heat to lowest possible setting, cover, and cook, stirring often, until grains of cornmeal are tender, about 30 minutes.

**2 Prep Vegetables** While polenta cooks, adjust oven rack 4 inches from broiler element and heat broiler. Brush rimmed baking sheet with 1 tablespoon oil. Trim and discard bottom 1 inch of broccoli rabe stems. Cut tops (leaves and florets) from stems, then cut stems into 1-inch pieces (keep tops whole). Grate Parmesan (¾ cup). Pat tomatoes dry and chop coarse. Mince garlic.

**3 Season Broccoli Rabe** Transfer broccoli rabe to prepared sheet, keeping leaves and stems separate. Combine pepper flakes, 3 tablespoons oil, garlic, and ¼ teaspoon salt in small bowl. Pour oil mixture over broccoli rabe and toss leaves and stems separately to coat.

**4** **Broil Broccoli Rabe** Broil broccoli rabe until half of leaves are well browned, 2 to 2½ minutes. Using tongs, toss to expose unbrowned leaves. Return sheet to oven and continue to broil until most leaves are lightly charred and stems are crisp-tender, 2 to 2½ minutes. Transfer to cutting board and cut tops (leaves and florets) into 1-inch pieces. Transfer to large plate along with stems and tent with aluminum foil.

**5** **Finish Polenta** Off heat, stir ½ cup Parmesan and chopped tomatoes into polenta and season with salt and pepper to taste. Cover and let sit for about 8 minutes. Crack eggs into 2 small bowls (2 eggs per bowl) and season with salt and pepper.

**6** **Fry Eggs and Finish Dish** Add remaining 2 teaspoons oil to 12-inch nonstick skillet and heat over medium-high heat until shimmering. Pour 1 bowl of eggs in 1 side of pan and second bowl in other side. Cover and cook for 1 minute. Remove from heat and let sit 15 to 45 seconds for runny yolks (white around edge of yolk will be barely opaque). Serve polenta with broccoli rabe and fried eggs, sprinkling with remaining ¼ cup Parmesan.

# Spiced Red Lentils with Cauliflower and Cilantro

serves 4; total time 1 hour

## notes for the cook

Earthy red lentils and nutty roasted cauliflower both take well to the Indian-spice flavor profile in this filling dish.

A two-stage cooking method for the cauliflower—on a sheet pan, first covered with aluminum foil and then uncovered in a hot oven—creates a well-browned exterior with a tender center.

You cannot substitute other types of lentils for the red lentils here; they have a very particular texture and break down more quickly than other lentils.

Note that you'll need ½ cup of cilantro, so shop accordingly.

1 ½ cups long-grain white rice

Salt and pepper

1 onion

4 garlic cloves

Fresh ginger

1 head cauliflower (2 pounds)

8½ ounces (1 ¼ cups) red lentils

3 tablespoons extra-virgin olive oil

1 tablespoon garam masala

1 ½ cups frozen peas

Fresh cilantro

1 lime

2 tablespoons unsalted butter

**1 Cook Rice** Adjust oven rack to lowest position and heat oven to 475 degrees. Rinse rice in fine-mesh strainer until water runs clear. Bring rice, 2¼ cups water, and ¼ teaspoon salt to simmer in large saucepan over medium heat. Reduce heat to low, cover, and simmer until rice is tender and liquid is absorbed, 16 to 18 minutes. Remove pot from heat, lay clean folded dish towel underneath lid, and let sit for 10 minutes.

**2 Prep Vegetables** While rice cooks, chop onion fine. Mince garlic. Peel and grate 1½ teaspoons ginger. Trim outer leaves of cauliflower and cut stem flush with bottom of head. Cut head into 8 equal wedges, keeping core and florets intact. Pick over and rinse lentils.

**3 Cook Aromatics** Heat 1 tablespoon oil in large saucepan over medium-high heat until shimmering. Add onion and ¾ teaspoon salt and cook until softened, about 5 minutes. Stir in garam masala, garlic, and ginger and cook until fragrant, about 30 seconds.

**4 Cook Lentils** Stir in lentils and 3 cups water into onion mixture and bring to boil. Reduce heat to low and simmer, uncovered, until lentils are tender and resemble coarse puree, 20 to 25 minutes. Off heat, stir in peas and cover to keep warm.

**5 Roast Cauliflower** While lentils cook, toss cauliflower with remaining 2 tablespoons oil and ¼ teaspoon salt. Place wedges cut side down on parchment paper–lined rimmed baking sheet. Cover tightly with aluminum foil and cook for 10 minutes. Remove foil. Continue to cook until bottoms of wedges are golden, 8 to 12 minutes. Remove from oven, flip wedges using spatula, and continue to cook until golden all over, 8 to 12 minutes.

**6 Finish Dish** While cauliflower cooks, mince ½ cup cilantro. Cut lime into wedges. Stir butter and 6 tablespoons cilantro into lentils and season with salt and pepper to taste. Serve lentils over rice with roasted cauliflower and lime wedges, sprinkling with remaining 2 tablespoons cilantro.

# Lentils with Roasted Broccoli, Goat Cheese, and Pine Nuts

serves 4; total time 1 hour

## notes for the cook

This supersavory bowl-based meal combines green lentils with roasted broccoli, toasted pine nuts, and creamy goat cheese.

*Lentilles du Puy* (or French lentils) hold their shape during cooking; we do not recommend substituting other types of lentils in this dish.

Roasting the broccoli on a preheated baking sheet in a 500-degree oven imparts deep, flavorful browning.

You can substitute ½ teaspoon dried thyme for the fresh thyme.

A final drizzle of balsamic reduction contributes sweet, fruity notes that pair well with the earthy lentils and rich goat cheese.

1 onion

2 garlic cloves

Fresh thyme

12 ounces (1¾ cups) lentilles du Puy

5 tablespoons extra-virgin olive oil

Salt and pepper

¼ cup pine nuts

½ cup balsamic vinegar

2 pounds broccoli

4 ounces goat cheese

**1 Sauté Aromatics** Adjust oven rack to lowest position and heat oven to 500 degrees. Chop onion fine. Mince garlic. Mince 1 teaspoon thyme. Pick over and rinse lentils. Heat 2 tablespoons oil in large saucepan over medium heat until shimmering. Add onion and ¼ teaspoon salt and cook until softened, about 5 minutes. Stir in garlic and thyme and cook until fragrant, about 30 seconds.

**2 Cook Lentils** Stir lentils and 3¾ cups water into onion mixture and bring to simmer over high heat. Reduce heat to low, cover, and simmer, stirring occasionally, until lentils are barely tender, about 25 minutes. Uncover, increase heat to medium and continue to cook until lentils are completely tender and most of liquid has evaporated, 10 to 15 minutes. Season with salt and pepper to taste, cover, and set aside.

**3 Toast Nuts** While lentils cook, place rimmed baking sheet on rack in oven to preheat. Toast pine nuts in 8-inch skillet over medium heat, shaking pan occasionally, until golden and fragrant, 3 to 5 minutes; transfer to small bowl.

**4** **Make Balsamic Reduction** Add vinegar to now-empty skillet and cook over medium heat, occasionally scraping bottom of skillet with rubber spatula, until reduced to 2 tablespoons, about 5 minutes.

**5** **Prep Broccoli** Cut broccoli florets from stalks. Halve florets. Using vegetable peeler, trim tough outer peel from stalks, then cut into ½-inch-thick planks about 2 to 3 inches long.

**6** **Roast Broccoli and Finish Dish** Toss broccoli with remaining 3 tablespoons oil, ¼ teaspoon salt, and pinch pepper in bowl. Working quickly, lay broccoli in single layer, flat sides down, on preheated sheet. Roast until florets are browned, 9 to 11 minutes. Divide lentils among individual serving bowls, top with broccoli, and sprinkle with pine nuts. Crumble goat cheese (1 cup) over top and drizzle with balsamic reduction. Serve.

# Skillet Burrito Bowl

serves 4; total time 45 minutes

## notes for the cook

This dish has all the appeal of a totally stuffed black bean burrito, but without the fuss of trying to contain it in a tortilla.

Cooking an onion with bloomed cumin, garlic, and chipotle chile creates an intense base that then infuses the beans and rice with deep flavor.

We don't skimp on the toppings; a quick, fresh tomato-cilantro salsa is balanced by chunks of ripe avocado and mounds of sour cream for richness and tang.

You can substitute fresh corn for the frozen corn (you'll need two ears) but the cooking time in step 2 will be shorter.

You will need a 12-inch nonstick skillet with tight-fitting lid for this recipe.

1 onion

4 garlic cloves

Canned chipotle chile in adobo sauce

1 cup long-grain white rice

2 (15-ounce) cans black beans

3 tablespoons extra-virgin olive oil

1½ cups frozen corn

Salt and pepper

1 teaspoon ground cumin

10 ounces cherry or grape tomatoes

Fresh cilantro

2 limes

1 avocado

½ cup sour cream

**1 Prep Ingredients** Chop onion fine. Mince garlic. Mince 1 tablespoon chipotle chile. Rinse rice in fine-mesh strainer until water runs clear. Drain and rinse black beans.

**2 Toast Corn** Heat 1 tablespoon oil in 12-inch nonstick skillet over medium-high heat until shimmering. Add corn and cook, stirring occasionally, until kernels begin to brown and pop, 6 to 8 minutes. Transfer corn to bowl and season with salt and pepper to taste.

**3 Cook Aromatics** Heat 1 tablespoon oil in now-empty skillet over medium-high heat until shimmering. Add onion and ½ teaspoon salt and cook until softened, about 5 minutes. Stir in cumin, garlic, and chipotle and cook until fragrant, about 30 seconds.

**4** **Cook Rice and Beans** Stir beans, rice, and 2 cups water into skillet and bring to simmer. Cover, reduce heat to low, and simmer gently, stirring occasionally, until liquid is absorbed and rice is tender, about 15 minutes.

**5** **Make Tomato Salsa** While rice and beans cook, quarter tomatoes. Mince ¼ cup cilantro. Grate ¼ teaspoon lime zest and squeeze 1 tablespoon juice from 1 lime. Cut remaining lime into wedges. Halve avocado, remove pit, and cut into ½-inch pieces. Combine remaining 1 tablespoon oil, tomatoes, cilantro, and lime zest and juice in bowl and season with salt and pepper to taste.

**6** **Finish Dish** Off heat, sprinkle corn over rice and beans. Cover and let sit for 5 minutes. Gently fluff rice and beans with fork and season with salt and pepper to taste. Sprinkle tomato mixture over rice and beans. Top individual portions with sour cream and avocado and serve with lime wedges.

# Black Bean and Sweet Potato Tacos

serves 4; total time 1 hour

## notes for the cook

These vegetarian tacos get their heft from satisfying black beans and their flavor from a combination of roasted sweet potatoes and poblano chiles seasoned with fragrant garlic, cumin, coriander, and oregano.

Instead of topping these tacos with the usual sour cream or queso fresco, we made a quick, refreshing avocado-lime spread.

If you have a few extra minutes, try our preferred tortilla-warming method: Using a dry skillet over medium-high heat, warm the tortillas one at a time until softened and speckled brown, 20 to 30 seconds per side.

You can substitute ¼ teaspoon dried oregano for the fresh oregano.

3 garlic cloves

Fresh oregano

1 pound sweet potatoes

4 poblano chiles

1 large onion

3 tablespoons extra-virgin olive oil

1½ teaspoons ground cumin

1½ teaspoons ground coriander

Salt and pepper

2 limes

Fresh cilantro

1 avocado

1 (15-ounce) can black beans

12 (6-inch) corn tortillas

**1 Prep Aromatics and Vegetables** Adjust oven racks to upper-middle and lower-middle positions and heat oven to 450 degrees. Mince garlic. Mince 1 teaspoon oregano. Peel sweet potatoes and cut into ½-inch pieces. Stem and seed poblanos, then cut into ½-inch-wide strips. Halve onion, then slice ½ inch thick.

**2 Season Vegetables** Whisk oil, cumin, coriander, garlic, oregano, 1 teaspoon salt, and ½ teaspoon pepper together in large bowl. Add potatoes, poblanos, and onion to oil mixture and toss to coat.

**3 Roast Vegetables** Spread vegetables in even layer over 2 aluminum foil–lined rimmed baking sheets (do not wash bowl). Roast vegetables until tender and golden brown, about 30 minutes, stirring vegetables and switching and rotating sheets halfway through baking.

**4 Prep Toppings** While vegetables roast, squeeze 1 tablespoon lime juice from 1 lime and cut remaining lime into wedges. Chop ¼ cup cilantro. Cut avocado in half, remove pit, then scoop flesh into bowl. Add lime juice and mash with fork until mostly smooth. Season with salt and pepper to taste. Drain and rinse beans.

**5 Add Beans to Roasted Vegetables** Return vegetables to now-empty bowl, add cilantro and black beans, and toss to combine.

**6 Warm Tortillas and Finish Dish** Place tortillas on plate, cover with damp dish towel, and microwave for 60 to 90 seconds until warm. Spread mashed avocado over tortillas, then top with roasted vegetable–black bean mixture. Serve with lime wedges.

# Corn and Green Chile Quesadillas with Romaine and Avocado Salad

serves 4; total time 1 hour

## notes for the cook

We precook the zesty vegetable filling for our crispy, cheesy quesadillas to avoid soggy results. Sautéed corn adds a deep sweetness while canned green chiles contribute bright, mild heat without requiring a ton of fussy prep.

Baking the quesadillas in the oven on a baking sheet let us make four at once so everyone's dinner is ready at the same time.

To counter the rich quesadillas, we make a refreshing, crunchy salad with romaine lettuce, fresh cilantro, roasted pepitas, and radishes.

Note that you'll need ½ cup of cilantro, so shop accordingly.

¼ cup extra-virgin olive oil
1 cup frozen corn
Salt and pepper
10 ounces Monterey Jack cheese
1 (4-ounce) can chopped green chiles
Fresh cilantro
2 scallions
1 lime
4 (10-inch) flour tortillas
2 romaine lettuce hearts (12 ounces)
1 avocado
4 radishes
¼ cup roasted pepitas

1 **Toast Corn** Adjust oven rack to middle position and heat oven to 450 degrees. Line rimmed baking sheet with aluminum foil and brush with 2 teaspoons oil. Heat 2 teaspoons oil in 12-inch nonstick skillet over medium-high heat until shimmering. Add corn and cook, stirring occasionally, until kernels begin to brown and pop, 6 to 8 minutes. Transfer corn to bowl and season with salt and pepper to taste; set aside to cool slightly.

2 **Prep Vegetables** While corn cooks, shred Monterey Jack (2½ cups). Pat green chiles dry. Chop ½ cup cilantro. Slice scallions thin. Grate 1½ teaspoons lime zest and squeeze 1½ tablespoons juice.

3 **Make Filling** Toss cooled corn, Monterey Jack, green chiles, ¼ cup cilantro, scallions, and 1 teaspoon lime zest together in bowl.

**4 Assemble Quesadillas** Divide cheese mixture evenly among tortillas, then spread in even layer over half of each tortilla, leaving ½-inch border around edge. Fold other half of each tortilla over top and press firmly to compact.

**5 Bake Quesadillas** Arrange quesadillas in single layer on prepared sheet, with rounded edges facing center of sheet. Brush tops with 2 teaspoons oil. Bake until quesadillas begin to brown, about 10 minutes. Flip quesadillas and press gently with spatula to compact. Continue to bake until crisp and golden brown on second side, about 5 minutes. Transfer sheet to wire rack and let quesadillas cool for 5 minutes.

**6 Finish Dish** Meanwhile, chop romaine. Halve and pit avocado, then cut into ½-inch pieces. Trim radishes and slice thin. Whisk remaining 2 tablespoons oil, remaining ½ teaspoon lime zest, lime juice, ½ teaspoon salt, and ¼ teaspoon pepper together in large bowl. Add pepitas, remaining ¼ cup cilantro, romaine, avocado, and radishes to bowl and toss to combine; season with salt and pepper to taste. Slice quesadillas into wedges. Serve with salad.

# Spicy Braised Chickpeas and Turnips with Couscous

serves 4 to 6; total time 1 hour

## notes for the cook

The flavors in this dish are inspired by Tunisian cuisine, which is known for being quite hot and spicy.

The combination of chickpeas and braised turnips may sound strange, but these earthy ingredients actually work quite well together and a base of fluffy couscous lets those components and our punchy sauce shine through.

Including the starchy, seasoned liquid from the canned chickpeas in the dish instead of throwing it away gives the sauce good flavor and body.

2 onions

2 red bell peppers

1 jalapeño chile

5 garlic cloves

12 ounces turnips

3 tablespoons extra-virgin olive oil

Salt and pepper

¼ cup tomato paste

¾ teaspoon ground cumin

¼ teaspoon cayenne pepper

2 (15-ounce) cans chickpeas

1½ cups couscous

Fresh parsley

2 lemons

**1  Prep Vegetables and Aromatics** Chop onions. Stem and seed bell peppers, then chop. Stem and seed jalapeño, then chop. Mince garlic. Peel turnips, then cut into ½-inch pieces.

**2  Cook Aromatics** Heat 2 tablespoons oil in Dutch oven over medium heat until shimmering. Add onions, bell peppers, ½ teaspoon salt, and ¼ teaspoon pepper and cook until softened and lightly browned, 5 to 7 minutes. Stir in tomato paste, cumin, cayenne, jalapeño, and garlic and cook until fragrant, about 30 seconds.

**3  Cook Chickpeas and Turnips** Stir in chickpeas and their liquid, turnips, and ¾ cup water. Bring to simmer and cook until turnips are tender and sauce has thickened, 25 to 35 minutes.

**4 Cook Couscous** While chickpeas cook, heat remaining 1 tablespoon oil in medium saucepan over medium-high heat until shimmering. Add couscous and cook, stirring frequently, until grains are just beginning to brown, 3 to 5 minutes. Stir in 1½ cups water and ¼ teaspoon salt. Cover, remove saucepan from heat, and let sit until couscous is tender, about 7 minutes. Fluff couscous with fork.

**5 Prep Garnishes** Chop ¼ cup parsley. Squeeze 2 tablespoons lemon juice from 1 lemon and cut remaining lemon into wedges.

**6 Finish Dish** Stir parsley and lemon juice into braised turnips. Season with salt and pepper to taste. Adjust consistency with hot water as needed. Serve chickpeas over couscous with lemon wedges.

# Spring Risotto with Peas, Asparagus, and Arugula

serves 6; total time 1 hour

## notes for the cook

Risotto has a reputation for being a laborious, fussy dish, but our method turns out perfectly al dente grains and tender spring vegetables in just an hour.

In a typical risotto recipe, you add the broth in small increments and stir constantly after each addition; we add most of the broth at once and then cover the pan and allow the rice to simmer until almost all the broth is absorbed. Stirring gently and constantly for just a few minutes towards the end of cooking releases the rice's starch and creates an extra-creamy dish.

Sautéing asparagus and stirring it into the rice right before serving keeps it vibrant green and perfectly crisp-tender.

4 cups vegetable broth
1 pound asparagus
1 large onion
1 garlic clove
5 tablespoons unsalted butter
Salt and pepper
2 cups Arborio rice
1 cup dry white wine
3 ounces Parmesan cheese
3 ounces (3 cups) baby arugula
1 lemon
1½ cups frozen peas

**1 Warm Broth and Prep Asparagus and Aromatics** Bring broth and 2½ cups water to boil in large saucepan over high heat. Cover and reduce heat to low to maintain bare simmer. Meanwhile, trim asparagus and cut on bias into 1½-inch lengths. Chop onion fine. Mince garlic.

**2 Cook Asparagus** Melt 1 tablespoon butter in Dutch oven over medium heat. Add asparagus and pinch salt and cook until crisp-tender, 3 to 5 minutes; transfer to bowl.

**3 Toast Rice** Melt 2 tablespoons butter in now-empty Dutch oven over medium heat. Add onion and ¾ teaspoon salt and cook until softened, about 5 minutes. Stir in garlic and cook until fragrant, about 30 seconds. Stir in rice and cook, stirring often, until grain edges begin to turn translucent, about 3 minutes.

**4** **Cook Risotto** Stir in wine and cook, stirring constantly, until fully absorbed, 2 to 3 minutes. Stir in 5 cups hot broth mixture. Reduce heat to medium-low, cover, and simmer until almost all liquid has been absorbed and rice is just al dente, 16 to 19 minutes, stirring twice during cooking.

**5** **Prep Parmesan, Arugula, and Lemon** While risotto cooks, grate Parmesan (1½ cups). Roughly chop arugula. Grate ½ teaspoon lemon zest and squeeze 1 teaspoon juice.

**6** **Finish Dish** When rice is just al dente, add ¾ cup hot broth mixture and peas and stir gently and constantly until risotto becomes creamy, about 3 minutes. Off heat, stir in 1 cup Parmesan, cover, and let stand for 5 minutes. Stir in remaining 2 tablespoons butter, asparagus, arugula, and lemon zest and juice. Season with salt and pepper to taste. Adjust consistency with remaining broth as needed. Serve with remaining ½ cup Parmesan.

# Vegetable and Orzo Tian with Garlic Toasts

serves 4; total time 1 hour

## notes for the cook

This colorful vegetable casserole has a striking look but a simple approach. Arranging slices of moisture-rich zucchini, summer squash, and tomatoes over the uncooked orzo and baking the dish all together lets us skip precooking the pasta and streamlines the recipe.

Garlic, shallots, oregano, and pepper flakes add punch to the fresh vegetables, while a topping of broiled Parmesan adds just the right finishing note.

Crisp garlic toasts are a perfect accompaniment to the creamy orzo.

Look for squash, zucchini, and tomatoes with similar-size circumferences so that they are easy to shingle into the dish.

3 ounces Parmesan cheese

2 shallots

4 garlic cloves

1 cup orzo

1 teaspoon dried oregano

⅛ teaspoon red pepper flakes

Salt and pepper

1 zucchini

1 yellow summer squash

12 ounces plum tomatoes

1¾ cups vegetable broth

1 loaf rustic bread

2 tablespoons extra-virgin olive oil

Fresh basil

**1 Prep Orzo** Adjust 1 oven rack to middle position and second rack 6 inches from broiler element and heat oven to 425 degrees. Grate Parmesan (1½ cups). Mince shallots. Mince 3 garlic cloves. Combine orzo, oregano, pepper flakes, ½ cup grated Parmesan, shallots, minced garlic, and ¼ teaspoon salt in bowl. Spread mixture evenly into broiler-safe 13 by 9-inch baking dish.

**2 Prep Vegetables** Slice zucchini and squash ¼ inch thick. Core tomatoes and slice ¼ inch thick. Alternately shingle zucchini, squash, and tomatoes in tidy rows on top of orzo.

**3 Bake Tian** Carefully pour broth over top of vegetables. Bake on lower rack until orzo is just tender and most of broth is absorbed, about 20 minutes. Meanwhile, slice four ¾-inch-thick slices of bread and spread out evenly over rimmed baking sheet; set aside.

**4** **Broil Tian** Remove dish from oven and heat broiler. Drizzle vegetables with 1 tablespoon oil, and sprinkle with remaining 1 cup Parmesan. Broil on lower rack until nicely browned and bubbling around edges, about 5 minutes. Remove dish from oven and let rest for 10 minutes.

**5** **Toast Bread** While tian rests, broil bread on upper rack, flipping as needed, until well toasted on both sides, about 4 minutes. Peel remaining 1 garlic clove and rub one side of each toast with garlic, then drizzle toasts with remaining 1 tablespoon oil and season with salt and pepper to taste.

**6** **Finish Dish** Chop 2 tablespoons basil and sprinkle over tian. Serve with toasts.

# Grilled Portobello Burgers with Smoky Red Potatoes

serves 4; total time 1 hour

## notes for the cook

These portobello burgers are robust and meaty. Lightly scoring the mushrooms not only helps them release their excess moisture on the grill, it also helps them suck up more of our simple, flavorful marinade.

The mushrooms marinate while the grill heats and our smoky potato side dish is prepared for a perfectly streamlined process.

Using wooden skewers allows the potatoes to go straight from the microwave to the grill. You will need 4 to 6 wooden skewers.

If the mushrooms absorb all the marinade, brush the onions with extra olive oil before grilling them in step 5.

3 garlic cloves

4 portobello mushrooms (4 to 5 inches in diameter)

10 tablespoons extra-virgin olive oil

3 tablespoons plus ½ teaspoon red wine vinegar

Salt and pepper

1½ pounds small red potatoes

Fresh basil

¾ cup sour cream

½ cup oil-packed sun-dried tomatoes

1 red onion

1 teaspoon smoked paprika

4 hamburger buns

1 cup baby arugula

**1 Prep and Marinate Portobellos** Mince garlic. Remove stems from mushrooms and use spoon to remove gills. Using tip of paring knife, cut ½-inch crosshatch pattern on tops of mushroom caps, ¹⁄₁₆ inch deep. Combine one-third of garlic, 6 tablespoons oil, 3 tablespoons vinegar, ½ teaspoon salt, and ½ teaspoon pepper in 1-gallon zipper-lock bag. Add mushrooms, seal bag, turn to coat, and set aside.

**2 Heat Grill, Prep Vegetable Skewers, and Make Garlic Oil** While mushrooms marinate, turn all grill burners to high, cover, and heat grill until hot, about 15 minutes. Turn all burners to medium-high. While grill heats, combine remaining ¼ cup oil, remaining garlic, and ¼ teaspoon salt in bowl and microwave until sizzling, about 1 minute. Halve potatoes and thread onto 4 to 6 wooden skewers. Brush with 1 tablespoon garlic oil.

**3 Parcook Potatoes and Prep Burger Toppings** Microwave potatoes until barely tender, about 8 minutes, turning halfway through cooking. While potatoes are microwaving, chop ¼ cup basil. Combine ¼ cup sour cream and basil in bowl; set aside. Pat sun-dried tomatoes dry, then chop. Slice onion into ½-inch-thick rounds.

**4** **Prep Vegetables** Brush microwaved potatoes with 1 tablespoon garlic oil. Remove mushrooms from marinade, reserving excess marinade. Brush onions all over with reserved mushroom marinade.

**5** **Grill Mushrooms, Onions, Potatoes, and Buns** Clean and oil cooking grate. Place onions, mushrooms (gill side up), and potatoes (cut side down) on grill and cook, covered, until grill marks appear, 4 to 6 minutes. Flip vegetables and continue to cook, covered, until charred and fully tender, 3 to 5 minutes; transfer to platter and cover with aluminum foil to keep warm. Grill buns, cut sides down, until lightly charred, about 1 minute.

**6** **Finish Dish** Remove potatoes from skewers. Toss with paprika, remaining ½ teaspoon vinegar, and remaining 2 tablespoons garlic oil. Season with salt and pepper to taste. Spread 1 tablespoon basil sour cream on each bun bottom, and top each with 1 mushroom, 2 tablespoons sun-dried tomatoes, and 1 onion round. Divide arugula evenly among burgers. Top with buns. Serve with potatoes and remaining ½ cup sour cream for dipping.

# Chickpea Cakes with Endive and Orange Salad

serves 6; total time 45 minutes

## notes for the cook

Buttery, nutty chickpeas make a great foundation for a light yet filling vegetarian patty. Here, we give them a flavor boost with a bit of garam masala and cayenne pepper and pair these spiced cakes with a crunchy, bright salad of endive and orange segments.

Avoid overmixing the chickpea mixture in step 4 or the cakes will have a mealy texture.

Be sure to excise all the peel and pith from the oranges; otherwise, their bitterness and tough texture will mar the salad.

2 (15-ounce) cans chickpeas

Fresh cilantro

1 shallot

1 large head Belgian endive (6 ounces)

1 orange

½ cup sliced almonds

2 large eggs

½ cup extra-virgin olive oil

1 teaspoon garam masala

⅛ teaspoon cayenne pepper

Salt and pepper

1 cup panko bread crumbs

½ cup plain Greek yogurt

2 tablespoons white wine vinegar

4 ounces (4 cups) mesclun greens

**1** **Prep Ingredients** Drain and rinse chickpeas. Mince 3 tablespoons cilantro. Mince shallot. Cut endive into 2-inch pieces. Cut away peel and pith from orange and cut into quarters. Slice quarters crosswise into ½-inch-thick pieces.

**2** **Toast Nuts** Toast almonds in 12-inch nonstick skillet over medium heat, shaking pan occasionally, until golden and fragrant, 3 to 5 minutes.

**3** **Make Chickpea Mixture** Pulse chickpeas in food processor until coarsely ground, about 8 pulses. Whisk eggs, 2 tablespoons oil, garam masala, cayenne, and ¼ teaspoon salt together in medium bowl.

4 **Shape Patties** Gently stir panko, yogurt, cilantro, shallot, and processed chickpeas into egg mixture until just combined. Divide mixture into 6 equal portions and shape into six 3½-inch-diameter patties, about ¾ inch thick.

5 **Cook Patties** Heat 2 tablespoons oil in now-empty skillet over medium heat until shimmering. Carefully lay 3 patties in skillet and cook until well browned and firm on both sides, 4 to 5 minutes per side. Transfer to plate and tent with aluminum foil. Return now-empty skillet to medium heat and repeat with 2 tablespoons oil and remaining 3 patties.

6 **Make Salad and Finish Dish** While patties cook, whisk vinegar, remaining 2 tablespoons oil, ¼ teaspoon salt, and ⅛ teaspoon pepper together in large bowl. Add mesclun, endive, orange pieces, and almonds and toss to combine. Serve with chickpea cakes.

# Black Bean Burgers with Roasted Carrots and Jalapeño Mayo

serves 4; total time 1 hour

## notes for the cook

We use an unconventional binder—ground tortilla chips—in our black bean burgers to hold the patties together without drying them out. This trick also infuses the burgers with the flavor of toasted corn.

An incredibly simple jalapeño mayo made by stirring the brine from pickled jalapeños into plain mayonnaise makes not only a punchy topping for the burgers but also a perfect dipping sauce for a side dish of sweet, caramelized roasted carrots.

Note that you need a 19-ounce can of black beans for this recipe. You can also use two 15-ounce cans and measure out 2 full cups of drained beans, but you'll have some extra beans.

4 scallions
1 (19-ounce) can black beans
2 ounces tortilla chips
1 large egg
1 tablespoon chili powder
Salt and pepper
1 jar pickled jalapeños
½ cup mayonnaise
2 pounds carrots
3 tablespoons extra-virgin olive oil
1 tablespoon honey
1 tomato
1 small head Bibb lettuce (6 ounces)
4 hamburger buns

**1** **Prep Ingredients** Adjust oven rack to middle position and heat oven to 450 degrees. Chop scallions coarse. Drain and rinse black beans. Process tortilla chips in food processor until very finely ground, about 1 minute. Add scallions and pulse until finely chopped, about 10 pulses. Add egg, chili powder, drained beans, and ½ teaspoon pepper and pulse until beans are finely chopped, about 15 pulses.

**2** **Make Burgers and Jalapeño Mayo** Divide bean mixture equally into four portions and shape into four 1-inch thick patties, about 3½ inches in diameter. Transfer burgers to plate and refrigerate for 20 minutes. Meanwhile, measure out ¼ cup pickled jalapeños; set aside. Measure out 1½ tablespoons pickled jalapeño brine. Combine jalapeño brine and mayonnaise in bowl; set aside.

**3** **Prep Carrots** While burgers chill, line rimmed baking sheet with aluminum foil. Peel carrots and cut into 2- to 3-inch lengths. Leave thin pieces whole, halve medium pieces lengthwise, and quarter thick pieces lengthwise. Toss carrots with 1 tablespoon oil, honey, and ¼ teaspoon salt on prepared sheet, and spread into single layer.

4 **Cook Carrots** Cover baking sheet tightly with foil and roast for 10 minutes. Remove foil and continue to roast until carrots are browned and tender but still hold their shape, 12 to 15 minutes. Season with salt and pepper to taste.

5 **Cook Burgers** After carrots have been uncovered, heat remaining 2 tablespoons oil in 12-inch nonstick skillet over medium heat until shimmering. Add burgers and cook until well browned and cooked through, about 4 minutes per side.

6 **Finish Dish** Core tomato then cut into 4 slices. Separate lettuce leaves. Spread 1 tablespoon mayonnaise mixture on each bun bottom. Place lettuce, burgers, tomato slices, jalapeños, and buns on top. Serve burgers with carrots and remaining ¼ cup mayonnaise mixture for dipping.

# Zucchini Noodles with Roasted Tomatoes and Cream Sauce

serves 4; total time 45 minutes

## notes for the cook

Spiralized veggie noodles help pack in the vegetables while still providing all the comfort food appeal of pasta. This dish coats zucchini noodles with a rich, creamy sauce and sweet, garlicky roasted tomatoes.

Roasting the zucchini noodles rids them of excess moisture and ensures that the sauce won't get washed out.

If possible use smaller, in-season zucchini, which have thinner skins and fewer seeds.

Store-bought zucchini "noodles" can be used here if you don't have a spiralizer. You'll need 2½ pounds of noodles.

A toasted loaf of ciabatta bread makes the perfect tool for wiping up every drop of cheesy sauce and roasted tomatoes.

1 shallot

5 garlic cloves

3 pounds zucchini or yellow summer squash

Fresh basil

1 pound cherry tomatoes

3 tablespoons extra-virgin olive oil

1 tablespoon tomato paste

1 teaspoon dried oregano

¼ teaspoon red pepper flakes

Salt and pepper

1½ ounces Parmesan cheese

1 cup heavy cream

2 tablespoons unsalted butter

1 medium loaf ciabatta bread

1 **Prep Vegetables** Adjust oven racks to upper-middle and lower-middle positions and heat oven to 375 degrees. Line 2 rimmed baking sheets with aluminum foil; set aside. Slice shallot thin. Mince garlic. Trim zucchini. Using spiralizer, cut zucchini into ⅛-inch-thick noodles, cutting noodles into 12-inch lengths with kitchen shears as you spiralize (about every 4 to 5 revolutions). Tear ¼ cup basil leaves into ½-inch pieces.

2 **Cook Tomatoes** Toss tomatoes, 2 tablespoons oil, tomato paste, oregano, pepper flakes, shallot, garlic, ½ teaspoon salt, and ¼ teaspoon pepper together in bowl. Spread tomato mixture on 1 prepared sheet and place on lower rack. Roast, without stirring, until tomatoes are softened and skins begin to shrivel, about 25 minutes.

3 **Cook Zucchini** While tomato mixture roasts, toss zucchini with remaining 1 tablespoon oil, ½ teaspoon salt, and ¼ teaspoon pepper, spread on second prepared sheet, and roast on upper rack until tender, 20 to 25 minutes. Transfer roasted zucchini to colander and shake to remove any excess liquid.

4 **Make Sauce** While vegetables cook, grate Parmesan (¾ cup). Bring cream and butter to simmer in large saucepan over medium heat. Reduce heat to low and simmer gently until mixture measures ⅔ cup, 12 to 15 minutes. Stir in Parmesan, ½ teaspoon salt, and ¼ teaspoon pepper and cook over low heat, stirring often, until Parmesan is melted.

5 **Warm Bread** Once vegetables are done roasting, place bread on upper rack to warm through, about 5 minutes.

6 **Finish Dish** While bread is in oven, add zucchini to cream sauce and gently toss to combine. Transfer to serving platter and top with roasted tomatoes. Season with salt and pepper to taste, and sprinkle with basil. Slice bread. Serve noodles immediately with warm bread.

# Broccoli and Feta Frittata with Watercress Salad

serves 4 to 6; total time 45 minutes

## notes for the cook

Frittatas are the lazy cook's omelet: all the flavor with almost none of the fussiness. In this version, we use a simple but satisfying combination of broccoli and feta to create a hearty dinnertime frittata.

If you're using broccoli heads instead of florets, you'll need about 1½ pounds of broccoli.

A hybrid stove-to-oven cooking approach creates a frittata that's nicely browned on the outside and tender inside.

Using crisp romaine lettuce gives our salad body and balances the delicate watercress. Briny kalamata olives add complex flavor.

The frittata can be served warm or at room temperature.

12 ounces broccoli florets

1 lemon

4 ounces feta cheese

12 large eggs

⅓ cup whole milk

Salt and pepper

3 tablespoons extra-virgin olive oil

Pinch red pepper flakes

¼ cup pitted kalamata olives

1 romaine lettuce heart (6 ounces)

3 ounces (3 cups) watercress

1 **Prep Ingredients** Adjust oven rack to middle position and heat oven to 350 degrees. Cut broccoli florets into ½-inch pieces (you should have about 4 cups). Grate ½ teaspoon lemon zest and squeeze 2½ teaspoons juice. Cut feta into ½-inch pieces (1 cup). Whisk eggs, milk, and ½ teaspoon salt in bowl until well combined.

2 **Cook Filling** Heat 1 tablespoon oil in 12-inch ovensafe nonstick skillet over medium-high heat until shimmering. Add pepper flakes, broccoli, and ¼ teaspoon salt; cook, stirring frequently, until broccoli is crisp-tender and spotty brown, 7 to 9 minutes. Add 3 tablespoons water, lemon zest, and ½ teaspoon lemon juice; continue to cook, stirring constantly, until broccoli is just tender and no water remains in skillet, about 1 minute longer.

3 **Start Frittata** Add egg mixture and feta to skillet with broccoli and cook, using rubber spatula to stir and scrape bottom of skillet until large curds form and spatula leaves trail through eggs but eggs are still very wet, about 30 seconds. Smooth curds into even layer and cook, without stirring, for 30 seconds.

4 **Bake Frittata** Transfer skillet to oven and bake until frittata is slightly puffy and surface bounces back when lightly pressed, 7 to 10 minutes.

5 **Make Salad** While frittata bakes, whisk remaining 2 tablespoons oil, remaining 2 teaspoons lemon juice, and ⅛ teaspoon salt together in large bowl. Cut olives in half. Tear romaine and watercress into bite-size pieces. Add olives, romaine, and watercress to bowl with dressing and toss to combine. Season with salt and pepper to taste.

6 **Finish Dish** Using rubber spatula, loosen frittata from skillet and transfer to cutting board. Let stand for 5 minutes before slicing. Serve frittata with salad.

# Baked Eggs with Tomatoes, Feta, and Croutons with Spinach Salad

serves 4; total time 1 hour

## notes for the cook

For this recipe, we were inspired by the classic Greek dish *avga feta domata*, which consists of eggs baked in a bed of savory tomato sauce and croutons and topped with tangy feta cheese. All this hearty dish needs to make it into dinner is a fresh spinach salad with complementary Greek flavors.

By baking the eggs in wide, shallow divots in the tomato-crouton mixture, we expose more of the egg whites' surface area to the heat, allowing the whites to cook through before the yolks completely solidify.

To ensure that the yolks stay runny, we let the eggs finish cooking gently off the heat. If you want your yolks fully cooked, bake until the whites are fully set before the resting period.

1 loaf French or Italian bread
5 tablespoons extra-virgin olive oil
Salt and pepper
6 garlic cloves
Fresh oregano
2 teaspoons tomato paste
1 teaspoon sugar
2 pounds cherry tomatoes
¼ cup pine nuts
1 shallot
1 lemon
8 large eggs
5 ounces (5 cups) baby spinach
2 ounces feta cheese

**1 Prep Croutons** Adjust oven racks to upper-middle and lower-middle positions and heat oven to 450 degrees. Grease 13 by 9-inch baking dish. Cut bread into ½-inch cubes (you should have about 4 cups). Toss bread with 1 tablespoon oil and season with salt and pepper. Spread bread into even layer in prepared dish and set aside.

**2 Prep Tomatoes and Aromatics** Slice garlic thin. Mince 2 tablespoons oregano. Whisk 1 tablespoon oil, tomato paste, sugar, garlic, 1 tablespoon oregano, ¾ teaspoon salt, and ¼ teaspoon pepper together in large bowl. Add tomatoes and toss to combine. Transfer mixture to aluminum foil–lined rimmed baking sheet. Scrape any remaining garlic and tomato paste from bowl into center of tomatoes.

**3 Bake Croutons and Roast Tomatoes** Bake croutons on upper rack and tomatoes on lower rack, stirring both sheets occasionally, until bread is golden and tomatoes begin to soften, 10 to 12 minutes. Remove croutons from oven and let cool in dish. Continue to bake tomatoes until blistered and browned, about 10 minutes.

**4** **Toast Nuts and Make Dressing**
Meanwhile, toast pine nuts in 8-inch skillet over medium heat, shaking pan occasionally, until lightly browned and fragrant, 3 to 5 minutes; set aside to cool. Mince shallot. Squeeze 1 tablespoon lemon juice. Whisk together 1 teaspoon oregano, remaining 3 tablespoons oil, shallot, lemon juice, ¼ teaspoon salt, and ⅛ teaspoon pepper in large bowl.

**5** **Bake Eggs** Add tomatoes to croutons, gently fold to combine, and smooth into even layer. Make 8 shallow indentations (about 2 inches wide) in surface of bread-tomato mixture using back of spoon. Crack 1 egg into each indentation and sprinkle with salt and pepper. Bake on lower rack until whites are just beginning to set, 8 to 12 minutes. Transfer dish to wire rack, tent with foil, and let sit for 5 minutes.

**6** **Make Salad and Finish Dish**
While eggs rest, add spinach and pine nuts to bowl with dressing and toss to coat. Crumble feta (½ cup) over eggs, sprinkle with remaining 2 teaspoons oregano, and drizzle with extra oil to taste. Serve immediately with salad.

# Individual Cheese Soufflés with Frisée and Strawberry Salad

serves 6; total time 1 hour

## notes for the cook

Cheese soufflé doesn't have to be intimidating. Our simple method mixes a cheese-béchamel sauce right into the beaten egg whites with no finicky folding.

Making individual-size soufflés cuts down on cooking time and makes for a simple, elegant presentation on the dinner table.

If you don't have six 10-ounce ramekins, you can bake the soufflé in one 8-inch round, 2-quart soufflé dish, extending the cooking time to 30 to 35 minutes.

Comté, sharp cheddar, or Gouda cheese can be substituted for the Gruyère.

A salad of sweet strawberries, slightly bitter frisée, and acidic balsamic vinegar is a perfect complement to the creamy soufflés.

1 ounce Parmesan cheese
6 ounces Gruyère cheese
6 large eggs
Fresh parsley
¼ cup all-purpose flour
¼ teaspoon paprika
Salt and pepper
4 tablespoons unsalted butter
1⅓ cups whole milk
¼ teaspoon cream of tartar
1 head frisée (6 ounces)
8 ounces strawberries
3 tablespoons extra-virgin olive oil
1 tablespoon balsamic vinegar
5 ounces (5 cups) baby spinach

**1 Prep Ramekins** Adjust oven rack to middle position and heat oven to 350 degrees. Grate Parmesan (½ cup). Shred Gruyère on large holes of box grater (1½ cups). Separate egg yolks and whites. Mince 2 teaspoons parsley. Spray six 10-ounce ramekins with vegetable oil spray, then sprinkle each with 1 teaspoon Parmesan. Place ramekins on rimmed baking sheet.

**2 Make Béchamel** Combine flour, paprika, ¼ teaspoon salt, and ⅛ teaspoon pepper in bowl. Melt butter in small saucepan over medium heat. Stir in flour mixture and cook for 1 minute. Slowly whisk in milk and bring to simmer. Cook, whisking constantly, until mixture is thickened and smooth, about 1 minute. Off heat, whisk in Gruyère and 5 tablespoons Parmesan until melted and smooth. Let cool for 10 minutes.

**3 Make Soufflé Batter** After béchamel has cooled for 5 minutes, using stand mixer fitted with whisk attachment, whip egg whites and cream of tartar on medium-low speed until foamy, about 1 minute. Increase speed to medium-high and whip until stiff peaks form, 3 to 4 minutes. Whisk egg yolks and 1½ teaspoons minced parsley into béchamel in saucepan. Add béchamel to egg whites in stand mixer and whip until fully combined, about 15 seconds.

**4 Bake Soufflés** Give soufflé batter a final stir by hand to fully incorporate cheese mixture. Pour batter into prepared ramekins, leaving ½ inch of space between top of batter and rims of dishes (discard any excess batter). Sprinkle ramekins evenly with remaining 1 tablespoon Parmesan. Bake until soufflés have risen above rims, tops are deep golden brown, and interiors register 170 degrees, 12 to 18 minutes.

**5 Prep Salad Ingredients and Make Dressing** While soufflés bake, chop frisée into 2-inch pieces. Hull and quarter strawberries. Whisk oil, vinegar, ½ teaspoon salt, and ¼ teaspoon pepper together in large bowl.

**6 Finish Dish** Add spinach, frisée, and strawberries to bowl with dressing, toss gently to coat, and season with salt and pepper to taste. Sprinkle soufflés with remaining ½ teaspoon minced parsley and serve immediately with salad.

# Cauliflower Tacos with Mango-Cabbage Slaw

serves 4; total time 45 minutes

## notes for the cook

These vegetarian tacos takes their inspiration from Baja-style fish tacos, a California classic. Battered and roasted cauliflower is a great stand-in for fried fish.

If you have a few extra minutes, try our preferred tortilla-warming method: Using a dry skillet over medium-high heat, warm the tortillas one at a time until softened and speckled brown, 20 to 30 seconds per side.

A slaw with juicy mango and spicy jalapeño provides balanced sweetness and heat.

You will only use half of the mango in the slaw; save the rest for another use.

For a spicier slaw, mince the jalapeño ribs and seeds and add them to the mix, or simply use more of the chile.

½ head cauliflower (1 pound)

1 cup unsweetened shredded coconut

1 cup panko bread crumbs

1 cup canned coconut milk

1 teaspoon garlic powder

1 teaspoon ground cumin

¼ teaspoon cayenne pepper

Salt and pepper

1 mango

2 limes

Fresh cilantro

1 jalapeño chile

3 cups (7½ ounces) coleslaw mix

12 (6-inch) corn tortillas

**1** **Prep Cauliflower** Adjust oven rack to middle position and heat oven to 450 degrees. Trim cauliflower, then cut into 1-inch pieces. Spray rimmed baking sheet with vegetable oil spray.

**2** **Coat Cauliflower** Combine coconut and panko in shallow dish. Whisk coconut milk, garlic powder, cumin, cayenne, and 1 teaspoon salt together in bowl. Add cauliflower to coconut milk mixture; toss to coat well. Working with 1 piece cauliflower at a time, remove from coconut milk, letting excess drip back into bowl, then coat well with coconut-panko mixture, pressing gently to adhere; transfer to prepared sheet.

**3** **Bake Cauliflower** Bake cauliflower until tender, golden, and crisp, 20 to 25 minutes, flipping cauliflower and rotating sheet halfway through baking.

**4 Prep Slaw** While cauliflower bakes, peel mango and cut in half, reserving half for another use. Cut remaining ½ mango into ¼-inch pieces (¾ cup). Squeeze 2 tablespoons lime juice from 1 lime and cut remaining lime into wedges. Chop 1 tablespoon cilantro. Stem and seed jalapeño, then mince 1 tablespoon. Reserve remaining jalapeño for another use.

**5 Make Slaw** Combine coleslaw mix, mango, lime juice, cilantro, jalapeño, and ¼ teaspoon salt in bowl; set aside.

**6 Warm Tortillas and Finish Dish** Place tortillas on plate, cover with damp dish towel, and microwave for 60 to 90 seconds until warm. Divide slaw evenly among warm tortillas and top with cauliflower. Serve with lime wedges.

# Barbecue Tempeh Skewers with Grilled Romaine

serves 4; total time 1 hour

## notes for the cook

Cooking protein-packed tempeh on the grill gives it great smoky flavor and char. We cut it into cubes and thread the cubes onto skewers with firm, sweet bell peppers and meaty mushrooms, then brush the whole thing with sweet barbecue sauce, which helps temper the slightly bitter tempeh.

A portion of the barbecue sauce, thinned with oil and water, also serves as a marinade for the tempeh, infusing it with barbecue flavor.

We took advantage of the grill being in use to create a simple but flavor-packed salad of grilled romaine and charred lemon.

You will need eight 12-inch metal skewers for this recipe.

1¾ cups barbecue sauce

6 tablespoons extra-virgin olive oil

1 pound tempeh

1 pound cremini mushrooms

2 red bell peppers

2 romaine lettuce hearts (12 ounces)

1 lemon

Salt and pepper

**1** **Heat Grill** Turn all burners to high, cover, and heat grill until hot, about 15 minutes. Leave all burners on high.

**2** **Marinate Tempeh and Mushrooms** While grill heats, combine 1 cup barbecue sauce, ¼ cup oil, and ¼ cup water in 1-gallon zipper-lock bag. Cut tempeh into 1½-inch pieces and add to bag with marinade. Trim mushrooms and add to bag. Press out air from bag, seal, and turn to coat; set aside.

**3** **Prep Vegetables** Stem and seed bell peppers, then cut into 1½-inch pieces. Halve each romaine heart lengthwise (do not core). Halve lemon crosswise.

**4 Prep Skewers and Lettuce** Remove tempeh and mushrooms from marinade and thread in alternating order with peppers onto eight 12-inch metal skewers. Pat dry with paper towels. Brush romaine with remaining 2 tablespoons oil and season with salt and pepper.

**5 Grill Skewers** Clean and oil cooking grate. Place skewers on grill and cook, covered, turning as needed, until tempeh is well browned and vegetables are tender and slightly charred, 10 to 12 minutes. Brush 1 side of skewers with ¼ cup barbecue sauce and turn sauced side down. Grill until sizzling and well browned, about 1 minute. Repeat on second side with additional ¼ cup barbecue sauce. Transfer to platter and tent with aluminum foil.

**6 Grill Lettuce and Finish Dish** Place romaine and lemon cut side down on now-empty grill and cook until lightly charred, 3 to 5 minutes. Flip romaine and cook until second side is lightly browned, 1 to 2 minutes. Transfer romaine to second platter and squeeze grilled lemon over lettuce. Slide tempeh and vegetables off skewers. Serve with remaining ¼ cup barbecue sauce and romaine.

# Pesto Flatbread with Artichokes, Olives, and Arugula

serves 4; total time 1 hour

## notes for the cook

Store-bought pizza dough makes this flatbread weeknight-friendly, and the perfect combination of salty and savory toppings plus a quick homemade pesto will make it a new staple in your rotation.

A hot water bath (120 degrees) brings the cold dough to room temperature quickly, making it easier to stretch and shape. If you have time, you can let the dough sit for 1 to 2 hours on the counter instead.

Parbaking the crust before adding the toppings ensures that it won't get soggy.

Be sure to use fresh mozzarella packed in water, not low-moisture mozzarella.

Note that you'll need 1 cup of basil, so shop accordingly.

1 pound refrigerated pizza dough
½ cup oil-packed sun-dried tomatoes, plus their oil
¼ cup pitted kalamata olives
6 ounces fresh mozzarella cheese
¾ cup jarred whole baby artichokes packed in water (4 ounces)
Salt and pepper
Fresh basil
¼ ounce Parmesan cheese
2 garlic cloves
¼ cup extra-virgin olive oil
2 tablespoons pine nuts
2 ounces (2 cups) baby arugula

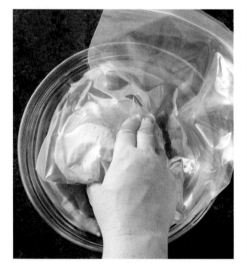

**1** **Prep Dough and Toppings** Adjust oven rack to lowest position and heat oven to 500 degrees. Place dough in zipper-lock bag and submerge in large bowl of hot water, squeezing periodically to warm through, about 10 minutes. Measure out and reserve 1 tablespoon sun-dried tomato oil. Pat sun-dried tomatoes dry and chop coarse. Cut olives in half. Slice mozzarella ¼ inch thick and pat dry. Drain artichokes, pat dry, and halve.

**2** **Shape and Parbake Crust** Spray rimmed baking sheet with vegetable oil spray. Press and roll dough into 15 by 11-inch rectangle on lightly floured counter. (If dough springs back, roll into as large a rectangle as possible, then let rest on counter for 5 minutes before continuing to roll out.) Transfer dough to prepared sheet and press to edges of sheet. Bake dough until bottom is just beginning to brown, about 5 minutes.

**3** **Top Flatbread** Remove crust from oven and press flat any large bubbles with spatula. Brush dough with sun-dried tomato oil, leaving ½-inch border around edge. Arrange olives, mozzarella, artichokes, and sun-dried tomatoes over crust and sprinkle with ¼ teaspoon salt and ¼ teaspoon pepper.

**4** **Bake Flatbread** Bake flatbread until mozzarella is melted and crust is golden around edges, 10 to 15 minutes, rotating sheet halfway through baking.

**5** **Make Pesto** While flatbread bakes, pick 1 cup basil leaves. Grate Parmesan (2 tablespoons). Mince garlic. Process olive oil, pine nuts, 2 tablespoons water, basil, and garlic in food processor until smooth, about 1 minute, scraping down sides of bowl as needed. Transfer to small bowl, stir in Parmesan, and season with salt and pepper to taste.

**6** **Finish Dish** Transfer flatbread to wire rack and let cool for 5 minutes. While flatbread cools, transfer 1 tablespoon pesto to large bowl. Add arugula to bowl, toss to coat, and season with salt and pepper to taste. Dollop remaining pesto over flatbread to taste, then arrange arugula over top. Slice flatbread and serve.

# Mushroom and Gruyère Crostata with Bibb Lettuce Salad

serves 4; total time 1 hour

## notes for the cook

Sautéed portobello mushrooms and leeks flavored with garlic and rosemary and topped with nutty Gruyère cheese transform store-bought pie crust into a rustic savory tart in under an hour.

The free-form style of a crostata is much less fussy than a traditional pie, and thus much more weeknight-friendly.

The test kitchen's favorite brand of pie crust is Pillsbury Refrigerated Pie Crusts.

A light salad with sliced pear and toasted almonds balances this hearty crostata.

Use a slightly firm pear for this salad; very ripe pears will fall apart.

6 portobello mushrooms

1 pound leeks

2 garlic cloves

Fresh rosemary

1 (9-inch) store-bought pie dough round

¼ cup extra-virgin olive oil

Salt and pepper

2 ounces Gruyère cheese

1 large egg

¼ cup sliced almonds

Fresh chives

1 tablespoon white wine vinegar

1 head Bibb lettuce (8 ounces)

1 Bosc pear

**1 Prep Vegetables** Adjust oven rack to middle position and heat oven to 425 degrees. Remove stems from mushrooms and use spoon to remove gills. Halve mushrooms, then slice crosswise into ¼-inch-thick slices. Cut dark green leaves from leeks and discard. Trim ends and halve leeks lengthwise, then slice thin and wash thoroughly. Mince garlic. Mince 1 teaspoon rosemary.

**2 Prep Dough** Line rimmed baking sheet with parchment paper. Roll dough into 14-inch circle on lightly floured counter; transfer to prepared sheet.

**3 Sauté Vegetables** Heat 2 tablespoons oil in 12-inch nonstick skillet over medium-high heat until shimmering. Add mushrooms, leeks, and ½ teaspoon salt and cook, stirring occasionally, until beginning to brown, about 10 minutes. Stir in garlic and rosemary and cook until fragrant, about 30 seconds.

**4** **Assemble and Bake Tart** While vegetables cook, grate Gruyère (½ cup). Lightly beat egg. Transfer cooked vegetables to prepared dough, leaving 2-inch border around edge. Sprinkle Gruyère over vegetables and fold border over filling around edge of tart, pinching pleated dough to secure. Brush dough with beaten egg. Bake until crust is deep golden brown, 15 to 18 minutes, rotating sheet halfway through baking.

**5** **Toast Nuts and Make Dressing** While tart bakes, wipe skillet clean with paper towels and toast almonds over medium heat, shaking pan occasionally, until golden and fragrant, about 3 minutes; transfer to bowl to cool. Mince 2 tablespoons chives. Whisk vinegar, remaining 2 tablespoons oil, 1 tablespoon chives, ¼ teaspoon salt, and ⅛ teaspoon pepper together in large bowl.

**6** **Make Salad and Finish Dish** Tear lettuce leaves into bite-size pieces. Halve and core pear, then slice thin. Add lettuce and pear to bowl with dressing and toss to coat. Sprinkle salad with toasted almonds. Sprinkle baked tart with remaining 1 tablespoon chives. Cut into wedges and serve with salad.

# Lavash Pizzas with Cauliflower, Fennel, and Coriander

serves 4; total time 45 minutes

## notes for the cook

Using the Middle Eastern flatbreads called lavash as the base of these quick pizzas gives them the perfect crispy, thin crust.

We start by brushing the lavash with oil and toasting them briefly in the oven before topping them with a hearty combination of nutty cauliflower and shredded mozzarella packed with flavor from garlic and red pepper flakes. A sprinkle of goat cheese provides the finishing touch.

Look for precut cauliflower florets for this recipe; if you can't find them, you'll need a little less than half a head of cauliflower to get 2 cups of florets.

Lavash can often be found near the tortillas in the supermarket.

2 cups cauliflower florets

1 fennel bulb

3 garlic cloves

1 scallion

4 ounces mozzarella cheese

2 ounces goat cheese

5 tablespoons extra-virgin olive oil

1 teaspoon ground coriander

Salt and pepper

2 (12 by 9-inch) lavash breads

¼ teaspoon red pepper flakes

1 lemon

6 ounces cherry tomatoes

5 ounces (5 cups) baby kale

**1 Prep Vegetables** Adjust oven racks to upper-middle and lower-middle positions and heat oven to 475 degrees. Chop cauliflower florets. Discard fennel stalks, halve bulb, core, and then chop. Mince garlic. Slice scallion thin. Shred mozzarella (1 cup). Crumble goat cheese (½ cup).

**2 Parcook Cauliflower** Heat 1 tablespoon oil in 12-inch skillet over medium heat until shimmering. Add coriander, 3 tablespoons water, cauliflower, fennel, and ½ teaspoon salt. Cover and cook, stirring occasionally, until vegetables are tender, 6 to 8 minutes; transfer to medium bowl and let cool.

**3 Parbake Lavash** While cauliflower cools, lay lavash on 2 rimmed baking sheets, then brush both sides of lavash with 2 tablespoons oil. Bake until golden brown, about 3 minutes, flipping lavash halfway through baking.

4 **Make Topping and Assemble Lavash Pizzas** Add pepper flakes, mozzarella, garlic, ¼ teaspoon salt, and ¼ teaspoon pepper to cauliflower mixture and stir to combine. Spread cauliflower mixture evenly over each lavash and sprinkle with goat cheese.

5 **Bake Lavash** Bake lavash pizzas until cheese is melted, 4 to 6 minutes, switching and rotating sheets halfway through baking.

6 **Make Salad and Finish Dish** While lavash bakes, squeeze 2 teaspoons lemon juice. Halve tomatoes. Whisk remaining 2 tablespoons oil, lemon juice, ¼ teaspoon salt, and ¼ teaspoon pepper together in large bowl. Add kale and tomatoes to bowl with dressing and toss to combine. Sprinkle pizzas with scallion, slice, and serve with salad.

# Eggplant and Mozzarella Panini with Simple Greens

serves 4; total time 1 hour

## notes for the cook

For a sophisticated take on this classic Italian sandwich, we combined broiled eggplant, a garlicky homemade tomato sauce, and fresh mozzarella cheese, which melted perfectly over the whole thing.

A grill pan and a heavy Dutch oven make a great stand-in for a traditional panini press.

Note that you'll need ½ cup of basil, so shop accordingly.

A simple salad of mixed greens, fennel, and sunflower seeds is a bright counterpoint to the rich panini.

We like the attractive grill marks that you get when you use a grill pan to press the panini in step 6, but if you don't have one, you can substitute a 12-inch nonstick skillet.

1 pound eggplant

2 garlic cloves

6 ounces mozzarella cheese

Fresh basil

10 ounces grape tomatoes

7 tablespoons extra-virgin olive oil

Salt and pepper

1 fennel bulb

2 tablespoon red wine vinegar

2 teaspoons Dijon mustard

¼ cup roasted sunflower seeds

8 (½-inch-thick) slices crusty bread

5 ounces (5 cups) mesclun greens

**1  Prep Ingredients** Adjust 1 oven rack 4 inches from broiler element and second rack to middle position. Heat broiler. Line rimmed baking sheet with aluminum foil and spray with vegetable oil spray. While broiler heats, slice eggplant into ¾-inch-thick rounds. Peel garlic. Shred mozzarella (1½ cups). Coarsely chop ½ cup basil.

**2  Broil Eggplant and Tomatoes** Spread tomatoes, eggplant, and garlic evenly over baking sheet and drizzle with 3 tablespoons oil. Sprinkle with ¼ teaspoon salt and ¼ teaspoon pepper. Broil until vegetables are browned and tomatoes have split open, 8 to 10 minutes, flipping eggplant once during broiling.

**3  Make Salad** While vegetables broil, discard fennel stalks, halve bulb, core, and slice thin. Whisk 1 tablespoon vinegar, mustard, ¼ teaspoon salt, and ¼ teaspoon pepper together in large serving bowl. Whisking constantly, slowly drizzle in 2 tablespoons oil. Add sunflower seeds and fennel; set aside.

**4** **Mash Tomatoes** When vegetables are done broiling, transfer tomatoes to small bowl and mash with fork. Mince roasted garlic and stir into tomatoes. Stir in remaining 1 tablespoon vinegar, ¼ teaspoon salt, and ¼ teaspoon pepper.

**5** **Assemble Sandwiches** Reduce oven temperature to 200 degrees. Set wire rack in clean rimmed baking sheet. Brush remaining 2 tablespoons oil evenly over 1 side of each slice of bread. Assemble sandwiches as follows between prepared bread (with oiled sides outside sandwich): half of mozzarella, tomato sauce, eggplant, basil, and remaining mozzarella. Press sandwiches gently to set. Add greens to bowl with dressing and toss to combine.

**6** **Finish Dish** Heat 12-inch nonstick grill pan over medium heat for 1 minute. Place 2 sandwiches in pan, place Dutch oven on top, and cook until bread is golden and crisp on first side, about 4 minutes. Flip sandwiches, replace Dutch oven, and cook until second side is crisp and cheese is melted, about 4 minutes. Transfer sandwiches to prepared wire rack and keep warm in oven. Wipe out grill pan and cook remaining 2 sandwiches. Serve with salad.

# Stir-Fried Eggplant with Garlic-Basil Sauce

serves 4; total time 45 minutes

## notes for the cook

Eggplant is a powerhouse vegetable that's especially good in stir-fries; it soaks up the flavor-packed sauce and softens to a melt-in-your-mouth consistency. We start by sautéing the eggplant with a bell pepper to develop browning and drive off excess moisture before adding our Thai-inspired garlic-basil sauce.

Do not peel the eggplant; leaving the skin on helps it hold together during cooking.

We like Bragg Liquid Aminos as a vegetarian substitute for fish sauce, but you can swap in an equal amount of fish sauce if you prefer.

Note that you'll need ½ cup of basil, so shop accordingly.

1 ½ cups long-grain white rice

Salt and pepper

1 lime

¼ cup Bragg Liquid Aminos

2 tablespoons packed brown sugar

2 teaspoons cornstarch

⅛ teaspoon red pepper flakes

1 pound eggplant

1 red bell pepper

6 garlic cloves

Fresh ginger

2 scallions

Fresh basil

2 tablespoons plus 1 teaspoon vegetable oil

**1 Make Rice** Rinse rice in fine-mesh strainer until water runs clear. Bring rice, 2¼ cups water, and ¼ teaspoon salt to simmer in large saucepan over medium heat. Reduce heat to low, cover, and simmer until rice is tender and liquid is absorbed, 16 to 18 minutes. Remove pot from heat, lay clean folded dish towel underneath lid, and let sit for 10 minutes.

**2 Make Sauce** While rice cooks, grate 2 teaspoons lime zest and squeeze 1 tablespoon juice. Combine liquid aminos, sugar, cornstarch, pepper flakes, lime zest and juice, and ½ cup water together in bowl.

**3 Prep Vegetables** Cut eggplant into ¾-inch pieces. Stem and seed bell pepper, then cut into 2-inch matchsticks. Mince garlic. Peel and grate 1 tablespoon ginger. Slice scallions thin. Tear ½ cup basil leaves.

4 **Cook Vegetables** Combine 1 teaspoon oil, garlic, and ginger in bowl. Heat remaining 2 tablespoons oil in 12-inch nonstick skillet over high heat until shimmering. Add eggplant and bell pepper and cook, stirring often, until well browned and tender, 8 to 10 minutes.

5 **Cook Garlic and Ginger** Clear center of skillet, add garlic mixture, and cook, mashing mixture into skillet, until fragrant, about 30 seconds. Stir garlic mixture into vegetables.

6 **Add Sauce and Finish Dish** Whisk sauce to recombine, then add to skillet. Cook, stirring constantly, until sauce is thickened, about 30 seconds. Off heat, stir in scallions and basil. Serve with rice.

# Tofu Banh Mi

serves 4; total time 45 minutes

## notes for the cook

*Banh mi* sandwiches inspired by Vietnamese street food have become hugely popular in the United States. This version features pan-fried tofu, quick-pickled vegetables, and a spicy mayo-based sauce.

Coating the tofu in cornstarch before cooking helps develop a crispy crust.

You will use only half of the cucumber in the pickles; save the rest for another use.

We like Bragg Liquid Aminos as a vegetarian substitute for fish sauce, but you can swap in an equal amount of fish sauce if you prefer.

You can use firm or extra-firm tofu in this recipe.

14 ounces firm tofu

Salt and pepper

2 carrots

1 cucumber

1 lime

1 tablespoon Bragg Liquid Aminos

¼ cup mayonnaise

1 tablespoon Sriracha sauce

4 (8-inch) Italian sub rolls

Fresh cilantro

⅓ cup cornstarch

3 tablespoons vegetable oil

**1** **Prep Tofu** Cut tofu crosswise into 8 equal slabs. Spread tofu over paper towel–lined baking sheet and let drain for 20 minutes. Gently press dry with paper towels and season with salt and pepper.

**2** **Prep Vegetables and Pickle** While tofu drains, peel and shred carrots. Peel cucumber and cut in half crosswise, reserving half for another use. Cut remaining ½ cucumber in half lengthwise, seed, and slice thin. Grate 1 teaspoon lime zest and squeeze 1 tablespoon juice. Combine liquid aminos, carrots, cucumber, and lime juice in bowl and let sit for 15 minutes.

**3** **Make Sauce and Toast Rolls** Adjust oven rack 8 inches from broiler element and heat broiler. Whisk mayonnaise, Sriracha, and lime zest together in small bowl. Split sub rolls lengthwise, place on rimmed baking sheet, and broil until lightly toasted, 3 to 5 minutes. While bread toasts, pick ⅓ cup cilantro leaves.

**4** **Dredge Tofu** Spread cornstarch in shallow dish. Coat tofu thoroughly in cornstarch, pressing gently to adhere; transfer to plate.

**5** **Cook Tofu** Heat oil in 12-inch nonstick skillet over medium-high heat until just smoking. Add tofu and cook until both sides are crisp and browned, about 4 minutes per side. Transfer to paper towel–lined plate.

**6** **Assemble Sandwiches and Finish Dish** Spread mayonnaise mixture evenly over cut sides of each roll. Assemble sandwiches by layering ingredients as follows between prepared rolls: tofu, pickled vegetables (leaving liquid in bowl), and cilantro leaves. Press gently on sandwiches to set. Serve.

# Sichuan Braised Tofu with Rice (Mapo Tofu)

serves 6; total time 1 hour

## notes for the cook

*Mapo* tofu is a renowned dish from China's Sichuan province that combines all the best qualities of hearty, spicy, rich dishes such as chili or ragu in a deeply flavorful, brothy dish.

This dish gets serious spiciness from the numbing heat of Sichuan peppercorns; consider yourself warned.

A small amount of chopped fresh and dried mushrooms add deep savory flavor, and poaching the tofu in the liquid used to soak the dried mushrooms helps the cubes stay intact in the braise.

Only soft tofu will work in this dish; do not use any other type.

Asian broad-bean chili paste is also known as *doubanjiang* or *toban djan*.

1½ cups long-grain white rice

Salt

28 ounces soft tofu

12 scallions

1 (3-inch) piece ginger

9 garlic cloves

4 ounces fresh shiitake mushrooms or oyster mushrooms

1 tablespoon Sichuan peppercorns

½ ounce dried shiitake mushrooms

⅓ cup Asian broad-bean chili paste

½ cup vegetable oil

2 tablespoons hoisin sauce

2 tablespoons soy sauce

1 tablespoon cornstarch

**1** **Cook Rice** Rinse rice in fine-mesh strainer until water runs clear. Bring rice, 2¼ cups water, and ¼ teaspoon salt to simmer in large saucepan over medium heat. Reduce heat to low, cover, and simmer until rice is tender and liquid is absorbed, 16 to 18 minutes. Remove pot from heat, lay clean folded dish towel underneath lid, and let sit for 10 minutes.

**2** **Prep Ingredients** While rice cooks, cut tofu into ½-inch cubes. Place in large bowl. Using side of chef's knife, crush whites of scallions, then cut greens into 1-inch pieces. Add to bowl with tofu. Peel ginger and cut into ¼-inch rounds. Peel garlic. Stem fresh shiitakes. Microwave peppercorns until fragrant, 15 to 30 seconds. Let cool completely, then grind with mortar and pestle or spice grinder (you should have 1½ teaspoons).

**3** **Microwave Mushrooms and Tofu** Microwave 2 cups water, dried shiitakes, and ½ teaspoon salt in covered bowl until steaming, about 1 minute. Let sit until softened, about 5 minutes. Drain mushrooms in fine-mesh strainer set over bowl of tofu and scallions. Set aside soaked mushrooms. Microwave tofu and scallions in bowl with mushroom liquid until steaming, 5 to 7 minutes.

**4 Make Spice Paste and Process Mushrooms** Meanwhile, process chili paste, garlic, and ginger in food processor until coarse paste forms, 1 to 2 minutes. Add ¼ cup oil and 1 teaspoon ground peppercorns. Process until smooth paste forms, 1 to 2 minutes longer. Transfer to bowl. Add reserved soaked shiitakes and fresh shiitakes to now-empty processor and pulse until finely chopped, 15 to 20 pulses.

**5 Cook Spice Paste and Tofu** Heat 2 tablespoons oil and spice paste in large saucepan over medium heat and cook, stirring frequently, until paste darkens and oil begins to separate from paste, 2 to 3 minutes. Add remaining 2 tablespoons oil and mushroom mixture to saucepan with paste and cook, breaking up mushrooms with wooden spoon, until mushrooms begin to brown and stick to bottom of saucepan, 3 to 5 minutes.

**6 Finish Dish** Gently add tofu-scallion mixture to mushroom mixture, then add hoisin. Cook, gently stirring frequently, until dish comes to simmer, 2 to 3 minutes. Whisk soy sauce and cornstarch together in small bowl and add mixture to saucepan. Continue to cook, stirring frequently, until thickened, 2 to 3 minutes. Transfer to serving dish, sprinkle with remaining ½ teaspoon ground peppercorns, and serve with rice.

# Crispy Tofu with Warm Cabbage Salad

serves 4 to 6; total time 45 minutes

## notes for the cook

Crispy pan-fried tofu, a zesty dressing, and a few key mix-ins transform bagged coleslaw into a light, flavorful dinner.

We prefer the texture of soft or medium-firm tofu here. Firm or extra-firm tofu will also work, but they will taste drier.

Note that you'll need ½ cup of both cilantro and mint, so shop accordingly.

Bags of coleslaw mix can vary in size, but a few ounces more or less won't make a difference here.

To make the dish spicier, use an extra teaspoon of Asian chili-garlic sauce in the dressing.

28 ounces soft or medium-firm tofu

Salt and pepper

4 scallions

Fresh cilantro

Fresh mint

¾ cup dry-roasted peanuts

3 tablespoons plus ¾ cup vegetable oil

5 tablespoons rice vinegar

2 tablespoons soy sauce

2 tablespoons sugar

1 teaspoons Asian chili-garlic sauce

1 (14-ounce) bag green coleslaw mix

¾ cup cornstarch

¼ cup cornmeal

**1 Prep Tofu** Cut tofu in half lengthwise, then slice crosswise into 3-inch-long by ½-inch-thick planks. Spread tofu over paper towel–lined baking sheet and let drain for 20 minutes, then gently press dry with paper towels. Season with salt and pepper.

**2 Prep Salad** While tofu drains, slice scallions thin. Pick ½ cup cilantro leaves. Chop ½ cup mint. Chop peanuts.

**3 Make Dressing** Whisk 3 tablespoons oil, vinegar, soy sauce, sugar, and chili-garlic sauce together in bowl, cover, and microwave until simmering, 1 to 2 minutes. Measure out and reserve 2 tablespoons dressing.

**4** **Toss Salad** Toss remaining dressing with coleslaw mix, scallions, cilantro, mint, and peanuts in large bowl.

**5** **Dredge Tofu** Combine cornstarch and cornmeal in shallow dish. Working with several tofu pieces at a time, coat thoroughly with cornstarch mixture, pressing gently to adhere; transfer to large plate.

**6** **Fry Tofu and Finish Dish** Heat remaining ¾ cup oil in 12-inch nonstick skillet over medium-high heat until shimmering. Working in 2 batches, cook tofu until both sides are crisp and brown, about 4 minutes per side. Gently lift tofu from oil, letting excess oil drip back into skillet, and transfer to paper towel–lined plate. Serve tofu with cabbage salad, drizzling with reserved dressing.

# Spicy Tofu and Basil Lettuce Cups

serves 4; total time 1 hour

## notes for the cook

This fresh, flavorful dish takes inspiration from Thai cuisine. A filling of mild tofu punched up with basil, garlic, and spicy Thai chiles gets served in crisp, cool lettuce cups.

Chewy rice vermicelli provides heft to this light meal, and quick pickled carrots make the perfect tangy foil to the spicy tofu.

You can use either red or green Thai chiles here. If fresh Thai chiles are unavailable, substitute two serranos or one jalapeño. For a milder version, remove the seeds and ribs from the chiles.

Note that you'll need 4 cups of basil, so shop accordingly.

28 ounces firm or extra-firm tofu

3 carrots

5 tablespoons distilled white vinegar

¾ teaspoon plus 2 tablespoons sugar

Fresh basil

6 Thai chiles

6 garlic cloves

6 shallots

¼ cup soy sauce

4 ounces rice vermicelli

1 teaspoon plus 3 tablespoons vegetable oil

½ cup dry-roasted peanuts

2 heads Bibb lettuce (1 pound)

**1 Prep Tofu** Cut tofu into 2-inch pieces and transfer to food processor. Pulse until coarsely chopped, about 5 pulses. Spread tofu over paper towel–lined baking sheet and let drain for 20 minutes. Gently press dry with paper towels and set aside.

**2 Pickle Carrots and Prep Vegetables** While tofu drains, peel and shred carrots. Combine 3 tablespoons vinegar, ¾ teaspoon sugar, and carrots in bowl and toss to combine; set aside. Pick 4 cups basil leaves. Stem chiles and peel garlic. Halve shallots lengthwise, then slice thin.

**3 Make Sauce** Bring 2 quarts water to boil in medium saucepan. Pulse 2 cups basil, chiles, and garlic in now-empty food processor until finely chopped, about 15 pulses, scraping down sides of bowl as needed. Transfer 2 tablespoons basil mixture to bowl and stir in soy sauce, 1 tablespoon vinegar, and remaining 2 tablespoons sugar; set aside. Transfer remaining basil mixture to 12-inch nonstick skillet.

4 **Soak Noodles** Off heat, add noodles to hot water, and let stand until tender, about 5 minutes. Drain noodles in colander and rinse under cold running water until water runs clear. Drain well then transfer to bowl; toss with remaining 1 tablespoon vinegar and 1 teaspoon oil.

5 **Cook Tofu** Stir drained tofu, shallots, and remaining 3 tablespoons oil into skillet with basil mixture. Cook over medium-high heat, stirring occasionally, until mixture starts to brown and tofu appears crumbly, about 15 minutes. While tofu cooks, chop peanuts and separate lettuce leaves.

6 **Finish Dish** Stir reserved basil–soy sauce mixture into skillet and cook, stirring constantly, until well coated, about 1 minute. Stir in remaining 2 cups basil and cook, stirring constantly, until wilted, 30 to 60 seconds. Off heat, stir in peanuts and transfer mixture to platter. Fill lettuce leaves with noodles and top with tofu mixture and pickled carrots. Serve.

# Nutritional Information for Our Recipes

To calculate the nutritional values of our recipes per serving, we used The Food Processor SQL by ESHA Research. When using this program, we entered all the ingredients, using weights for important ingredients such as most vegetables. We also used our preferred brands in these analyses. When the recipe called for seasoning with an unspecified amount of salt and pepper, we added ½ teaspoon of salt and ¼ teaspoon of pepper to the analysis. We did not include additional salt or pepper for food that's "seasoned to taste." If there is a range in the serving size, we used the highest number of servings to calculate the nutritional values.

| | Servings/ Portions | Calories | Total Fat (g) | Sat Fat (g) | Chol (mg) | Sodium (mg) | Total Carbs (g) | Fiber (g) | Total Sugar (g) | Added Sugar (g) | Protein (g) |
|---|---|---|---|---|---|---|---|---|---|---|---|
| **Dinner Salads** | | | | | | | | | | | |
| Chicken and Arugula Salad with Figs and Warm Spices | 6 | 440 | 24 | 3 | 85 | 460 | 26 | 6 | 14 | 1 | 31 |
| Kale Caesar Salad with Chicken | 4 | 510 | 32 | 6 | 75 | 930 | 25 | 2 | 2 | 0 | 29 |
| Beet and Carrot Noodle Salad with Pan-Seared Chicken | 4 | 420 | 21 | 3.5 | 60 | 860 | 35 | 8 | 20 | 5 | 28 |
| Chicken Salad with Whole-Grain Mustard Vinaigrette | 4 | 400 | 17 | 2.5 | 125 | 710 | 13 | 2 | 9 | 0 | 41 |
| Grilled Thai Beef Salad | 4 | 360 | 15 | 6 | 115 | 750 | 16 | 5 | 4 | 1 | 40 |
| Wedge Salad with Steak Tips | 4 | 540 | 35 | 15 | 155 | 990 | 7 | 1 | 5 | 0 | 46 |
| Arugula Salad with Pears, Prosciutto, and Chickpeas | 4 | 420 | 27 | 5 | 20 | 810 | 30 | 6 | 14 | 4 | 17 |
| Arugula Salad with Steak Tips and Gorgonzola | 4 | 670 | 51 | 18 | 155 | 1160 | 8 | 2 | 4 | 1 | 47 |
| Salmon, Avocado, Grapefruit, and Watercress Salad | 4 | 540 | 39 | 7 | 60 | 550 | 23 | 11 | 11 | 0 | 27 |
| Smoked Salmon Niçoise Salad | 4 | 450 | 19 | 6 | 295 | 480 | 25 | 4 | 5 | 0 | 45 |
| Mediterranean Couscous Salad with Smoked Trout | 6 | 360 | 16 | 2.5 | 30 | 950 | 37 | 3 | 1 | 0 | 17 |
| Fennel and Bibb Salad with Scallops and Hazelnuts | 4 | 430 | 31 | 4 | 40 | 1180 | 15 | 4 | 4 | 0 | 24 |
| Shrimp and Wilted Spinach Salad with Bacon-Pecan Vinaigrette | 4 | 450 | 31 | 7 | 170 | 1420 | 17 | 6 | 8 | 2 | 24 |
| Shrimp and White Bean Salad with Garlic Toasts | 4 | 510 | 19 | 3 | 145 | 1490 | 55 | 8 | 6 | 0 | 29 |
| Farro Salad with Sugar Snap Peas and White Beans | 6 | 310 | 9 | 1 | 0 | 460 | 50 | 4 | 6 | 0 | 11 |
| Quinoa Taco Salad | 4 | 410 | 22 | 3.5 | 5 | 560 | 43 | 13 | 4 | 0 | 14 |
| Bistro Salad with Fried Egg | 4 | 440 | 38 | 11 | 225 | 870 | 8 | 2 | 3 | 1 | 16 |
| Pita Bread Salad with Tomatoes, Cucumber, and Chickpeas (Fattoush) | 4 | 440 | 30 | 4 | 0 | 440 | 36 | 6 | 6 | 0 | 9 |
| Marinated Tofu and Vegetable Salad | 4 | 360 | 22 | 3 | 0 | 510 | 21 | 2 | 12 | 3 | 21 |
| Chopped Winter Salad with Butternut Squash | 4 | 400 | 28 | 5 | 15 | 460 | 35 | 7 | 13 | 0 | 8 |
| **Soups and Stews** | | | | | | | | | | | |
| Thai Chicken Soup | 4 | 320 | 10 | 4.5 | 85 | 1040 | 23 | 3 | 7 | 0 | 32 |
| Garlicky Chicken and Orzo Soup | 6 | 230 | 7 | 1 | 55 | 740 | 18 | 2 | 4 | 0 | 21 |
| Chicken Tortilla Soup with Greens | 6 | 260 | 8 | 1 | 55 | 1150 | 23 | 1 | 4 | 0 | 21 |

| | Servings/ Portions | Calories | Total Fat (g) | Sat Fat (g) | Chol (mg) | Sodium (mg) | Total Carbs (g) | Fiber (g) | Total Sugar (g) | Added Sugar (g) | Protein (g) |
|---|---|---|---|---|---|---|---|---|---|---|---|
| Quick Turkey Chili | 4 | 420 | 15 | 5 | 50 | 820 | 40 | 11 | 6 | 1 | 35 |
| Ginger Beef and Ramen Noodle Soup | 4 | 550 | 12 | 4 | 75 | 2130 | 68 | 1 | 6 | 0 | 42 |
| Rioja-Style Potatoes with Chorizo and Peas | 4 | 580 | 29 | 9 | 50 | 1150 | 45 | 3 | 5 | 0 | 21 |
| Kimchi Beef and Tofu Soup | 6 | 270 | 14 | 3.5 | 50 | 1090 | 11 | 0 | 8 | 0 | 22 |
| Sicilian Fish Stew | 6 | 330 | 16 | 3 | 75 | 770 | 17 | 2 | 10 | 0 | 25 |
| Thai-Style Hot and Sour Soup with Shrimp and Rice Vermicelli | 4 | 230 | 2 | 0 | 145 | 1470 | 32 | 1 | 5 | 1 | 20 |
| Chickpea and Kale Soup | 4 | 220 | 10 | 2 | 5 | 1110 | 23 | 7 | 7 | 0 | 12 |
| Turkish Tomato, Bulgur, and Red Pepper Soup | 6 | 310 | 6 | 0.5 | 0 | 1290 | 52 | 5 | 8 | 0 | 8 |
| Quinoa and Vegetable Stew | 8 | 280 | 12 | 3 | 10 | 760 | 36 | 6 | 4 | 0 | 9 |
| Caribbean-Style Swiss Chard and Butternut Squash Stew | 4 | 320 | 20 | 11 | 0 | 1030 | 35 | 7 | 9 | 0 | 7 |
| African Sweet Potato and Peanut Stew | 6 | 360 | 19 | 4.5 | 10 | 850 | 38 | 8 | 12 | 0 | 11 |
| Black Bean Soup | 6 | 230 | 6 | 0 | 0 | 1250 | 35 | 11 | 4 | 0 | 12 |
| **Beef, Pork, and Lamb** | | | | | | | | | | | |
| Sichuan-Style Orange Beef with Sugar Snap Peas and Rice | 4 | 660 | 22 | 7 | 115 | 1410 | 70 | 3 | 10 | 4 | 44 |
| Grilled Cumin-Rubbed Flank Steak with Mexican Street Corn | 4 | 480 | 28 | 8 | 125 | 1230 | 20 | 3 | 5 | 0 | 41 |
| Grilled Flank Steak with Vegetables and Salsa Verde | 4 | 510 | 33 | 9 | 115 | 610 | 13 | 6 | 6 | 0 | 40 |
| Skirt Steak with Pinto Bean Salad | 4 | 570 | 28 | 8 | 120 | 1010 | 33 | 9 | 2 | 0 | 48 |
| Grilled Skirt Steak and Poblano Tacos with Lime Crema | 6 | 530 | 22 | 7 | 105 | 670 | 47 | 3 | 6 | 0 | 38 |
| Skillet Steak Tips with Roasted Feta Potatoes and Mesclun Salad | 4 | 680 | 40 | 11 | 130 | 700 | 33 | 1 | 2 | 0 | 42 |
| Grilled Beef Skewers with Arugula Salad and Heirloom Tomatoes | 6 | 460 | 30 | 8 | 105 | 590 | 10 | 2 | 6 | 0 | 35 |
| Easy Steak Frites | 4 | 850 | 45 | 13 | 150 | 1020 | 52 | 0 | 1 | 0 | 59 |
| Thick-Cut Steaks with Broiled Asparagus and Brown Butter Sauce | 4 | 550 | 33 | 12 | 150 | 790 | 9 | 5 | 4 | 0 | 58 |
| Perfect Cheeseburgers with Easy Grilled Coleslaw | 4 | 760 | 53 | 16 | 125 | 1040 | 32 | 4 | 9 | 0 | 35 |
| Fennel-Crusted Pork Chops with Apples, Shallots, and Brown Rice | 4 | 780 | 22 | 7 | 90 | 680 | 92 | 7 | 24 | 0 | 37 |
| Roasted Pork Chops and Vegetables with Parsley Vinaigrette | 4 | 810 | 36 | 8 | 190 | 1440 | 40 | 6 | 8 | 0 | 79 |
| Pan-Seared Thick-Cut Boneless Pork Chops with Peaches and Spinach | 4 | 460 | 20 | 3.5 | 145 | 610 | 14 | 4 | 8 | 0 | 54 |
| Sesame Pork Cutlets with Wilted Napa Cabbage Salad | 6 | 580 | 31 | 4.5 | 160 | 340 | 30 | 5 | 4 | 0 | 43 |
| Stir-Fried Pork with Green Beans and Cashews | 4 | 620 | 18 | 2.5 | 75 | 1510 | 75 | 3 | 8 | 0 | 33 |
| Grilled Pork Tenderloin with Tomato-Onion Salad | 4 | 310 | 15 | 2.5 | 110 | 920 | 6 | 2 | 3 | 0 | 37 |
| Roasted Pork Tenderloin with Green Beans and Potatoes | 4 | 580 | 25 | 10 | 140 | 1080 | 48 | 7 | 11 | 0 | 41 |
| Pork Milanese with Arugula, Parsley, and Parmesan Salad | 4 | 530 | 30 | 6 | 175 | 760 | 27 | 1 | 1 | 0 | 36 |
| Sausage and White Beans with Mustard Greens | 4 | 380 | 17 | 4.5 | 35 | 1370 | 26 | 7 | 6 | 0 | 28 |
| Polenta with Sausage, Peppers, and Olives | 4 | 490 | 21 | 9 | 65 | 1800 | 43 | 1 | 6 | 0 | 32 |

| | Servings/ Portions | Calories | Total Fat (g) | Sat Fat (g) | Chol (mg) | Sodium (mg) | Total Carbs (g) | Fiber (g) | Total Sugar (g) | Added Sugar (g) | Protein (g) |
|---|---|---|---|---|---|---|---|---|---|---|---|
| Bratwurst Sandwiches with Red Potato and Kale Salad | 4 | 850 | 59 | 11 | 90 | 1740 | 53 | 4 | 9 | 0 | 23 |
| Thai-Style Pork Burgers with Sesame Green Beans | 4 | 720 | 48 | 12 | 120 | 770 | 36 | 3 | 9 | 0 | 38 |
| Spicy Korean-Style Pork Tacos with Red Cabbage Slaw | 4 | 370 | 13 | 2.5 | 85 | 350 | 34 | 1 | 6 | 1 | 28 |
| Chorizo, Corn, and Tomato Tostadas with Lime Crema | 4 | 850 | 49 | 20 | 90 | 1760 | 73 | 8 | 12 | 0 | 30 |
| Lamb Meatballs with Couscous and Yogurt Sauce | 4 | 770 | 43 | 19 | 140 | 590 | 59 | 5 | 3 | 0 | 35 |
| Lamb and Summer Vegetable Kebabs with Grilled Focaccia | 6 | 530 | 25 | 5 | 115 | 840 | 36 | 2 | 6 | 0 | 43 |
| Grilled Harissa Lamb Burgers with Cucumber and Olive Salad | 4 | 640 | 46 | 15 | 85 | 630 | 31 | 3 | 7 | 0 | 26 |
| Sumac Lamb Loin Chops with Carrots, Mint, and Paprika | 4 | 370 | 22 | 6 | 85 | 740 | 15 | 4 | 5 | 0 | 30 |
| Grilled Lamb Shoulder Chops with Zucchini and Corn Salad | 4 | 590 | 44 | 11 | 105 | 990 | 16 | 3 | 7 | 0 | 33 |
| Spicy Lamb with Lentils and Yogurt | 4 | 730 | 39 | 16 | 90 | 990 | 58 | 8 | 7 | 0 | 38 |
| **Poultry** | | | | | | | | | | | |
| Poached Chicken with Quinoa and Warm Tomato-Ginger Vinaigrette | 4 | 560 | 19 | 3 | 125 | 670 | 46 | 6 | 5 | 0 | 48 |
| Parmesan Chicken with Wilted Radicchio Salad | 4 | 880 | 50 | 10 | 275 | 1050 | 36 | 4 | 6 | 0 | 69 |
| Chicken Katsu with Tonkatsu Sauce, Cabbage Salad, and Rice | 6 | 680 | 25 | 3 | 175 | 700 | 66 | 1 | 6 | 0 | 43 |
| Pan-Seared Chicken with Warm Mediterranean Bulgur Pilaf | 4 | 580 | 23 | 7 | 150 | 850 | 45 | 8 | 3 | 0 | 50 |
| Stir-Fried Chicken and Broccoli with Herbs and Scallion Rice | 4 | 510 | 12 | 1.5 | 85 | 1010 | 64 | 3 | 3 | 0 | 35 |
| Easy Chipotle-Orange Chicken Tacos with Radish-Cilantro Salad | 4 | 520 | 18 | 4 | 140 | 440 | 42 | 1 | 5 | 0 | 45 |
| Chicken and Cauliflower Tikka Masala with Basmati Rice | 4 | 680 | 18 | 5 | 140 | 1010 | 79 | 4 | 10 | 0 | 50 |
| Crispy Chicken with Moroccan Carrot Salad | 4 | 690 | 39 | 11 | 165 | 1220 | 30 | 7 | 13 | 0 | 55 |
| Apricot-Glazed Chicken with Chickpeas, Chorizo, and Spinach | 4 | 750 | 42 | 12 | 185 | 1020 | 28 | 4 | 11 | 0 | 62 |
| Lemon-Thyme Roasted Chicken with Ratatouille | 4 | 540 | 32 | 8 | 145 | 920 | 13 | 4 | 7 | 0 | 50 |
| Pomegranate-Glazed Chicken with Warm Farro Salad | 4 | 830 | 34 | 8 | 145 | 810 | 76 | 2 | 17 | 0 | 58 |
| Chicken with Creamy Butternut Squash Orzo | 4 | 720 | 32 | 12 | 170 | 1210 | 46 | 3 | 5 | 0 | 62 |
| Za'atar Chicken with Pistachios, Brussels Sprouts, and Pomegranate | 4 | 680 | 44 | 9 | 145 | 760 | 17 | 6 | 6 | 0 | 53 |
| Oven-Roasted Chicken Breasts with Chickpeas, Fennel, and Chermoula | 4 | 700 | 38 | 8 | 145 | 1130 | 34 | 10 | 9 | 0 | 56 |
| Chicken Thighs with White Beans, Pancetta, and Baby Kale | 4 | 750 | 47 | 13 | 245 | 1320 | 27 | 8 | 3 | 0 | 53 |
| Roasted Chicken Thighs with Brussels Sprouts and Carrots | 4 | 770 | 56 | 14 | 240 | 1180 | 24 | 6 | 10 | 0 | 45 |
| Cumin-Crusted Chicken Thighs with Cauliflower Rice | 4 | 630 | 44 | 11 | 235 | 990 | 13 | 5 | 4 | 0 | 45 |
| Thai-Style Chicken and Sweet Potato Curry | 4 | 750 | 25 | 13 | 160 | 1360 | 83 | 6 | 8 | 0 | 45 |
| Chicken Mole with Cilantro-Lime Rice and Beans | 4 | 750 | 19 | 4 | 215 | 1360 | 87 | 6 | 14 | 0 | 57 |

| | Servings/ Portions | Calories | Total Fat (g) | Sat Fat (g) | Chol (mg) | Sodium (mg) | Total Carbs (g) | Fiber (g) | Total Sugar (g) | Added Sugar (g) | Protein (g) |
|---|---|---|---|---|---|---|---|---|---|---|---|
| Nepali-Style Chicken Curry with Basmati Rice | 4 | 560 | 16 | 3 | 165 | 1010 | 60 | 3 | 5 | 0 | 41 |
| Chicken Leg Quarters with Cauliflower and Shallots | 4 | 590 | 38 | 9 | 190 | 830 | 22 | 7 | 9 | 0 | 42 |
| Crispy Chicken with Sautéed Radishes, Spinach, and Bacon | 4 | 640 | 42 | 12 | 240 | 960 | 6 | 3 | 2 | 0 | 56 |
| Roasted Chicken with Harissa and Warm Bulgur Salad | 4 | 850 | 49 | 15 | 170 | 1360 | 51 | 8 | 7 | 0 | 53 |
| Honey-and-Garlic Roasted Chicken with Pearl Couscous Salad | 4 | 810 | 36 | 9 | 160 | 920 | 68 | 2 | 11 | 8 | 51 |
| Mustard-Roasted Chicken with Warm Green Bean and Potato Salad | 4 | 830 | 51 | 12 | 230 | 1180 | 32 | 5 | 4 | 0 | 57 |
| Paprika and Lime–Rubbed Chicken with Grilled Vegetable Succotash | 4 | 850 | 54 | 12 | 230 | 1150 | 35 | 8 | 10 | 2 | 60 |
| Indian-Spiced Chicken with Grilled Naan and Radicchio | 4 | 760 | 44 | 12 | 235 | 1100 | 29 | 1 | 4 | 0 | 59 |
| Teriyaki Chicken with Grilled Bok Choy and Pineapple | 4 | 780 | 44 | 11 | 235 | 1820 | 51 | 5 | 41 | 13 | 44 |
| Turkey Cutlets with Barley and Swiss Chard | 4 | 650 | 18 | 3 | 75 | 1070 | 65 | 14 | 2 | 0 | 57 |
| Crispy Skillet Turkey Burgers with Tomato-Feta Salad | 4 | 660 | 37 | 11 | 70 | 1120 | 44 | 2 | 8 | 0 | 41 |

## Fish and Seafood

| | Servings/ Portions | Calories | Total Fat (g) | Sat Fat (g) | Chol (mg) | Sodium (mg) | Total Carbs (g) | Fiber (g) | Total Sugar (g) | Added Sugar (g) | Protein (g) |
|---|---|---|---|---|---|---|---|---|---|---|---|
| Roasted Salmon and Broccoli Rabe with Pistachio Gremolata | 4 | 510 | 36 | 7 | 95 | 580 | 6 | 4 | 1 | 0 | 40 |
| Sesame Salmon with Grapefruit Slaw | 4 | 580 | 39 | 7 | 95 | 770 | 19 | 7 | 10 | 0 | 38 |
| Black Rice Bowls with Roasted Salmon and Miso Dressing | 4 | 720 | 33 | 6 | 95 | 590 | 64 | 9 | 7 | 0 | 43 |
| Glazed Salmon with Black-Eyed Peas, Walnuts, and Pomegranate | 4 | 720 | 44 | 8 | 95 | 960 | 37 | 7 | 11 | 0 | 44 |
| Salmon Tacos with Collard and Radish Slaw | 4 | 570 | 31 | 5 | 70 | 700 | 43 | 6 | 2 | 0 | 31 |
| Salmon Burgers with Asparagus and Lemon-Herb Sauce | 4 | 550 | 34 | 6 | 70 | 870 | 30 | 2 | 6 | 0 | 31 |
| Braised Halibut with Coriander Carrots and Pearl Couscous | 4 | 670 | 22 | 13 | 135 | 620 | 67 | 3 | 8 | 0 | 42 |
| Lemon-Poached Halibut with Roasted Fingerling Potatoes | 4 | 360 | 9 | 1.5 | 85 | 710 | 33 | 5 | 3 | 0 | 35 |
| Cod in Saffron Broth with Chorizo and Potatoes | 4 | 340 | 13 | 4 | 95 | 800 | 12 | 1 | 2 | 0 | 37 |
| Pan-Seared Cod with Herb-Butter Sauce and Roasted Green Beans | 4 | 590 | 37 | 11 | 105 | 860 | 26 | 5 | 7 | 1 | 35 |
| Thai Curry Rice with Cod | 4 | 550 | 14 | 9 | 75 | 1120 | 65 | 2 | 4 | 0 | 39 |
| Cod Cakes with Garlic-Basil Aïoli and Arugula-Celery Salad | 4 | 590 | 40 | 6 | 105 | 920 | 30 | 1 | 5 | 0 | 26 |
| Blackened Snapper with Sautéed Spinach and Black Rice | 4 | 530 | 17 | 2.5 | 65 | 760 | 57 | 8 | 2 | 0 | 44 |
| Roasted Trout with White Bean and Tomato Salad | 4 | 700 | 41 | 6 | 115 | 870 | 30 | 9 | 6 | 0 | 51 |
| Seared Tuna Steaks with Wilted Frisée and Mushroom Salad | 4 | 520 | 31 | 4.5 | 65 | 790 | 12 | 3 | 6 | 0 | 47 |
| Swordfish Kebabs with Zucchini Ribbon Salad | 4 | 680 | 46 | 10 | 165 | 1180 | 8 | 2 | 4 | 0 | 56 |
| Grilled Swordfish with Eggplant, Tomato, and Chickpea Salad | 4 | 560 | 34 | 6 | 110 | 780 | 25 | 9 | 7 | 0 | 40 |
| Pan-Seared Scallops with Sugar Snap Pea Slaw | 4 | 310 | 18 | 2.5 | 45 | 1200 | 13 | 2 | 4 | 0 | 23 |

| | Servings/ Portions | Calories | Total Fat (g) | Sat Fat (g) | Chol (mg) | Sodium (mg) | Total Carbs (g) | Fiber (g) | Total Sugar (g) | Added Sugar (g) | Protein (g) |
|---|---|---|---|---|---|---|---|---|---|---|---|
| Lemony Shrimp with Orzo, Feta, and Olives | 4 | 620 | 18 | 6 | 240 | 2140 | 71 | 1 | 7 | 0 | 43 |
| Seared Shrimp with Tomato, Avocado, and Lime Quinoa | 4 | 530 | 20 | 3 | 215 | 1420 | 53 | 10 | 5 | 0 | 35 |
| Garlicky Roasted Shrimp with Napa Cabbage and Orange Salad | 4 | 550 | 38 | 6 | 285 | 1590 | 18 | 4 | 11 | 0 | 33 |
| Quick Paella | 4 | 690 | 32 | 9 | 220 | 2040 | 52 | 2 | 4 | 0 | 45 |
| Clams with Pearl Couscous, Chorizo, and Leeks | 6 | 740 | 19 | 5 | 115 | 2240 | 72 | 2 | 6 | 0 | 61 |
| **Pasta and Noodles** | | | | | | | | | | | |
| Grown-Up Macaroni and Cheese with Swiss Chard | 4 | 640 | 31 | 15 | 75 | 1120 | 56 | 2 | 9 | 0 | 32 |
| Bucatini with Peas, Kale, and Pancetta | 6 | 430 | 8 | 2.5 | 10 | 610 | 66 | 2 | 3 | 0 | 18 |
| Linguine with Broccoli Rabe, Capers, and Lemon | 6 | 410 | 13 | 3.5 | 10 | 880 | 59 | 2 | 2 | 0 | 16 |
| Skillet Penne with Chickpeas and Cauliflower | 4 | 600 | 15 | 2.5 | 5 | 1500 | 94 | 5 | 13 | 0 | 25 |
| Garlicky Spaghetti with Basil and Broiled Tomatoes | 6 | 420 | 15 | 3 | 5 | 520 | 60 | 1 | 4 | 0 | 14 |
| Spaghetti with Spring Vegetables | 6 | 450 | 16 | 2.5 | 0 | 430 | 64 | 3 | 5 | 0 | 14 |
| Spaghetti with Fried Eggs, Asparagus, and Bread Crumbs | 4 | 760 | 30 | 6 | 195 | 1040 | 95 | 2 | 5 | 0 | 29 |
| Penne with Butternut Squash and Radicchio | 6 | 580 | 26 | 11 | 45 | 500 | 74 | 3 | 7 | 1 | 14 |
| Penne with Chicken, Artichokes, Cherry Tomatoes, and Olives | 4 | 600 | 20 | 4.5 | 95 | 1260 | 56 | 6 | 6 | 0 | 44 |
| Farfalle with Crispy Prosciutto and Peas | 4 | 600 | 17 | 4.5 | 45 | 2010 | 79 | 3 | 8 | 0 | 33 |
| Pasta with Sausage, Kale, and White Beans | 4 | 580 | 20 | 6 | 40 | 1330 | 65 | 6 | 5 | 0 | 38 |
| "Baked" Ziti with Spinach and Sausage | 4 | 770 | 27 | 15 | 85 | 2800 | 86 | 4 | 11 | 1 | 45 |
| Ricotta Gnocchi with Garlicky Cherry Tomato Sauce and Arugula | 4 | 490 | 25 | 12 | 110 | 1270 | 41 | 2 | 5 | 2 | 23 |
| Fideos with Chickpeas, Fennel, and Kale | 4 | 470 | 12 | 1.5 | 0 | 800 | 74 | 9 | 11 | 0 | 16 |
| Garlicky Shrimp Pasta with Cherry Tomatoes and Tarragon | 6 | 500 | 17 | 6 | 165 | 1140 | 60 | 1 | 4 | 0 | 26 |
| Linguine with Mussels and Fennel | 6 | 530 | 12 | 1.5 | 40 | 900 | 73 | 2 | 7 | 0 | 29 |
| Scallops Fra Diavolo with Fennel and Linguine | 6 | 570 | 16 | 2 | 25 | 1330 | 75 | 4 | 9 | 0 | 26 |
| Soba Noodles with Roasted Eggplant and Sesame | 4 | 710 | 28 | 3 | 0 | 2410 | 101 | 9 | 33 | 17 | 18 |
| Sesame Noodles with Snow Peas, Radishes, and Bell Peppers | 6 | 480 | 20 | 3.5 | 10 | 1070 | 62 | 3 | 11 | 7 | 17 |
| Japanese-Style Yakisoba Noodles with Beef | 6 | 390 | 7 | 1.5 | 55 | 1520 | 53 | 2 | 7 | 0 | 27 |
| Rice Noodles with Crisp Tofu and Cabbage | 4 | 550 | 19 | 1.5 | 0 | 1080 | 80 | 2 | 15 | 12 | 16 |
| One-Pan Shrimp Pad Thai | 4 | 510 | 14 | 1.5 | 145 | 1360 | 75 | 2 | 21 | 18 | 25 |
| Pad Kee Mao with Pork (Drunken Noodles) | 4 | 780 | 28 | 9 | 80 | 1660 | 108 | 4 | 24 | 15 | 24 |
| Vietnamese Lemon Grass Beef and Rice Noodles | 4 | 520 | 18 | 4.5 | 75 | 820 | 60 | 2 | 7 | 3 | 32 |
| Red Curry Noodles with Shrimp, Summer Squash, and Bell Peppers | 4 | 680 | 25 | 12 | 145 | 1440 | 92 | 4 | 9 | 3 | 23 |
| Rice Noodle Bowl with Pork and Scallions | 4 | 620 | 36 | 10 | 80 | 1540 | 51 | 1 | 3 | 0 | 24 |

| | Servings/ Portions | Calories | Total Fat (g) | Sat Fat (g) | Chol (mg) | Sodium (mg) | Total Carbs (g) | Fiber (g) | Total Sugar (g) | Added Sugar (g) | Protein (g) |
|---|---|---|---|---|---|---|---|---|---|---|---|
| **Vegetarian Dinners** | | | | | | | | | | | |
| Farro Bowl with Tofu, Mushrooms, and Spinach | 4 | 420 | 18 | 1.5 | 0 | 660 | 51 | 1 | 6 | 2 | 15 |
| Hearty Pearl Couscous Bowl with Eggplant, Spinach, and Beans | 4 | 370 | 12 | 1.5 | 0 | 650 | 55 | 5 | 5 | 0 | 11 |
| Quinoa Bowl with Mushrooms, Swiss Chard, and Tahini-Lemon Dressing | 4 | 590 | 36 | 5 | 0 | 820 | 53 | 7 | 6 | 0 | 15 |
| Crispy Falafel Pitas with Chopped Salad | 4 | 590 | 43 | 9 | 65 | 980 | 41 | 5 | 8 | 0 | 13 |
| Polenta with Broccoli Rabe and Fried Eggs | 4 | 400 | 23 | 5 | 190 | 1170 | 36 | 4 | 1 | 0 | 16 |
| Spiced Red Lentils with Cauliflower and Cilantro | 4 | 720 | 19 | 5 | 15 | 820 | 114 | 18 | 9 | 0 | 26 |
| Lentils with Roasted Broccoli, Goat Cheese, and Pine Nuts | 4 | 700 | 32 | 7 | 15 | 520 | 77 | 20 | 12 | 0 | 33 |
| Skillet Burrito Bowl | 4 | 590 | 24 | 5 | 15 | 750 | 80 | 12 | 6 | 0 | 14 |
| Black Bean and Sweet Potato Tacos | 4 | 560 | 21 | 2.5 | 0 | 880 | 85 | 14 | 14 | 0 | 12 |
| Corn and Green Chile Quesadillas with Romaine and Avocado Salad | 4 | 790 | 54 | 18 | 20 | 1410 | 55 | 8 | 7 | 0 | 27 |
| Spicy Braised Chickpeas and Turnips with Couscous | 6 | 400 | 9 | 1 | 0 | 760 | 66 | 9 | 9 | 0 | 13 |
| Spring Risotto with Peas, Asparagus, and Arugula | 6 | 470 | 15 | 8 | 35 | 1060 | 64 | 6 | 6 | 0 | 18 |
| Vegetable and Orzo Tian with Garlic Toasts | 4 | 510 | 15 | 4.5 | 15 | 1040 | 73 | 2 | 8 | 0 | 22 |
| Grilled Portobello Burgers with Smoky Red Potatoes | 4 | 690 | 46 | 9 | 20 | 740 | 61 | 6 | 10 | 0 | 12 |
| Chickpea Cakes with Endive and Orange Salad | 6 | 670 | 48 | 21 | 100 | 520 | 36 | 6 | 11 | 0 | 25 |
| Black Bean Burgers with Roasted Carrots and Jalapeño Mayo | 4 | 700 | 37 | 6 | 55 | 1340 | 78 | 13 | 19 | 4 | 17 |
| Zucchini Noodles with Roasted Tomatoes and Cream Sauce | 4 | 610 | 43 | 21 | 90 | 1320 | 45 | 5 | 14 | 0 | 16 |
| Broccoli and Feta Frittata with Watercress Salad | 6 | 290 | 22 | 7 | 390 | 700 | 6 | 2 | 3 | 0 | 18 |
| Baked Eggs with Tomatoes, Feta, and Croutons with Spinach Salad | 4 | 530 | 37 | 8 | 385 | 1180 | 29 | 4 | 10 | 1 | 21 |
| Individual Cheese Soufflés with Frisée and Strawberry Salad | 6 | 410 | 32 | 14 | 245 | 700 | 12 | 2 | 5 | 0 | 20 |
| Cauliflower Tacos with Mango-Cabbage Slaw | 4 | 580 | 29 | 23 | 0 | 870 | 78 | 6 | 11 | 0 | 12 |
| Barbecue Tempeh Skewers with Grilled Romaine | 4 | 590 | 29 | 4.5 | 0 | 800 | 36 | 1 | 17 | 0 | 26 |
| Pesto Flatbread with Artichokes, Olives, and Arugula | 4 | 660 | 38 | 10 | 10 | 850 | 62 | 1 | 6 | 0 | 20 |
| Mushroom and Gruyère Crostata with Bibb Lettuce Salad | 4 | 580 | 36 | 10 | 70 | 850 | 56 | 7 | 14 | 0 | 14 |
| Lavash Pizzas with Cauliflower, Fennel, and Coriander | 4 | 300 | 18 | 6 | 20 | 530 | 23 | 3 | 5 | 0 | 10 |
| Eggplant and Mozzarella Panini with Simple Greens | 4 | 830 | 42 | 11 | 10 | 1450 | 90 | 7 | 14 | 0 | 25 |
| Stir-Fried Eggplant with Garlic-Basil Sauce | 4 | 430 | 9 | 1 | 0 | 850 | 78 | 5 | 12 | 7 | 9 |
| Tofu Banh Mi | 4 | 580 | 29 | 3.5 | 5 | 1000 | 66 | 1 | 11 | 0 | 18 |
| Sichuan Braised Tofu with Rice (Mapo Tofu) | 6 | 500 | 24 | 1.5 | 0 | 1390 | 53 | 2 | 4 | 0 | 15 |
| Crispy Tofu with Warm Cabbage Salad | 6 | 480 | 31 | 2.5 | 0 | 540 | 35 | 4 | 8 | 4 | 16 |
| Spicy Tofu and Basil Lettuce Cups | 4 | 630 | 32 | 3.5 | 0 | 1300 | 57 | 6 | 17 | 7 | 32 |

# Conversions and Equivalents

Some say cooking is a science and an art. We would say that geography has a hand in it, too. Flours and sugars manufactured in the United Kingdom and elsewhere will feel and taste different from those manufactured in the United States. So we cannot promise that the pie crust you bake in Canada or England will taste the same as a pie crust baked in the States, but we can offer guidelines for converting weights and measures. We also recommend that you rely on your instincts when making our recipes. Refer to the visual cues provided. If the pie dough hasn't "come together," as described, you may need to add more water—even if the recipe doesn't tell you to. You be the judge.

The recipes in this book were developed using standard U.S. measures following U.S. government guidelines. The charts below offer equivalents for U.S. and metric measures. All conversions are approximate and have been rounded up or down to the nearest whole number.

*Example*
1 teaspoon = 4.9292 milliliters, rounded up to 5 milliliters
1 ounce = 28.3495 grams, rounded down to 28 grams

| Volume Conversions | |
|---|---|
| **U.S.** | **Metric** |
| 1 teaspoon | 5 milliliters |
| 2 teaspoons | 10 milliliters |
| 1 tablespoon | 15 milliliters |
| 2 tablespoons | 30 milliliters |
| ¼ cup | 59 milliliters |
| ⅓ cup | 79 milliliters |
| ½ cup | 118 milliliters |
| ¾ cup | 177 milliliters |
| 1 cup | 237 milliliters |
| 1¼ cups | 296 milliliters |
| 1½ cups | 355 milliliters |
| 2 cups (1 pint) | 473 milliliters |
| 2½ cups | 591 milliliters |
| 3 cups | 710 milliliters |
| 4 cups (1 quart) | 0.946 liter |
| 1.06 quarts | 1 liter |
| 4 quarts (1 gallon) | 3.8 liters |

| Weight Conversions | |
|---|---|
| **Ounces** | **Grams** |
| ½ | 14 |
| ¾ | 21 |
| 1 | 28 |
| 1½ | 43 |
| 2 | 57 |
| 2½ | 71 |
| 3 | 85 |
| 3½ | 99 |
| 4 | 113 |
| 4½ | 128 |
| 5 | 142 |
| 6 | 170 |
| 7 | 198 |
| 8 | 227 |
| 9 | 255 |
| 10 | 283 |
| 12 | 340 |
| 16 (1 pound) | 454 |

## Conversion For Common Baking Ingredients

Baking is an exacting science. Because measuring by weight is far more accurate than measuring by volume, and thus more likely to produce reliable results, in our recipes we provide ounce measures in addition to cup measures for many ingredients. Refer to the chart below to convert these measures into grams.

| Ingredient | Ounces | Grams |
|---|---|---|
| **Flour** | | |
| 1 cup all-purpose flour* | 5 | 142 |
| 1 cup cake flour | 4 | 113 |
| 1 cup whole-wheat flour | 5½ | 156 |
| **Sugar** | | |
| 1 cup granulated (white) sugar | 7 | 198 |
| 1 cup packed brown sugar (light or dark) | 7 | 198 |
| 1 cup confectioners' sugar | 4 | 113 |
| **Cocoa Powder** | | |
| 1 cup cocoa powder | 3 | 85 |

*U.S. all-purpose flour, the most frequently used flour in this book, does not contain leaveners, as some European flours do. These leavened flours are called self-rising or self-raising. If you are using self-rising flour, take this into consideration before adding leavening to a recipe.*

## Converting Temperatures from an Instant-Read Thermometer

When a recipe includes a doneness temperature, we recommend an instant-read thermometer for the job. Refer to the table below to convert Fahrenheit degrees to Celsius. Or, for temperatures not represented in the chart, use this simple formula:

Subtract 32 degrees from the Fahrenheit reading and then divide the result by 1.8 to find the Celsius reading.

*Example*
"Churn until mixture has consistency of soft-serve ice cream and registers 22 to 23 degrees."

To convert:
22°F − 32 = -10°
-10° ÷ 1.8 = -5.56°C, rounded to -6°C

| Oven Temperatures | | |
|---|---|---|
| **Fahrenheit** | **Celsius** | **Gas Mark** |
| 225 | 105 | ¼ |
| 250 | 120 | ½ |
| 275 | 135 | 1 |
| 300 | 150 | 2 |
| 325 | 165 | 3 |
| 350 | 180 | 4 |
| 375 | 190 | 5 |
| 400 | 200 | 6 |
| 425 | 220 | 7 |
| 450 | 230 | 8 |
| 475 | 245 | 9 |

## Meat Doneness at a Glance

Using a reliable instant-read thermometer is one of the best ways to ensure that your food will turn out delicious. In meat, poultry, and fish recipes we almost always use temperature to indicate when food is done. The temperatures listed in a particular recipe reflect the test kitchen's preferred doneness, but if you like your food more or less done, you can use the temperature guidelines listed here to adjust your cooking. Since the temperature of cooked beef and pork will continue to rise as they rest, they should be removed from the oven, grill, or pan when they are 5 to 10 degrees below the desired serving temperature. Use the temperatures below to figure out when to remove the food from the heat. Carryover cooking doesn't apply to poultry and fish, so they should be cooked to the desired serving temperatures (although they should still be rested afterwards to allow the juices to redistribute and to cool the food enough that it won't burn your mouth). To keep meat warm while it rests, tent it with foil.

| Meat Doneness at a Glance |
|---|
| **Beef and Lamb** |
| **Rare:** 115 to 120 degrees (120 to 125 degrees after resting) |
| **Medium-Rare:** 120 to 125 degrees (125 to 130 degrees after resting) |
| **Medium:** 130 to 135 degrees (135 to 140 degrees after resting) |
| **Medium–Well:** 140 to 145 degrees (145 to 150 degrees after resting) |
| **Well-Done:** 150 to 155 degrees (155 to 160 degrees after resting) |
| **Pork** |
| **Medium-Well:** 145 degrees (150 degrees after resting) |
| **Well-Done:** 160 degrees |
| **Poultry** |
| **White Meat:** 160 degrees |
| **Dark Meat:** 175 degrees |
| **Fish** |
| **Rare:** 110 degrees (for tuna only) |
| **Medium-Rare:** 125 degrees (for tuna or salmon) |
| **Medium:** 140 degrees (for white-fleshed fish) |

# Index